Beyond HR

Beyond HR

The New Science of
Human Capital

John W. Boudreau

Peter M. Ramstad

HARVARD BUSINESS SCHOOL PRESS
BOSTON, MASSACHUSETTS

Library of Congress Cataloging-in-Publication Data
Boudreau, John W.
   Beyond HR: the new science of human capital / John W. Boudreau, Peter M. Ramstad.
     p. cm.
   Includes bibliographical references.
   ISBN: 978-1-4221-0415-6 (hardcover: alk. paper)
   1. Intellectual capital. 2. Knowledge management. 3. Knowledge workers 4. Decision making. 5. Human capital. 6. Personnel management. I. Ramstad, Peter M. II. Title. III. Title: Beyond human resources.
   HD53.B646 2007
   352.3'8—dc22

2006038272

I dedicate this book to my family,
who provide a perpetual source of support and joy,
and to the students in my university and executive classes.

—JWB

I dedicate this book to Jan, Jenny, and Christine
for supporting this effort, so much of which came
from time that otherwise would have been theirs,
and to the consultants at Personnel Decisions International,
who welcomed me into their field and
taught me a great deal along the way.

—PMR

Contents

Preface and Acknowledgments

This book describes our vision of a future where the issues of talent and how it is organized get the attention they deserve, the kind of deep and logical attention worthy of a resource that's vital to strategic success. In 1995 we began working together on the ideas that eventually produced this book. It was a unique collaboration between a professor with fifteen years of scholarship and consulting on HR, human capital measurement, staffing, and strategy and a consultant with significant expertise and experience in accounting, finance, and strategy and a strong interest in research. The colleagues who introduced us said that we were pursuing a similar vision—greater clarity connecting talent to strategy—but from different ends of the discipline. Boudreau had begun studying the HR profession, working outward through measurement, finance, and strategy. Ramstad had started in strategy and finance, working inward to the role of people in driving financial and economic outcomes. It turned out to be a good match and has produced more than a decade of collaborative research, writing, and consulting.

In this book we've attempted to capture the insights that emerged as we were fortunate enough to work with HR and line leaders in the world's top organizations. Our hope is that this book will be read both by leaders within HR and their counterparts outside HR. Our work repeatedly shows that revolutionary opportunities for competitive advantage emerge when these two groups work together with a common logic and approach to talent. We are pleased to see the ideas we have developed appearing in the work of academics, companies, organizations, and consulting firms. When we first suggested the concept of a decision science for human capital about five years ago, we were often met with quizzical reactions. The idea is now well established, and the challenge is to make it come alive.

We hope this book helps organizations meet that challenge.

Acknowledgments

We are indebted to our students and colleagues at the University of Southern California, Personnel Decisions International, and Cornell University, and to the HR and business leaders in the many companies and organizations we have had the great privilege to advise, teach, and collaborate with. While it is not possible to mention them all here, their generosity of ideas and enthusiasm for the notion of a talent decision science gave us confidence in the early years and provided a valuable touchstone as the frameworks, tools, and teaching and consulting techniques developed. We received particularly valuable assistance on the book itself from Gale Adcock, John Bronson, Wayne Cascio, Jeff Chambers, Peter Dowling, Kelly Frank, Lisa Haines, Alan May, Steve Milovich, Toyin Ogun, Dave Pace, and Brian Smith. The field experience gained from working with consulting colleagues such as Terry Gray, Joy Hazucha, Jennise Henry, Shawn Lancaster, Dave McMonagle, and Donna Neumann has provided insight we never could have obtained without their hands-on applications. Melinda Merino and Brian Surette at Harvard Business School Publishing provided valuable editorial support, and Lauren Byrne's production editing was also significant. Finally, we are grateful to the PDI publications team that worked so hard on this project—including Lora Alexander, Susan Gebelein, Katie Mulinix, Kristie Nelson-Neuhaus, and Linda Van-Denboom—who each made important contributions to refining the manuscript and managing the project.

1

The Essential Evolution

Personnel, Human Resources, Talentship

Corning, like many high-tech organizations, traditionally emphasized excellence in its R&D scientists, primarily in the United States.[1] Globalization was recognized as important, but the connection between globalization and people remained fuzzy. By the early twenty-first century, Corning's HR and business leaders discovered that global expansion, particularly in emerging economies, demanded flexible production capability that depended on a specific type of production engineer. The organization realized that there were only a few such engineers in many global regions and that it took years to train them. If Corning could hire these engineers before other companies realized their importance, it would have several years' head start on its competition. This would force the organization's potential competitors into a difficult choice: lacking necessary talent, they could staff their factories with very expensive expatriates, or they could wait years to begin production, which is how long it would take to train regional engineers or build a new cadre of engineering graduates with these skills. The idea of locking up key engineering talent was a far cry from traditional workforce planning, which focused on filling vacancies. Corning had identified a tangible opportunity to exploit its superior knowledge about human capital to provide a significant competitive advantage.

The Uncharted Talent Strategy

Would your organization have been the first to realize this talent pivot-point and exploit it so adeptly? In companies, as well as government and nonprofit organizations, we've found that out of all the jobs, a small number are *pivotal* like this—the performance of talent and organization in these roles moves the strategic needle far more significantly than in other roles. Unfortunately, most organizations don't know which jobs are pivotal (they are not always leaders, salespeople, or technical professionals). Most strategy and planning processes leave these roles virtually uncharted. It's a dangerous blind spot.

This book is about revealing these opportunities in *talent*. We define talent as the resource that includes the potential and realized capacities of individuals and groups and how they are organized, including those within the organization and those who might join the organization.

Reading this book will encourage you to ask tough questions—ones you may have never considered before: Do you know where your pivotal talent is?[2] Do you invest differentially in the most pivotal talent? Or do you adopt a "peanut-butter" approach, spreading the same investments over the entire organization (such as paying for performance in all jobs just because it is good for some of them)?

Right beneath the surface of virtually every organization's formal strategy are opportunities for competitive advantage that are overlooked and untapped every single day. Such uncharted opportunities exist because most organizations make decisions about their people's talents and how those people are organized with far less rigor, logic, and distinctiveness than their decisions about other resources, like money and technology.

HR Strategies Must Become Truly Distinctive

Pull out the strategy document from your HR function. Most HR strategies contain the same things that appear in every other competitor's strategy, such as "build the leadership pipeline," "deal with the brain drain of an aging workforce," "increase the available candidates in technical positions," and "reduce health care costs." How concerned would you be if your HR strategy fell into the competition's hands? If your answer is "not very," can your organization be making world-class decisions where talent matters most to your strategic success? You can bet that Corning would have been very concerned if its strategy for hiring the available production engineers had become known to its competitors before implementation!

Find the Uncharted Talent Opportunities

This isn't just about your HR strategy. It's about how well your entire organization connects decisions about talent, and how it is organized, to your vital strategic interests. At your next strategy meeting, ask your top organizational leaders to provide their best answers to questions like:

- Where does our strategy require that our talent and organization be better than our competitors' to work?

- Where do our talent and organization systems need to be different from competitors', and why?

- Where should we pay more than the fiftieth percentile of the salary survey for pivotal talent pools?

- Where should we spend more on pivotal talent programs and practices than our competitors, and why?

- If we shifted our strategic goals, which of our employees or organizational structures would have to change the most?

Our experience shows that too often the answer is "That's HR's problem, not mine." Yet business leaders don't abdicate decisions about where to invest more in pivotal customer segments by calling it a "marketing department issue" or where to invest more in strategic technologies by calling it a "technology department issue."

Leaders Must Make Talent Decisions
Like Any Vital Resource

Take a look at your competency framework for your leaders. It likely contains such things as "communication," "vision," "execution," and "finding and developing talent." But try asking your high-potential leaders questions like these: What are the necessary and sufficient conditions for motivation or learning? What are the elements of an effective organizational change? What are the requirements of an effective talent pipeline? What defines *critical* jobs or competencies? Their answers will far too often be based on opinion, fads and fashions, half-truths, or outdated traditions, as in other management areas.[3] Such theories are often implicit, based on the last motivational speaker the leader saw or drawn from that leader's own limited experiences. Far too frequently these theories are simply wrong. If you don't allow managers to have their own theory of cash flow, why let them invent their own theory of motivation? If you don't tolerate this kind of ambiguity in decisions about money, technology, and brands, why navigate with ambiguity when it comes to a resource as important as talent?

The Essential Evolution Beyond HR to Talentship

So you have a choice. You can continue to navigate your strategic territory with inadequate talent and organization tools, or you can embrace and build a new decision science that illuminates the hidden opportunities that lie in great decisions about your talent and how it is organized—where those decisions matter most and wherever they are made. This is an essential evolution, because once your competitors figure it out, you can no longer compete effectively unless you evolve too.

This evolution requires changes in the way companies use the perspective of talent and organization to form their strategies, the way business leaders are held accountable for their decisions about the talent and organization resources under their stewardship, the way HR professionals teach principles about optimizing talent and organization, and the way the HR function is organized, rewarded, and evaluated. We call the decision science for talent and organization that drives this evolution "talentship," and its emergence will change the game just as the emergence of finance and marketing changed the game in their eras.

Talentship builds organization effectiveness by improving decisions that affect or depend on human capital, where they make the biggest strategic difference, and wherever they are made.

The Importance of Human Capital

Whether it is called "people," "labor," "intellectual capital," "human capital," "human resources," "talent," or some other term, the resource that lies within employees and how they are organized is increasingly recognized as critical to strategic success and competitive advantage. This observation is so common today that it almost goes without saying. Digitization, labor shortages, growth through acquisitions, simultaneous downsizing and expansion, constant hypercompetition and change, workforce demographic changes, and globalization are just a few of the trends that have made what we call "talent" a top priority.[4] Writers in business, academia, and public policy note that business decisions must happen more quickly at the same time as those decisions increasingly depend on talent and its organization and as the employment relationship is under unprecedented pressure to adapt.[5]

Business leaders recognize that managing people is vital to organizational success, and it is among their top concerns. Top HR officers are respected by boards of directors. Successful CEOs write memoirs that note the connection between their success and their talent management processes. Financial research shows that increasing amounts of market value are driven by intangibles, including human capital. Researchers from disciplines as diverse as accounting, consumer research, finance, political science, and operations management compete to define the latest metrics for human capital within organizations. Academics and consulting firms provide a barrage of evidence that HR practices correlate with financial performance. Consulting firms that built their reputations on disciplines such as strategy, operations, and finance now have leadership and talent management practices. Enterprise software companies routinely integrate human capital applications (including competency databases, performance management, and selection and development systems) into their enter-prisewide solutions. Being one of the best places to work is a goal of top management, not just HR leaders.

For example, GE is widely revered for the depth of its management talent and its ability to apply a deep and shared management logic across a wide array of businesses. This is one of the essential reasons why these businesses are more valuable inside GE than individually. GE can grow through acquisitions in no small part because, compared to its competitors, it can more reliably place good managers in newly acquired companies. This allows GE to consider acquisitions that others might forgo.

By all accounts, the HR profession should be among the most influential and strategically important. We would expect significant advancements in the sophistication with which HR leaders drive organizational effectiveness and create sustainable strategic success. Yet survey research and our own field experience with top HR leaders suggest that this is not the typical reality for HR, even in organizations that highly value their HR leaders. Instead, HR scorecards focus on costs and activities, and typical goals involve achieving benchmark levels of lowest HR cost per revenue dollar or lowest HR headcount to total headcount. The increasing sophistication of benchmarking and outsourcing accelerates this trend by making costs more apparent and offering many ways to shift massive amounts of HR staff activity and costs out of organizations.[6]

For all the evidence that the quality of talent and organization matters, it is still frustratingly difficult for most business leaders to know precisely where and how investments in employees' talent and organization actually drive strategic success. Academics call this gap the "black box."[7] Business leaders are frustrated with traditional HR, even when it is executed with best-in-class programs at benchmark cost levels. One CFO (now the CEO of his organization) said to us, "I value the hard work of HR, but I worry that our organization may not know which talent issues are the important ones versus which are mostly tactical. I know how to answer that question in finance, marketing, and operations. I'm not sure how to do it for talent. I wish HR had more to offer here."[8] Relentless HR cost cutting can easily become the only way that such frustrated CEOs see to create economic impact through people, even as they wish for something more strategic.

In this chapter we'll show why HR's full potential hasn't been achieved. Our purpose, however, is not to demean HR's potential—it's quite the opposite. We wrote this book in part because it has become simply too common to describe HR's shortcomings without offering solutions. We will describe the factors that limit HR and use them to show how they hold the key to its evolution into a strategic discipline that is as valued and fundamental as finance or marketing.

The implications go well beyond HR. This evolution is not only essential; it is inevitable. Organizations that ignore it will suffer as their competitors figure it out first.

Stubborn Traditionalism in HR Management

In 2005 an article appeared in *Fast Company* entitled "Why We Hate HR."[9] It chronicled many of the all-too-common symptoms of a profession that focuses on administrative activities, requires compliance with rules, demonstrates little logical connection to strategic value, and works diligently on functional programs and practices that have no clear connection to business goals. The article has received a lot of attention. In 2006 a Web search on the title produced over twelve thousand hits, and its author asserts that it got more response than any *Fast Company* article in the prior two years.[10]

What many people don't remember is that in 1981 there was a similar article in the *Harvard Business Review* entitled "Big Hat, No Cattle."[11] The title referred to a "tall, well-dressed businessman" in the Dallas, Texas, airport "wearing a large and immaculate Stetson hat." Nearby, two middle-aged, sunburned men in faded jeans looked him up and down and said to each other, "Big hat, no cattle." The businessman dressed like a cattleman but really had no herd. The sunburned men were the real cattle ranchers, and they didn't need to prove it with a big hat. In 1981 HR had the executive title and the executive offices, and looked and dressed like other business leaders, but the article asserted that all too often there was no evidence of real contribution to business success.

It's the same story twenty-five years apart. As we'll see, this doesn't mean that the HR profession hasn't progressed. It has. It doesn't mean that business leaders don't want to compete better for and with talent and organization resources. They do. It *does* suggest that after twenty-five years of admonishments that HR professionals become strategic business partners and calls for business leaders to tap the potential in their people, organizations still have not produced the kind of change we'd expect. There is an answer to this problem, but it's not to continue doing the same thing better, and it isn't achieved by the HR function alone.

Evidence from many sources confirms that the HR profession has made many technical advances, but in many ways it has changed little. Perhaps the most vivid evidence comes from a unique survey done by the Center for Effective Organizations. Beginning in 1995, HR professionals were asked how much time they spent on strategic pursuits compared to administrative pursuits. They noted the time they remembered spending on various activities five to seven years ago, and then they noted the time they currently spend. Every year the responses suggested that HR professionals perceived a statistically significant shift toward more strategic activities, with the most recent data shown in table 1-1.

Yet when we examine what HR leaders said were their actual activities across the years, the picture is much different. HR leaders in every survey since 1995 have provided virtually the same percentages! There has been very little change over time, as shown in table 1-2.

Obviously, today's arsenal of HR activities is very different and more sophisticated than it was in the mid-1990s, and of course, HR professionals are doing different things and doing many things better. There

TABLE 1-1

How HR professionals believe they spend their time

Percentage of time spent on . . .	5–7 years ago	Current
Maintaining records Collect, track, and maintain data on employees	25.9	13.2
Auditing and controlling Ensure compliance to internal operations, regulations, and legal and union requirements	14.8	13.3
Providing HR services Assist with implementation and administration of HR practices	36.4	32.0
Developing HR systems and practices Design HR programs, policies, and supporting systems	12.6	18.1
Serving as strategic business partner Serve as member of the management team; involved with strategic HR planning, organizational design, and strategic change	9.6	23.5

Source: Edward E. Lawler III, John W. Boudreau, and Susan Mohrman, *Achieving Strategic Excellence* (Palo Alto, CA: Stanford University Press, 2006).

TABLE 1-2

How HR professionals actually spent their time, 1995–2004

Percentage of time spent on . . .	1995	2001	2004
Maintaining records	15.4	14.9	13.4
Auditing and controlling	12.2	11.4	13.4
Providing HR services	31.3	31.3	31.7
Developing HR systems and practices	18.5	19.3	18.2
Serving as strategic business partner	21.9	23.2	23.3

Source: Edward E. Lawler III, John W. Boudreau, and Susan Mohrman, *Achieving Strategic Excellence* (Palo Alto, CA: Stanford University Press, 2006).

are improved information systems, scorecards, benchmarks, outsourcing contracts, and competency models. Workforce plans can now track the headcount moving between jobs using computerized databases and forecasting algorithms. Selection testing is done through kiosks or online surveys. These are better versions of the same tools that HR has been using for decades, and they have made important differences in the efficiency and effectiveness of the HR function. Yet by their own reports, the tables show that HR professionals' focus is still largely on administrative and service-related goals, not on strategic decisions. The data vividly reveals a profession that is getting better and better at the traditional paradigm— but as we shall see, the opportunities for breakthrough strategic successes lie in a new, extended paradigm.

The Essential Evolution: A Paradigm Extension

At the same time that the article titled "Big Hat, No Cattle" appeared in 1981, executives at Pepsi were building an internal HR function that was a significant force in changing the organization from the bottom up. In 1987 Andrall Pearson, a former Pepsi top executive, chronicled the story, which was notable for its rarity. Pearson didn't just note the excellence of the HR function at Pepsi. He correctly understood that the paradigm shift was as much about what business leaders expected from HR and how they worked with HR professionals as it was about what HR did. Pearson said, "Unfortunately, business leaders rarely recognize the potential of the personnel function, so they often fail to staff the department with high-caliber people. Their low expectations then become a self-fulfilling prophecy."[12]

This vicious cycle is still quite common today. The key to breaking it can be seen through the evolution of professions like finance and marketing. HR's mission can typically be summarized by the following statement (which we constructed using several actual examples of company HR missions): *the mission of the HR function is to be a respected business partner, helping the company achieve its goals by providing outstanding services to help manage the company's most important asset, its people.*

This statement defines the value proposition as providing high-quality services in response to client needs. Even strategic HR management is often defined as delivering the HR services that are deemed important to internal clients (such as leadership development, competency systems, incentive pay, etc.). This traditional paradigm of service delivery and client satisfaction is fundamentally limited because it assumes that clients know what they need. Market-based HR and accountability for business results are now recognized as important, but in practice they are typically enacted by using marketing techniques or business results to assess traditional HR services' popularity and perceived association with financial outcomes.[13]

To break out of the traditional focus, or the current paradigm, HR must extend its focus from the services it provides to the decisions that it supports. If it did, the new mission statement would be: *the mission of the HR function is to increase the success of the organization by improving decisions that depend on or impact people.*

This sounds deceptively simple. Yet, when leading organizations make this paradigm shift, things change dramatically—and not just inside the HR management function. Business leaders, HR leaders, and employees are all affected. This shouldn't be surprising. In earlier eras it sounded simple to say, "Technology companies focused only on making great products need to shift to delivering solutions." But this simple insight transformed companies like IBM and GE and marked the demise of competitors that didn't see it or couldn't execute on it. The paradigm extension we describe in this book is similar in its significance to the extension from a product-based focus to a solutions-based focus. Here we apply it to talent. Such a change has significant implications for the HR profession and for everyone who makes decisions about talent and organization resources.

This evolution is as much about business strategy as it is about talent and organization management, and it's as much about organizational strategic leadership as it is about the HR profession. This transformation is inevitable, and we shall see that history suggests the evolution has already begun. However, like organisms that fail to adapt quickly enough, organizations that choose passively to await the evolution may not be around to capitalize on it. It is an essential evolution because those who adapt first will have a significant advantage, and it's an inevitable evolution because the talent resource is simply too important.

The paradox just described is something that HR and organization leaders experience every day. Organizations respect their HR professionals, and HR professionals are working harder than ever and achieving great things. In many ways today's sophisticated service and information platforms provide enormous potential on which to build the new paradigm. Today's HR leaders are generally well respected for the work that they do and for the professional standards they embrace. Business leaders have great admiration for the individual HR leaders they work with, but less for the HR function than for such functions as finance, marketing, and operations. These leaders typically find value in the contributions of their HR leaders but have difficulty articulating the value of the function in driving business success.

This is one reason that, even among very well-respected HR functions, we hear top HR officers say, "We will do great things in the coming year, but the first question my CEO will ask is whether I've reduced the HR budget." Likewise, implementing useful, professional HR programs is important, but it's not the same as having a deep and consistent effect on the organization's vital strategic decisions. The solution to the paradox is that the current paradigm is and will remain valuable and important, so it is not a matter of a paradigm shift, but rather a paradigm extension.

Once the paradigm extension begins, it permeates the organization. It's often seen in a subtle but profound shift in conversations about talent or in the day-to-day relationship between HR leaders and their colleagues. Most organizations have no systematic way to identify when talent strategies that worked in the past must be changed. For example, companies often persist in recruiting only at the same top schools year after year, in an effort to hire the best talent. Yet this often means trolling in exactly the same waters as their competitors, going after exactly the same limited pool of students.

In the 1970s this created significant competitive challenges not only getting enough candidates but also achieving the goals of a racially and gender-diverse pool of hires. Procter & Gamble (P&G) chose a different path. P&G could certainly compete effectively even at the top schools, but a careful analysis of the cost and quality of applicants led it to cut in half the number of schools where it recruited and to pay increased attention to key regional campuses, such as the University of Wisconsin. P&G realized that it could use its proprietary testing technology, called the "M-test" to find the high-potential future leaders more accurately than its competitors. P&G applied the same marketing principles it used for products to the recruiting process. P&G was often the first company on campus to prescreen and prerecruit promising students to sign up for interviews, rather than just waiting to see who applied. P&G nurtured relationships with deans and faculty who could help identify the promising future leaders. The company applied the same techniques to schools where candidates of color or promising female candidates were likely to be found. It provided incentives to the schools in the form of research grants or donations, based on how quickly and how far students progressed through the leadership ranks. The result was a significant increase in candidate quality, retention, and diversity, and a reduction in recruiting costs—all from a policy to stop doing what everyone else was doing and to emphasize logic, analysis, and basic marketing principles in recruitment.[14]

In an organization we worked with in the mid-1990s, the typical approach to workforce planning was for HR to wait until the business strategy and planning were completed, translate the business goals into headcount gaps, and propose HR programs and a budget to address those gaps (such as improved recruiting, staffing, or compensation). Using the decision-focused approach, HR leaders tried something different. They guided the annual headcount review with the following questions:

- What do these employees do that makes the biggest difference to our business?

- How does their activity blend with others in the organization to create that value?

- What are the key processes in the business where these activities have their biggest effect?

- How does improving these processes contribute most to our ability to build and sustain an advantage in the marketplace?

After this encounter, line managers said, "This is a different conversation than I have ever had with someone from HR. I never before saw headcount planning as so strategic! This is causing us to evaluate elements of our strategy that we had missed before." In this book we will describe the logical framework that provided the foundation for these questions.

By the way, the HR professionals asking the questions were moved to line management positions to reflect their business and strategic savvy. We envision a future in which line leaders will likewise move into HR roles precisely so that they can learn how to generate this kind of strategic insight.

The implications of shifting to a decision focus go beyond HR plans and strategies. The paradigm shift has profound implications for employees throughout the organization. *Employee engagement* is a popular term. Yet most organizations are remarkably vague when they explain what employees are engaged with.

One financial services organization we worked with in the 1990s was acquiring companies to build out a complete portfolio of financial services offerings, including credit cards, loans, investment advice, and investment services.[15] Everyone inside and outside the organization knew the strategic objective was to use the brand and the established reputation as a basis to cross-sell other services to consumers and thus create strategic success through synergy. Everyone in the industry was focusing on building a sales force that was good at cross-selling, not just selling one particular product. This organization was investing heavily in sales training just like everyone else. It surveyed salespeople to track their engagement with the synergy strategy, and it held sales managers accountable for raising those engagement scores.

Yet, guided by the new extended paradigm, this company's HR professionals encouraged sales managers to step back from the traditional logic that enhancing sales means making salespeople better and to examine the full array of processes involved in cross-selling. They realized that past training investments had already vastly improved sales processes but that product integration lagged. Salespeople were getting better at selling products and services that weren't well integrated!

Armed with this insight, the organization took a fresh look at the "product integrator" job and discovered that it was defined as the clerical task of recording product features in technical sales documents. Realizing the significance of the product integrators, the organization redefined the product integrator role to emphasize excellence in discovering and implementing product synergies, not just recording product features. Training and other investments for such product integrators were increased, and employees in the product integrator role developed a much clearer idea about where they could make their greatest contributions. Product integrators had always been engaged, but now they knew precisely where to engage. The organization had seen its synergy strategy differently through the perspective of the talent resource.

In this book we'll show that opportunities like this exist in roles as diverse as aircraft engineers, street sweepers at theme parks, and Web designers at specialty retail organizations. The opportunities go untapped because, when it comes to talent and how it is organized, today's guiding models are still rudimentary and focused largely on the programs, not the decisions. Extending the paradigm illuminates these untapped opportunities. As noted earlier, they represent an uncharted strategy that is just waiting to be discovered.

How Talent Decisions Are Made Today

Organizations make decisions about talent all the time. Such decisions are often driven by one of four approaches. The first approach is compliance, which states the rules, regulations, or standards that must be met. This is powerful because often it is directly linked to reducing the risk of penalties, fines, or lawsuits. Decisions based solely on compliance, however, provide little guidance for the increasing array of situations that are not specifically governed by such standards.

The second approach is fads and fashions. Some evidence suggests that HR innovations follow patterns more akin to fashions than to rational strategic logic.[16] For example, between 2001 and 2003, organizations spanning a vast array of sizes, industries, and maturities simultaneously adopted a performance management system that required leaders to rate their employees so that 20 percent were rated top performers, 70 percent were rated middle performers, and 10 percent were rated bottom performers. What was the underlying strategic and economic shift that applied to all these organizations at precisely the same time?

Of course, it was not an economic shift of any kind, but rather a book by Jack Welch (*Jack: Straight From the Gut*) that appeared on the best-seller lists beginning in 2001.[17] Business leaders everywhere read how Welch credited GE's success to its "20-70-10" system. HR leaders tell us that it was not uncommon for a CEO, board member, or head of a division to walk into their offices, place the book on their desk, and say, "This performance management system worked for GE. Why don't we have one?" Few realized that the same performance management system was also applied at Enron! Without a logic, following the fads and fashions will not necessarily lead to good results.

In contrast, business leaders didn't ask their chief marketing officers to adopt GE's approach to advertising or their chief financial officers to adopt GE's approach to debt structure. Marketing and finance are more mature professions with frameworks that business leaders have learned they must use for such decisions. In the absence of such frameworks for human capital, well-meaning and smart business leaders have little choice but to follow fads and fashions, even when the HR practices in vogue don't fit the organization's strategic needs. Even when substantial ROI is associated with practices in other organizations, marketing and finance conduct rigorous analysis to examine whether those results are relevant to their organization.

For example, NASCAR has research showing that the stock price of the average NASCAR sponsor increases the day that a new sponsorship is announced.[18] This does not mean, however, that every company should sponsor a NASCAR team. The marketing decision science dictates that companies consider whether sponsoring a team fits their particular strategic context. It also dictates that marketing practices be applied differently, depending on the market segment. Contrast this with the peanut-butter approach of applying the same performance management system to all employees, regardless of their roles.

The third approach for making talent and organization decisions is equality. Organizations say, "All our employees are important. It would be unfair to treat some of them differently, so everything we do must be fair and applied equally to everyone." Similar debates have ensued regarding revenue management. Over time, decision principles on customer segmentation have guided the development of sophisticated revenue management systems that treat customers differently based on their significance to strategic objectives. Coca-Cola has experimented with vending machines that price soft drinks based on the outside temperature, and Wal-Mart stocks more Pop-Tarts when weather models indicate an area is in for bad weather.[19] Studies in the hotel industry suggest that providing information about the logical basis for differential pricing increases fairness perceptions.[20] Fairness and equality are not the same, but the key to simultaneously achieving both is an effectively communicated, logical basis for differentiation.

The same thing is happening with regard to talent. Equity is important (both in terms of process and outcomes) when it comes to employment, but equity is not the same as equal treatment for all employees, just as it does not mean equal treatment of all customers. Maturing professions make this distinction. We have found this to be one of the most difficult distinctions for organizations to make, but it's one of the most important. We'll describe a logical framework that has helped organizations meet this challenge.

Finally, the fourth basis for talent and organization decisions is strategic logic, which is the decision framework that we will advocate and develop in this book. It is important that leaders inside and outside the HR profession evolve to make more of the vital talent decisions with a deep logical connection to organizational effectiveness and strategic success. Just as with marketing and finance, not every decision will be equally rigorous, but the essential evolution requires that organizations systematically consider such connections more rationally and logically and use them for more of the important talent decisions. Over time and with continued use, the logic and precision will improve, just as it has with finance and marketing. This will not just advance the HR profession; more important, it will advance the organization's strategic capability.

Conditions That Mark the Emergence of a Decision Science

Historical conditions suggest that a talent decision science must emerge soon and that organizations using it will prosper. These conditions include:

- The resource is important for business success.

- The resource is constrained.

- There is a well-developed professional practice supporting the resource, providing the ability to implement decisions and monitor their effects.

Similar conditions existed at the genesis of finance and marketing. In addition, there were business processes in place to implement the decisions, largely through the accounting and sales functions. When these new sciences emerged, there was tremendous competitive advantage in their early application. However, as they became more commonly used and understood, it became increasingly difficult to create breakthrough competitive advantages with the new scientific principles. They became standard practice.

Consider how difficult it is to create and sustain breakthrough competitive advantage through new approaches to decisions about financial resources. The finance decision science has become so mature and well developed that there is increasingly little variation across organizations. Not only are additional innovations difficult to create, but they also get copied quickly—because the importance of financial decisions is widely recognized, and mature decision systems in organizations detect and absorb such innovations fast.

For example, at one time currency valuation anomalies that present arbitrage opportunities lasted days; now they last milliseconds. Financial systems have evolved to detect them and move massive amounts of capital to exploit them quickly. Markets correct in seconds, and currency valuation anomalies disappear. The same thing can be seen in marketing, with so many companies adopting a "fast-follower" model that allows advantages to be more quickly duplicated and differentiators more difficult to sustain.

The point is that the first organizations to recognize the emergence of a decision science frequently find massive opportunities for improved sustainable strategic success. As we'll show, the conditions for the emergence of a decision science for talent and organization resources exist today.

Distinctions Between Markets, Decision Sciences, and Professional Practices

If we want to understand how a profession becomes strategic, we can't do it by looking within the profession or by asking internal customers whether it is strategic. Rather, we must begin where strategy is formed and enacted, in the markets where organizations compete and thrive.

There are at least three markets vital to organizational success: the financial market, the customer/product market, and the talent market. In the financial and customer/product markets, there is a clear distinction between the professional practice that defines how organizations operate in the market and the decision science used to analyze and deploy the resources there. For example, there is a clear distinction between accounting (the professional practice) and finance (the decision science). Accounting is vital for management reporting and external requirements, while finance develops tools used to make decisions about appropriate debt structure, internal rate-of-return thresholds, and so forth. There is an equally clear distinction between the professional practice of sales and the decision science of marketing. Excellent sales practices and measures are vital, but they're very different from the tools used to make decisions about customer segmentation, market position, and the product portfolio.

Today the differences between accounting and finance are so clear that we seldom even consider them. The competencies to be a successful accountant are related but clearly quite distinct from those for a successful financial executive (CFO, treasurer, etc.), and professional curricula reflect this. The industry itself has segmented this way—large accounting firms are very different from investment banking firms that focus on finance. Similarly, the competencies and activities of sales are clearly distinct from those of marketing.

This does not mean that the professional practice is merely administrative or less important. The decision science cannot exist without the professional practice; the professional practice must, in fact, precede the decision science. Few organizations survive with great marketing and ineffective sales, or with great finance and unprofessional accounting. Today the synergy between accounting and finance, or between sales and marketing, is so strong that it is easy to overlook how the decision sciences evolved from the professional practices and how they are both inextricably related yet distinct. Taking a closer look at this symbiotic relationship between the professional practice and the decision science reveals insights about the evolution of HR and the talent decision science that will change it.

Like finance and marketing, HR helps the firm operate within a critical market—in this case, the market for talent. Organizations cannot succeed in the financial and customer markets without both effective decisions and professional practices, but they are two distinct elements. Organizations will increasingly compete through the synergy of effective decisions aligned with professional practices in the talent market. When we see this distinction applied to HR and talent, we see that organizational decision processes in the talent market are less mature and refined than those used in finance or marketing, while the HR professional practices are more mature. Today the distinction between professional practices and effective decision systems is less clear in the talent market. Yet a clear understanding of this difference reveals the path for the coming evolution.

Decision Sciences Evolve from Professional Practices

While accounting and finance are clearly distinct, as are sales and marketing, perhaps the most valuable insights can be drawn from their synergy and how the decision science evolved from the professional practice. Accounting is about five hundred years old and was a well-developed profession long before the decision science of finance showed how accounting measures could support decisions based on concepts (such as relative returns on capital) and how different factors (margin, asset productivity, and leverage) affect those returns.

Finance emerged in the early 1900s and is largely credited to the DuPont organization, with the DuPont model still in wide use today.[21] Why the early 1900s? Because that is when capital acquisition and deployment became an important source of competitive advantage, and when the ability to differentiate which businesses could generate an appropriate return on capital became vital to effective decisions. Before that, organizations consisted of business units that, even if quite large, had generally consistent capital returns. With advancing industrial production, capital investment decisions took on more importance within companies and across capital markets, and the tools of finance evolved to improve these decisions.[22] For example, Sears was a large organization, but its capital model varied little from location to location.

Similarly, sales is as old as trade itself, and sales practices were a well-developed profession long before the decision science of marketing used sales information to create decision models such as customer segmentation and product life cycles. Alfred Sloan restructured GM by aligning brands to specific customer segments and charted a new course. This strategy meant, for example, that the Chevrolet division would make

midmarket cars, not Cadillacs. In the years that followed, the decision
science of marketing made rapid advancements as the size and sophistication of customer and product markets made systematic decisions—
about market segmentation, product line management, branding, and so
forth—a competitive factor for organizations. Marketing evolved from focusing almost exclusively on advertising practices to recognizing advertising as only one of many tools to be synergistically deployed to achieve
strategic success and increased value.[23] During the 1950s decisions about
the competitive customer moved from being advertising-research oriented
to being decision oriented.[24] Top management became accountable and
was provided tools to integrate marketing with the overall business objectives through strategic deployment decisions.[25] Today, in packaged goods
companies like Pepsi and Kraft, products or packaging are segmented by
the type of retail outlet where they'll be sold. You'll find single-serve
Pepsi in a bucket of ice in a small convenience store and six-packs on the
shelf at room temperature in supermarkets.

As figure 1-1 shows, the historical lessons from finance and marketing
suggest that today's HR challenges will not be addressed merely through
incremental improvements in the professional practices of HR, as important as such practices will remain. Today's HR functions typically create
value by focusing on delivery of HR practices (staffing, development,
compensation, labor relations, etc.), based on professional and often
well-researched principles. These practices are important, and studies in-

FIGURE 1-1

Evolution from professional practice to the decision science

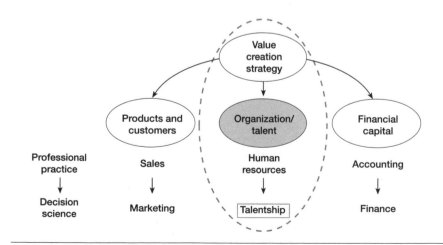

dicate that when they are done well, they add value to the organization.[26] Yet professional practices alone do not systematically address the increasing sophistication and importance of talent markets and today's competitive challenges.

Finance frameworks create organizational value by enhancing decisions that depend on or impact financial resources. Marketing frameworks create organizational value by enhancing decisions that depend on or impact customer or product resources. Finance and marketing provide reliable and profoundly logical frameworks that connect financial and customer capital to the organization's sustainable strategic success. Strategic decisions must go beyond generic best practices to create a unique and sustainable competitive position for the organization.[27]

Talentship: The New Decision Science

The lessons from marketing and finance tell us that the goal of a talent decision science would be to increase the organization's success by improving decisions that impact or depend on talent resources. We have coined the term *talentship* to describe the new decision science and to reflect the notion of stewardship of employee talent resources. Figure 1-1 shows that talentship is to HR what finance is to accounting, and what marketing is to sales. The talentship decision science provides a logic that connects human capital, organizational design, organizational effectiveness, and ultimately, strategic success.

The talent resource as we define it includes not just the talents that your organization knows about and manages but all those talents that are potentially available and valuable, if only you knew about them. It includes not just the people you have and how they are organized but the people you potentially could get and the organizing decisions you could make. For example, in the earlier example of product integration, the organization knew and tracked the clerical talent among its product integrators through its system of job descriptions and performance tools. What it didn't track was their capacity to discover and implement new product integration approaches. That uncharted human capacity was the key to a game-changing product integration strategy.

Improving the decisions about this resource is the domain of talentship. The talent resource not only includes the abilities of individuals; it also includes their motivations and the opportunities they encounter. It includes concepts such as human capital and knowledge. The decision science of talentship also includes a structure for improving decisions about how to enhance individual contributions, as well as how to enhance the way individuals interact in formal and informal organizational designs, structures, and so on. Talentship is concerned with improving decisions about the talents of people and how they organize and interact.

The Talent War Shows the Need for Talentship

The *war for talent* refers to the need for organizations to effectively attract, develop, and retain necessary human resources, particularly where they are going to be scarce, paying most attention to HR practices that get and keep more of the scarce talent. The talent war illustrates the conditions that we described earlier: the talent resource is critical for success and increasingly constrained. In addition, there is wide variation in how well the talent resource is managed, which provides the conditions necessary for significant competitive shifts and sustained competitive advantage.

Much of the talent war debate, however, still revolves around identifying the HR professional practices that enable organizations to get and keep the scarce talent. Talentship is relevant to the talent war because it addresses decisions about how to compete more effectively in vital human capital markets, but talentship encourages an expanded perspective.

Talentship suggests the first question should be "In what vital human capital markets does winning the talent war make the biggest difference to our strategic success?" Talentship helps organizations identify where winning the talent war matters most. It provides a strategic logic to determine unique ways to compete for scarce talent, not just mimic the practices that have worked for others.

Most writing about the talent war presumes that winning means getting and keeping more of the scarce talent. A talentship perspective, however, reveals that this is only one option for the strategic management of these resources. For example, shortages of high-quality fossil fuels make it prudent to invest in electrical generation facilities that operate effectively with a wider range of fuel quality. Talentship defines similar alternatives for talent resources. The best response to a shortage of high-quality call-center talent may be to redefine the role so that automated systems provide more guidance and can operate with a wider variety of talent quality. You don't need a human being to tell you whether a flight is delayed or to take your frequent-flier number, but you may well need one to determine whether you can take your fifteen-pound cat in the cabin.

A second alternative for scarce resources is to deploy them where they have the greatest effect. An organization routinely analyzes its manufacturing operations to ensure they are devoted to the mix of products that generates the highest overall margin. Talentship suggests a similar approach to talent and organization resources. If leaders or engineers are in short supply, it is vital to allocate them where they can have the greatest impact. The talent war debate largely focuses on only one of the options—getting more talent—and the traditional HR response is to design ever more creative programs for acquiring, developing, and retaining talent.

Recognizing that there is a talent war is akin to DuPont recognizing that there was a "war for capital" and GM's Alfred Sloan recognizing that there was a "war for customers." Both organizations responded to this insight not simply by searching for practices to get more capital or customers, but with some of the first sophisticated systems to guide optimal decisions about capital and customers. In today's talent war, organizations must go beyond the traditional paradigm of building ever more sophisticated HR practices to attract and keep talent. They must address talent as a competitive resource through a decision science.

The Essential Evolution and the HR Professional's Role

It is a commonly held fallacy that the future of the HR profession lies exclusively in the realm of roles such as "strategic business partner," "organizational architect," or "human capital change agent." The idea seems to be that if HR professionals aren't in one of these roles, they are irrelevant, outsourced, or obsolete. Of course, these roles are important, but history shows that mature professions extend their role, rather than leaving earlier roles behind. When finance emerged, all accountants didn't have to become financial analysts. When marketing emerged, all salespeople didn't have to become chief marketing officers. Figure 1-2 shows that this is a paradigm extension, not a substitution.

Finance and marketing have evolved from an exclusive focus on control, first extending the focus to providing value-adding services and finally

FIGURE 1-2

Extending the HR paradigm

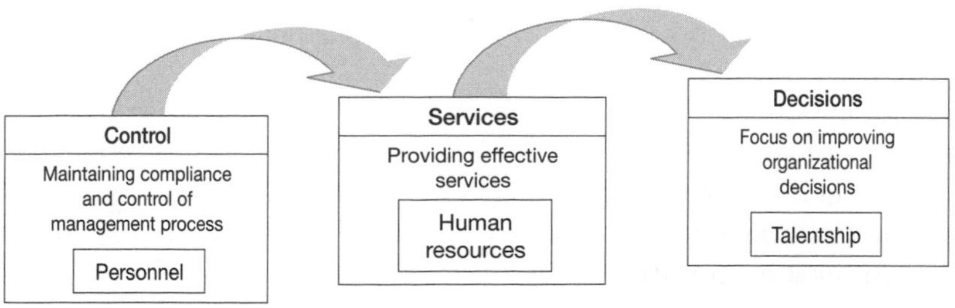

extending it to improve key decisions. In its control role, a profession creates value through assuring compliance with important rules, regulations, or standards. The Sarbanes-Oxley Act in the United States recently increased control activities in accounting functions.[28] Likewise, regulations governing advertising content reflect this focus in marketing. Regarding talent, this focus is associated with the personnel function (often seen as administrative). However, compliance remains important, such as adhering to legal requirements or international labor standards.

The services role is also important. In finance it means there must be timely and accurate management of accounting and reporting, and in marketing it means there must be strong advertising or sales services. Similarly, it will always be important to provide strong HR services, such as compensation, succession planning, staffing, and training.

However, fields such as finance and marketing have augmented their service delivery model with a decision science that teaches frameworks that allow those inside and outside the profession to make better decisions. For example, a service delivery approach in marketing would provide excellent advertising where and when business leaders requested it. The more modern decision-focused approach teaches business leaders about the principles of customer segments and customer response to advertising, and then holds leaders accountable for their success in creating a strategy that increases sales and profits in key customer segments.

In this book we describe a decision science for talent and organization resources and how organization leaders must learn the principles of that decision science to improve their talent decisions, just as they learned principles of marketing and finance. As we shall see, a significant new role for the HR profession will be to develop, articulate, and teach these principles. This does not mean simply applying finance and accounting formulas to HR programs and processes. Rather, it means learning the principles that defined the evolution of these fields into powerful, decision-supporting functions. Those evolutionary principles provide a blueprint for what's next for HR.

Objectives of the Book

In the chapters that follow, we strive to:

- Provide a manifesto for business leaders who realize there is something more than today's definition of HR as a strategic partnership and want to elevate the quality and rigor of decisions about human capital in their organization

- Provide a specific logical framework that connects human capital to organizational effectiveness and strategic success

- Articulate how the same logic that historically created breakthrough insights in finance and marketing can be applied to competing with and through talent

- Describe a new science of human capital decisions, analogous to the finance and marketing decision sciences for money and customers/offerings

- Demonstrate tangibly how HR and line leaders can compete with and through human capital just as strategically as they compete with and through technology, money, and brands

Organization of the Book

Chapter 1 has introduced talentship, the essential evolution that extends the HR paradigm from services toward decisions. Chapter 2 defines a decision science and its supporting elements and shows how more mature decision sciences like finance and marketing guide the path toward a decision science for talent. We see that a logical decision framework is a fundamental pillar of a decision science. Chapter 3 describes the decision framework called the "HC BRidge model" and shows how its elements provide a logical connection between organization and talent decisions, and strategic success. This model is the organizing framework for the book and shows how investments in talent and organization are connected through efficiency, effectiveness, and impact. Chapters 4 through 8 use the decision framework to show how organizations can more purposely identify their strategic pivot-points, identify the organization and talent pivot-points that matter most, and then identify the programs, policies, and investments that will make those pivot-points happen. Chapter 9 describes the implications of talentship for human capital and organizational measurement. Chapter 10 describes what we have learned about implementing talentship organizations during our ten years of working with organizations and explores what's next for HR.

2

A Decision Science
Applied to Talent

Understanding the Necessary Components

Chapter 1 defined the goal of the talentship decision science: "to increase the success of the organization by improving decisions that depend on or impact talent resources." In this chapter we define the concept of a decision science and its necessary components. We concentrate here on the elements that characterize all successful decision sciences and how they apply to talent. Chapter 3 will more fully describe the specific decision framework that we use as a pillar of the talentship decision science—the framework that is the basis for much of the rest of this book.

Why a "Decision Science"?

In about 1999 we began using the term *decision science* to capture the nature of the essential evolution for HR. Since then, its use has become increasingly common among HR executives, thought leaders, and academics. The 2005 book of essays by thought leaders on the future of HR that was copublished by the Society for Human Resource Management contains an entire section entitled "See HR as a Decision Science and Bring Discipline to It."[1] This section includes a chapter from us that applies talentship concepts to the sustainable enterprise.[2] It also includes other chapters, such as "Science Explodes Human Capital Mythology"; "Human Resource Accounting, Human Capital Management, and the Bottom Line"; "Improving Human Resources' Analytical Literacy"; and "The Dual Theory of Human Resource Management and Business Performance."

Yet there is no widely accepted definition of a talent decision science. For decades there has been a general science of decisions and decision making, producing insights about how decision makers behave and the factors that enhance and reduce their rationality and accuracy. Our concept of a decision science for talent draws on this research. As we shall see, the components of a decision science help define the necessary elements for improving talent decisions and the relevance of the HR profession. First, let's consider the power of combining *decisions* and *science*.

Decisions

Why do we focus on decisions? As we saw in chapter 1, marketing and finance evolved to the strategically influential functions they represent today in large part by extending their paradigm from compliance to services to decisions. Functional service excellence alone cannot achieve strategic success through these resources because they are integral to the ongoing success of the organization, not isolated within a single function. The majority of decisions that depend on or impact financial capital or customers are made by those in general leadership roles outside the finance and marketing functions. This is true for talent decisions as well.

When we ask line or HR leaders to think of a decision that depended on or affected talent resources but in retrospect was not made well, even companies with best-in-class HR functions can describe numerous examples. Many of the examples are remarkably consistent. The talent decision mistakes are *not* typically made by HR professionals. Poor talent decisions seldom have poor HR programs as the root cause; instead, they're made by well-intentioned leaders with unintended talent implications.

For example, one highly specialized high-tech firm made a decision to relocate to be closer to its key customer, one that accounted for well over 50 percent of revenues. The decision logic was that the organization could more efficiently and quickly serve this large customer by locating its operations closer. What was overlooked was that the key services required several sophisticated and highly specialized experts. When the move was announced, more experts than anticipated left the organization, creating a disruption that was far more damaging to client relationships and the company's reputation than the benefits of proximity. The decision required integrating three perspectives: financial, marketing, and talent. The financial and marketing elements were logically considered, but the failure to accurately consider the talent implications undermined the intended benefits.

Several senior executives we have worked with have noted that HR strategies often reflect traditionally critical industry needs, such as "avoid employee strikes" in companies where heavy manufacturing is vital and where leaders often worked in labor relations before advancing to top HR roles. In many sales organizations the rallying cry is "reduce turnover" because turnover costs are so apparent. HR leaders point out that without a logical decision framework, such goals can become so prominent that they mask other significant organizational needs.

The greatest opportunity to improve talent and organization decisions is by improving those decisions that are made outside the HR function. Just like with decisions about financial and customer resources, talent decisions reside with executives, managers, supervisors, and employees who make decisions that impact talent, including their own as well as those they are responsible for or interact with. Even in core HR processes—such as succession planning, performance management, selection, and leadership development—potential improvements in effectiveness rely far more heavily on improving the competency and engagement of non-HR leaders than on anything that HR typically controls directly.

The relocation example is typical in that most significant business decisions impact multiple resources, so the objective should be to equip leaders with more comprehensive decision frameworks. It's not a matter of choosing between people versus profits, with the organization's financial controller arguing for profits and the HR leader acting as the employee advocate. Instead, the goal is a decision science that enables leaders to integrate talent resources with other vital resources. To be sure, this improves talent and organization decisions, but its ultimate goal is to improve strategic decisions more broadly.

Science

Why use the term *science*? Because the most successful professions have decision systems that follow scientific principles and that have a strong capacity to quickly incorporate new scientific knowledge into practical applications. Disciplines such as finance, marketing, and operations not only provide leaders with frameworks and concepts that describe how those resources affect strategic success; they also reflect the findings from universities, research centers, and scholarly journals. Their decision models are compatible with the language and structure of the scholarly science that supports them.

For example, in operations research there is often a very close connection between the technical tools used in industry and the scholarly research that informs them. In the arena of total quality management (TQM), the decision frameworks used by managers reflect fundamental logical elements—such as plan, do, check, and act—that translate into logical connections with such processes as inspection, maintenance, adjustment, and equipment replacement. This logic allows managers' decision models to be quickly informed by research on topics like statistical process control, control charts, and time-series statistical analysis. It also provides a context for researchers, who frame their research questions consistently with the logic and practical issues facing leaders who apply TQM.[3]

With talent and organization, the logical frameworks used by leaders often bear distressingly little similarity to the scholarly research in HR and human behavior at work.[4] As we will see throughout this book, this is regrettable because there is much that leaders can learn from scholarly findings and much that scholars can learn by better incorporating business leaders' insights into their research.[5] Compare the approach to bond ratings in finance and employee assessment practices in HR. Both strive to provide a valid and reliable measure of the future performance of an asset with some risk. A treasury department is expected to purchase information on scientifically rigorous bond ratings in its investment decisions. HR functions often lack support for scientific employee assessment investments (valid tests, interviews, assessment centers, surveys, etc.) because they don't see the value. In fact, frameworks for comparing the costs of employment testing to their benefits have existed since the 1940s, but they are not widely used, in part because organizations' decision frameworks have few connections to the logical principles of these models.[6]

A decision science also approaches decisions through a scientific method, which means that questions are framed so that they are testable and falsifiable with data-based results. It means that the logic supporting the decision science is modified when new findings make old ideas obsolete. It means that the decision framework clearly translates new scientific findings into practical implications. This scientific method includes, but goes well beyond, a fact-based approach to HR. Many articles that carry the label of "decision science" are about improved analytics, measurement, or scorecards. Data is certainly an element of a decision science, as we will describe later, but much of the data being used by HR lacks the logical framework and the analysis required to use it to advance either decisions or science.

A true decision science does more than just incorporate facts and measures. A decision science draws on and informs scientific study related to the resource. There is a vast array of research about human behavior at work, labor markets, and how organizations can better compete with and for talent and organization resources. Such disciplines as psychology, economics, sociology, organization theory, game theory, and even operations management and human physiology all contain potent research frameworks and findings. Unfortunately, the transfer of such findings into actual decisions is often woefully slow or nonexistent. A decision science connects research to the practical dilemmas facing decision makers in organizations. It also provides a means to apply research on talent and organization to other fields and to bring insights from other scientific fields (such as operations, strategy, marketing, etc.) to bear on talent decisions within organizations.

Components of a Decision Science for Talent

To implement a decision science for talent, it is important to consider what is required. Based on what we have learned from fields outside HR and our experience in implementing a decision science for HR within organizations, we find that there are five important elements in a mature decision science:

- Decision framework

- Management systems integration

- Shared mental model

- Data, measurement, and analysis

- Focus on optimization

Decision Framework

The decision framework defines the logical connection between the decisions about a resource and the organization's ultimate goals. It defines how the organization should think about the talent and organizational implications of business decisions in a common and consistent way. It provides the basis for evaluating and improving the decisions that involve the resource.

An effective decision framework provides a consistent logical model of the chain of causal connections divided into independent elements. The DuPont return on equity (ROE) model is a good illustration.[7] There is a goal ROE segmented into three elements (margin, asset productivity, and leverage), as shown in figure 2-1.

ROE is a consistent and logical model that can be expressed as an algebraic formula. It also depicts the causal chain of capital:

$$\text{Equity} \rightarrow \text{Assets} \rightarrow \text{Sales} \rightarrow \text{Profits}$$

Starting at the denominator in the right corner of the model, the causal chain can be described as follows:

FIGURE 2-1

DuPont return on equity model

| | Margin | Asset productivity | Leverage |

- Equity (investment) is used to acquire assets (the ratio of assets to equity is leverage).

- Assets are used to generate sales (the ratio of sales to assets is the asset productivity).

- Sales generate profits (the ratio of profits to sales is the margin).

There is a significant amount of independence between margin, asset productivity, and leverage. While there is almost never complete independence between the elements, a good decision framework will achieve as much as possible. Within the DuPont model, lowering the cost of goods sold could increase margins without affecting asset productivity or leverage. Increasing the accounts receivable could improve asset productivity without affecting margin or leverage. Finally, reducing equity by increasing debt could increase leverage without affecting asset productivity or operating margin.

The same standard chain of causal connections can also be seen in the decision frameworks from marketing. While there can be many variations, a typical decision framework for marketing is:

Investments → Mix (such as the "four P's" of product, price, promotion, and placement) → Targets (typically customer or market segments, such as males 18–25 years old) → Lifetime Profits

HC BRidge: The decision framework for talentship. The causal chain for talent and organization decisions can be described as:

Investments → Program and Practices (efficiency) → Performance of Organization Elements and Talent Pools (effectiveness) → Organization's Sustainable Strategic Success (impact)

Figure 2-2 illustrates the causal logic of finance, marketing, and talentship that we have described. While the analogy is not perfectly precise, you can see that the underlying logic is similar. The point is not that the talentship logic maps perfectly against marketing and finance, but rather that it is logically consistent with them. Resources are expended on activities or assets; those activities or assets produce changes in targets, such as sales, customers, and talent pools; those targets produce changes in financial outcomes or other sustainable strategic success factors.

The segments are also independent. You can spend the same amount to produce training activities (efficiency) and get far different results from the training programs and practices (effectiveness). Likewise, you can enhance skills in different talent pools (effectiveness), but the outcomes achieved through the new skills can vary significantly. The same level of efficiency can produce different levels of effectiveness. The same level of effectiveness can produce significantly different impact. As we shall see, when organizations lack such a framework, they mistakenly consider only one part of the logical chain (such as squeezing HR budgets to produce more efficiency without considering effectiveness or impact), or they mistakenly assume that improving one element improves the others (such as assuming that if employees have more training, the organization will compete better on its unique knowledge).

We call this decision framework for organization and talent the "HC BRidge framework" and refer to impact, effectiveness, and efficiency as "anchor points." (The "HC" stands for "Human Capital" and the "BRidge" reflects the metaphor of three anchor points supporting a set of linking

FIGURE 2-2

Finance, marketing, and talentship progressions

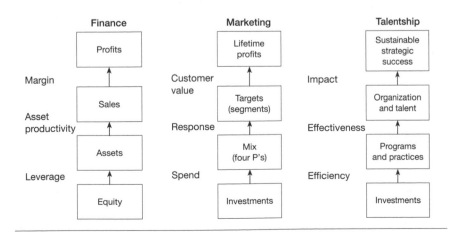

elements that collectively span the logical connections between investments in talent and organization programs and practices and the ultimate goal of sustainable strategic success. The capitalized letters B and R
in HC BRidge symbolize Boudreau and Ramstad.) This framework will be
described in more detail in chapter 3, and each anchor point and linking element will be used throughout the book to describe how the decision
framework reveals new insights about competing for and with talent.

Traditional HR Decision Frameworks. HR leaders' common first reaction to talentship and the need for a decision framework for HR is "We already have many systems designed to help leaders outside HR make
decisions, like salary structures and competency systems." Consider salary
structures. Virtually everyone knows their salary grade, and employees
and managers routinely use salary structures in their decisions about
budgeting, headcount planning, merit pay, and other rewards. Because
salary grades are often the only available framework for mapping the organization's talent resources, they can become the default framework for
things such as signature authority, participation in leadership programs,
parking space allocation, and many other decisions unrelated to the original purpose. The salary grade system certainly affects decisions, but it is
not a decision framework in the way that we have defined it. It is an organizing framework for the delivery of an HR system, not a decision framework for the resource.

Competency systems that span an enterprise serve a similar purpose.
When done well, they provide a common architecture for defining, measuring, and developing capabilities within an organization, including not
only the requirements for a job but also the logical progression and important transition points between jobs. Such systems can be used to align
key talent management systems, and individual measurement to help develop both individuals and the talent pool overall. Like salary grade structures, they are very important and useful, supporting both decisions and
data analysis. Even well-developed versions of competency systems, however, do not provide necessary insight into important business questions
such as the talent implications of alternative business models, organizational structures and design, competing talent market value propositions,
and the value of HR investments.

Salary structures and competency systems are very similar to the organizing frameworks such as the "chart of accounts" in accounting that
existed before the decision science of finance emerged.[8] The chart of accounts provides a classification system to organize large amounts of data,
and it certainly improves the consistency of decisions. Like the chart of

accounts, the salary grade system provides its primary value through systematic management control, and it emerged during the control era of personnel that we described earlier. It often creates more value in restraining excessive investment than in identifying areas where increased compensation would optimize organizational value. Competency models emerged more recently, during the services stage of the HR profession, to integrate and align HR services. When compensation and competency systems are integrated within a decision science framework, they become even more powerful and offer potentially greater impact on the organization, because they can be deployed in a more strategically relevant and integrated perspective.

Management Systems Integration

The next component of a decision science is the integration of its decision framework and key principles into the general management systems. The decision framework must be integrated so that decisions about different resources seamlessly support the overall organization and business processes. When this is done well, it induces decisions that consider all the key resources, including talent, rather than focusing on resources in isolation. This integration also requires more alignment between the general business planning processes and functional planning processes. For example, planning for the finance and marketing functions is closely tied to planning for the overall organization.

Financial frameworks are well integrated into general management systems in most organizations. In fact, one challenge to improving talent and organization decisions is that companies only have financial management systems and lack well-developed decision systems for other important resources. For example, many organizations have strategic-planning processes that seem to be far more focused on preparing the long-range financial plan than on optimizing the strategic position. It is not so much that the finance function intentionally dominates but rather that its processes and frameworks are much more mature and integrated. The same integrated attention is rare in strategic planning for the leadership capabilities that support the financial plan.

Two types of management systems must be integrated with a mature decision science for organization and talent:

- Management systems outside the HR function, where talent issues should be considered and addressed, which include strategic planning, product line management, corporate development (e.g., mergers and acquisitions), operational budgeting, and capital budgeting

- Talent management systems (often within the HR function) that must consider the strategic context of the organization, including workforce planning, staffing, development, performance management, compensation, and succession planning

Perhaps the most difficult way to change organizations is to impose new decision frameworks that compete with useful management processes already in place. Too often, HR organizational effectiveness leaders roll out their planning and decision systems as distinct additions to existing processes. In our experience we've encountered workforce planning systems that have little commonality and integration with the long-range planning processes. HR leaders would often better serve the organization by improving the business planning process in partnership with other leaders rather than deploying new HR processes that are potentially poor substitutes. We find that the more HR and talent planning processes are separate and distinct from the core management processes, the less they are strategically effective.

Let us illustrate how talent decision frameworks can integrate with management systems using the capital budgeting system, which is well refined in most organizations. One of the basic financial assumptions is to expect a higher return on investments with higher risk. Many of the potential risk factors in capital investments are linked to talent resources. One way that capital budgeting could be more integrated with talent resource decisions is to specifically identify the talent and organization risk factors associated with capital investments (availability and quality of leadership, degree of organizational change required, experience in the organization with the technology, etc.) and then set a higher return hurdle rate for investments that are higher risk due to organizational factors.

Integration of talent and organization systems with management systems must also consider the sequence of planning processes. It is not unusual to encounter organizations where the talent planning process occurs long after the organizational planning process has concluded, and where the HR budget basically distributes the allotted budget for headcount or training. In some organizations HR planning couldn't possibly affect organizational strategic decisions because the HR process occurs *after* all the key strategic decisions are made. Even something as simple as timing the HR planning process so its results are available to the broader budgeting and planning process can significantly enhance integration with the management processes and the quality of decisions that result.

Leaders at Pepsi in the 1980s referred to decisions about hiring and training levels as the "human capex," meaning the human capital expenditure plan. They believed that organizations should treat the human capex process as equally important as the financial capex. As John Bronson, former executive vice president of HR at Pepsicola Worldwide, recalls:

> One of the legacies of Andrall [Andy] Pearson at PepsiCo was the MRPA, the management resources planning audit. It was his audit of the talent of the organization. He was unabashed that it was his process, not HR's process, and not even the division presidents' process. He expected leaders to treat their human capex with the same importance as the more traditional financial capex. Andy believed that blue-chip companies required blue-chip players. He was relentless in driving the process through the PepsiCo organization. He was like a merchant banker reviewing a financing plan. If the business-unit CEO couldn't explain how the talent plan supported the growth, budget, and financial capex, not only would his plan be in jeopardy; he might lose his job. To Andy, if you didn't have a solid plan for how talent supported both superior business performance and growth, you weren't a serious contender for larger jobs.[9]

A fundamental requirement for this kind of business leader accountability is a shared decision science that aligns functional and general management systems. HR is a less mature profession, so there is often less consistency in the decision models used within the profession when compared to more mature fields like finance. Here is one of our favorite discussion questions for business and HR leaders: suppose you asked ten controllers to address a specific financial challenge, and you asked ten HR professionals to address a specific organizational or talent challenge. Where would the responses be more consistent and aligned, among the controllers or the HR professionals?

The answer is nearly always that there will be less consistency and alignment on the people issues than the financial ones. In addition, HR leaders' different backgrounds, experiences, and perspectives will drive variation among their responses. This can be seen when there is significant misalignment between HR professionals at headquarters and the business-unit HR professionals. Examples include different approaches to goal setting in performance management and compensation, and different assumptions and models for individual development from the professionals who drive the design of succession-planning and development systems.

This is a symptom of HR functions operating without a common point of view. Without a consistent decision framework connecting the various elements of the talent management systems and decisions, they lack a consistent message to integrate their core systems, much less affect the broader management systems outside the HR function.

Thus, aligning HR systems, such as talent planning and HR functional planning, with the decision framework is a vital requirement of a mature and effective decision science and a platform for integrating talent decisions within the broader management systems.

Shared Mental Model

A successful decision science is used by organizational leaders as a natural part of their work. Its logic elements are a part of the mental models and mind-set of key decision makers inside and outside the profession. All organizational leaders are expected to be conversationally competent in the basic principles of the decision framework and are required to have the skills and professional support to use the systems that require their direct involvement. Every business leader must be conversant with principles from the finance decision science, such as net present value and assets and liabilities. Likewise, they must be familiar with marketing decision science concepts, such as customer segments and product life cycles. The marketing and finance functions provide support and deeper professional capabilities, but all managers know that they cannot abdicate the basic knowledge of finance and marketing principles to others. These same principles operate in management systems like budgeting, so leaders not only understand why they are important, but they routinely use the fundamental decision science concepts. So there is less resistance and more opportunity to improve decision making with those systems. It doesn't seem strange if marketing or finance suggests enhancements to the decision systems for general managers because those managers are already accustomed to working with marketing and finance principles.

Today, individual leaders too often approach talent and organization decisions with vastly different mental models, divergent logical principles, and a focus on very different factors. The sources of principles vary—from motivational speakers and high-profile executives to successful athletes and an occasional college professor. Without a common understanding of the key principles, talent and organization management systems lack context and are seen as administrative or bureaucratic. As the talent and organization decision science matures, its principles will become more consistent and a more natural part of the mind-set of both line leaders and HR leaders, with the appropriate level of sophistication.

To achieve this goal, HR leaders will need to focus more on teaching than telling, a significant change. Finance and marketing are effective in part because their principles have been taught to business leaders in business school, followed up with executive development, and reinforced with real-world practice and career experiences in which leaders are usually coached by functional specialists. Even with very mature and strong staff functions within finance and marketing, the need for senior leaders with well-developed competencies in finance and marketing is seen as important. Talentship will produce decision frameworks that will be consistently taught to organization leaders, becoming a natural part of their work and decisions.

The need for a talentship mind-set is also vital for HR functional leaders. In our experience there are almost always some HR professionals in any organization who effectively understand, teach, and enhance decisions based on how talent connects to strategic success. These HR professionals typically admit that they learned to provide this kind of support in their own way, with little systematic instruction or development. One HR professional put it well: "This capability is critical to our future, but it doesn't scale because everyone does it and learns it differently."[10]

A decision framework contributes to scale by developing, using, and teaching a consistent, logical point of view about how to connect talent resources to strategic success. A logical point of view provides a consistent script for an ongoing dialogue about talent and strategy, allowing more reliable and consistent diagnosis, analysis, and action on talent issues throughout the organization.

Data, Measurement, and Analysis

A mature decision science has data, measurement, and analysis aligned with its decision framework principles. These are refined and deployed through management systems, used by leaders who understand the principles, and supported by professionals who add insight and expertise. Today finance reflects this level of maturity almost everywhere, and marketing approaches this level of maturity, particularly in industries where competitive dynamics hinge on marketing sophistication, such as consumer products and multilocation retail.

These systems have evolved over decades, and today we hardly notice how well integrated financial measurement and analysis processes are with financial decision models. It seems to have always been that way. For example, as described in table 2-1, today the ratios commonly measured in financial decisions and the structure of accounting statements link directly to the DuPont decision framework. Similarly, marketing decision frameworks provide the logical structure for customer relationship management and customer analysis systems, which use vast amounts of data mining and advanced analytics to produce competitive insights.[11]

In stark contrast, HR data, information, and measurement face a paradox today. Although there is increasing sophistication in technology,

TABLE 2-1

Ratios measured in financial decisions

	Common supporting analysis ratios	Source of data for the numerator and denominator
Margin	Gross margin	Both are from the operating statement (profit and losses)
	Cost of goods sold	
	Sales, general, and administrative expense ratio	
	HR as a percentage of revenue	
	Operating margin	
Asset productivity	Accounts receivable (in days)	One is from the operating statement, and the other is from the balance sheet
	Accounts payable (in days)	
	Inventory turns	
	Cash operating cycle	
Leverage	Debt-to-equity ratio	Both are from the balance sheet

data availability, and the capacity to report and disseminate HR information, frustration increases when investments in HR data systems, scorecards, and integrated enterprise resource systems fail to create the strategic insights needed to drive organizational effectiveness. One reason for this paradox is that the technological advances have outpaced the fundamental logic connecting talent and organization decisions to strategic success. Major elements of marketing and finance are well over fifty years old, so those decision sciences were far more mature by the time technology advanced. The computer-enhanced systems could build on well-developed decision frameworks, integrated management systems, and shared mental models, making information technology much more valuable.

HR has no such decision science and no decision framework to organize information technology. Thus, technology has found its greatest value in automating areas with more established organizing frameworks, such as payroll, but has not reached the level of impact in supporting more strategic decisions. For example, HR functions often brainstorm their own unique employee turnover classifications when installing a new software system. It's not surprising that even after years of using such systems, there remains too little insight into the factors that affect employee turnover, how it affects the organization, and what to do about it.

As we will discuss later, HR measures exist mostly in areas where the accounting systems require information to control labor costs or monitor functional activity. Efficiency gets a lot of attention, but effectiveness and impact are often unmeasured. While there have been significant advances in applying analytics to the field of HR management—including high-level data analysis approaches like social network analysis and multivariate regression—such methods often suffer from the lack of a more comprehensive decision framework. For example, a statistical method from marketing, called "conjoint analysis," has been applied to employee survey data to see which work elements most significantly associate with employee engagement or turnover.[12] This provides insights about how HR programs might enhance those work elements, but it often fails to identify where engagement and retention matter most and why. Advanced analytics hold great promise for enhancing talent decisions, but as we shall see later, it is often the logic, not the analytics, that creates the big breakthroughs.

A decision framework provides the logical structure to organizational data, measures, and analytics, and identifies gaps in existing measurement systems. Armed with such a decision science and framework, organizations can avoid investing in sophisticated data and analysis that fails to achieve its potential because the tools don't address the important questions.

Focus on Optimization

The final pillar of a mature decision science is that its logic reveals how decisions can optimize the returns from a resource, rather than simply describing them or only partially maximizing them. A mature decision science reveals how to optimize results by balancing trade-offs instead of assuming that more is better.

Finance provides a good illustration. Before the DuPont model (which marks the beginning of the decision science of finance), the goal was simply to maximize profits. Disproportionate amounts of capital were directed to businesses with large profits, often resulting in high margins but low return on capital. Instead of maximizing profits in isolation, the DuPont model strove to optimize profits by recognizing the constraints on financial capital resources.[13] As the finance decision science matured, other factors were integrated. Financial decision models now not only maximize returns but use decision frameworks, such as portfolio theory, to optimize return in the context of risk and liquidity. Further refinements revealed how to balance liquidity in the broader strategy, by investing in ways that consider the range of future strategic options that investment might enable.

By contrast, many HR decisions often try to increase learning, engagement, or retention without limit or context. This is very different from optimizing a portfolio of HR practices against the organization's unique resource opportunity costs and constraints.[14] For example, if more sales training increases product knowledge, which increases selling success, a less mature decision framework might apply training more broadly. Having proved the value of training by linking it to increased sales, the right decision seems to be to acquire more training. Several executives we have worked with have termed this the "peanut-butter" approach, because it spreads something equally across the entire organization.

In fact, considering the necessary investments (time, money, etc.) to achieve increased selling success through training, enhancing product knowledge from an already high level may be very expensive. The optimal solution might involve less product knowledge and more motivation, and thus less training and more incentives. The key point is that a mature decision science frames the question in terms of optimal solutions rather than just describing relationships or increasing one desired outcome out of context. Even when optimal decisions can't be precisely defined, the logic that a focus on optimization provides will often lead to insights that are missed by a less comprehensive approach.

Distinguish Average from Marginal Value. A core principle in optimization is the difference between average and marginal (or incremental) impact. Although something can be highly valuable, increasing or decreasing the amount of it may not have a big effect. For example, suppose an organization has a hundred sales representatives and total revenue of $50 million, making the average sales per sales representative $500,000. What is the optimal number of sales representatives? You can't tell from the average. Optimizing requires that you know the potential effects of increasing or decreasing the sales force. If the same $50 million in revenue could be generated by forty representatives, then the marginal value of the last ten representatives would actually be zero. On the other hand, if these sales representatives were working to their capacity and there were available sales territories without adequate sales coverage, additional reps would create significant incremental sales.

A mature decision science clearly articulates the difference between resources or activities that provide high average value and those that provide high marginal value. We use the word *pivotal* to describe the marginal effect of resources, activities, and decisions. *Pivotal* captures the idea of a lever, where a small change at the fulcrum causes very large changes on the other end. Highly pivotal areas are those where a small change makes a big difference to strategy and value. A resource, decision, or activity can be highly valuable and important, even if it is not pivotal.

Some resources, decisions, or activities are both important (highly valuable on average) and pivotal (small changes make a big difference).

A good example is product design. Consider how two components of a car relate to a consumer's purchase decision: tires and interior design. Which adds more value on average? The tires. They are essential to the car's ability to move, and they impact both safety and performance. Yet tires generally do not influence purchase decisions, because safety standards guarantee that all tires will be very safe and reliable. Differences in interior features—optimal sound system, elegant upholstery, portable technology docks, number and location of cup holders—likely have far more effect on the consumer's buying decision. In terms of the overall value of an automobile, you can't drive without tires, but you can drive without cup holders and an iPod dock. Interior features, however, clearly have a greater impact on the purchase decision. In our language, the tires are important, but the interior design is *pivotal*.

Figure 2-3 shows this example in the form of what we call a "performance yield curve," a fundamental idea underlying talentship that is used throughout the book. The performance yield curve for tires is much higher than for interior features, which reflects tires' importance. The yield curve for tires is relatively flat across a large range of performance levels, and it drops quickly on the left if tire performance falls below a certain level. Tires create tremendous value and are very important, but once they reach a certain level, increasing their performance does not add value to the consumer's purchasing decision. Yet, if they fall below the

FIGURE 2-3

Yield curves for automobile components: Tires vs. interior design

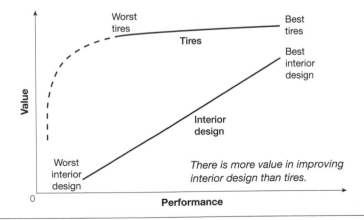

minimum standard (as happened with the Firestone tires on Ford SUVs, resulting in a massive recall in 2000), the result is very bad indeed. The key to optimizing tires against their effect on the initial purchase decision is to get them to standard, not significantly higher. Beyond this point the incremental cost of increasing tire performance exceeds the incremental value in customer purchases.

The marketing and finance decision sciences have sophisticated systems to exploit the distinction between marginal and average value. As the marketing decision science evolved, the concept of segmentation was applied at multiple levels, including markets, customers within markets, products, and as we just discussed, product features within products. Conjoint analysis and other statistical tools use data from extensive consumer research to produce deep insights about the incremental value of features, which informs decisions about product designs. They carefully isolate those attributes (such as safe tires) that are core or expected (sometimes referred to as "table stakes") from those where differences drive perceptions of value (such as the interior design of a new car). Optimization requires investing based on the incremental contribution, not the average contribution. To do this, features must be segmented on their marginal value (pivotalness), not their average value (or importance). Failing to segment based on pivotalness often results in equal investments, even when the potential marginal return is significantly different, as shown in figure 2-4.

FIGURE 2-4

Segmentation and the dangers of equal investments

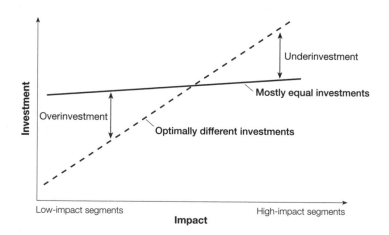

This seems fundamental, but it is frequently misapplied in organization and talent decisions. What we have called "talent segmentation" is still very rudimentary.[15] We see this in the frequent tendency to do the same thing across a wide range of jobs or talent pools. Examples include: "If stock options are good for executives, then they should be expanded to all employees" and "If it's important to increase attention given to our customers, then everyone should have thirty hours of training in customer awareness" and "If weeding out the bottom 10 percent of performers makes sense in our sales force, let's weed out the bottom 10 percent in every job."

Effective segmentation based on marginal value in talent and organization decisions helps answer questions such as "Where does my strategy require increasing the performance of our talent, and how it is organized?" The answer cannot be "everywhere," because that is cost prohibitive. The answer also cannot be "nowhere," because competitive advantage must have some source—one or more multi-incumbent roles, or talent pools, where superior talent quality makes a significant strategic difference. Lacking a decision science that guides this kind of talent segmentation, organizations typically invest too little in talent pools that are most pivotal and too much in talent pools that are important but far less pivotal. The idea that talent and organization decisions are vital to competitive advantage is a virtual truism today, as we noted earlier, yet the very essence of competitive advantage is finding unique and different ways to advance a particular value proposition, seize specific market opportunities, or leverage distinctive strategic resources. Still, today's decisions about organization and talent are often made with an eye toward duplicating the practices of other successful companies, rather than in-depth internal analysis to find the appropriate investments for specific contexts. The absence of a decision science that distinguishes marginal from average value is a significant cause.

Segmentation in Auto Insurance. Segmentation based on marginal impact produced a competitive advantage for Allstate Insurance Company. Allstate (then a division of Sears) was one of the first companies to adjust rates based on age, auto usage, and claims history—a revolution at the time.[16] This easily described idea had massive implications for virtually all aspects of the auto insurance business. Allstate was able to extract much more value from the insurance market and provide much greater value to its customers by adjusting what it charged according to customer characteristics related to the probability of accidents and other factors. Allstate has continued its tradition of innovative differentiation in its pricing models by bringing in a variety of new factors that it now markets

under the brand "Your Choice Auto Insurance," which is based on sophisticated pricing models. This changed the game from a product definition perspective by providing customers a much wider variety of choices.
Before, customers could choose their level of coverage and size of de-
ductibles. Now they can customize policies on features such as accident
forgiveness and what type of rewards they would like associated with
good driving records.

Allstate's research revealed interesting and surprising patterns in auto
safety among different consumer groups. A *BusinessWeek* item noted:

> For decades, Allstate had lumped customers into three main pricing cat-
> egories, based on basic details such as a customer's age and place of resi-
> dence. It now has more than 1,500 price levels. Agents used to simply
> refer to a manual to give customers a price; now they log on to a com-
> puter that uses complex algorithms to analyze 16 credit report variables,
> such as late payments and card balances, as well as data such as claims
> history for specific car models. Thus, [drivers who are safe bets] are re-
> warded, saving up to 20% over the old system, and high-risk drivers are
> penalized, paying up to 20% more. It has worked well enough that All-
> state now applies it to other lines, such as homeowners' insurance.[17]

Thinking Differently Using
Decision Science Principles

A decision is an invitation to think differently. Historically, as decision
sciences become embedded within organizations, natural synergies
emerge across the five decision science elements. This creates tangible but
very organic changes in the way business and HR leaders, employees, investors, and potential employees converse about a strategic resource.
Consider the power of just three changes in the way your organization
approaches its talent and organization decisions.

First, clearly distinguishing between pivotalness and importance motivates a focus on the marginal value of talent decisions. This is as important
for talent as the distinction between the marginal value of advertising
and the overall importance of advertising, for example. It helps decision
makers avoid getting lost in a sea of important initiatives and set priorities correctly.

Second, consistently use performance yield curves to identify the nature of pivot-point slopes and shapes. Not only does this kind of discipline help identify where decisions should focus on achieving a standard
versus improving performance, it also provides a way to think about the
risks and returns to performance at different levels. It helps people avoid

making decisions based on well-meaning but rudimentary rules such as "get the best person in every job."

Third, focus on optimization, not just maximization. This creates an environment in which trade-offs can be discussed with less of the emotion that usually prevents good decisions and often leads to decisions like "Let's just do the same thing for everyone to be fair." Optimization presumes that talent investments will be unequal but also creates a high standard for analyzing and communicating good reasons for such unequal investments.

Thus, even in the early stages of implementing a decision science, tangible changes occur in how talent and organizations are understood and made. History shows that it is from these small tangible steps that significant untapped strategic success flows.

Conclusion

When new decision sciences emerge, they typically present difficult changes in social, organizational, and personal traditions. Before the new logic is used by competitors, a failure to make decisions more optimally doesn't create any relative disadvantage, so less sophisticated decision systems still allow organizations to stay competitive. Before Allstate applied the decision science principle of customer segmentation and optimization, no one did any worse by following the old model. Yet first movers who apply a new decision science often create formidable competitive advantages. Once Allstate generated value by adopting a more sophisticated decision science, its competitors were at a disadvantage. Soon everyone began to realize the power of the new decision framework and tried to catch up.

We believe that HR, and the larger domain of organization and talent decisions, is at precisely this historical point. A few organizations are beginning to develop some elements of a more mature decision science. For example, at Corning, HR leaders who support key divisions use talent-focused strategy analysis during their annual strategy sessions.[18] At The Hartford Financial Services Group, Inc., investments in HR programs are allocated in part based on where they will have the most pivotal effect.[19]

Still, because the effects are so isolated, there is not yet an urgent need to evolve. The vast majority of organizations can compete effectively, even while making more traditional talent and organization decisions. A new decision science, however, will emerge for talent, just as surely as it emerged for other resources. The first organizations to apply the new decision framework will achieve significant first-mover advantages, forcing others to react. In time we envision the talent decision science becoming as natural a part of management thinking as finance and marketing are today, but before that happens there are opportunities for game-changing strategic decisions by organizations that apply it first.

The remainder of this book describes this emerging decision science: talentship. It rests on the pillars of management systems integration, shared mental models, and aligned data, analytics, and measures. The decision framework based on impact, effectiveness, and efficiency is the core pillar around which all these decision science components revolve. So we have organized the book around the decision framework and its vital core elements. Next, we describe those core elements.

3

The HC BRidge Framework

Pivot-Points in Impact, Effectiveness,
and Efficiency

Which talent pools at a Disney theme park make the biggest difference to strategic success? Would it be the characters (such as Mickey Mouse), the ride designers, the cast members on the street, the executive leadership team, or a host of other roles that Disney employees play every day? As we saw in chapter 2, the answer may well depend on a clear distinction between what's important versus what is pivotal. It requires thinking about strategy at a much deeper level than simply asking, "Which talent pools help make Disney theme parks 'The Happiest Place on Earth'?" Clearly, everyone tries to contribute to that. When we ask questions like this in any organization, the answers vary widely and the reasons for the answers vary even more! Becoming clearer and more consistent about the answers is vital to strategic success.

Chapter 2 showed how a decision science produces that clarity using a framework that describes the logical connections between decisions about a vital resource and how they affect strategic success. The other elements of the decision science (mind-set, systems, and optimization) rely on the logic of the decision framework. This chapter describes the decision framework that underpins talentship. It articulates the logical connections between decisions about talent and strategic success and organizes them so they can be applied consistently across different strategic and business situations. We will introduce the decision framework using the relatively simple example of talent in a theme park and use the decision framework as the guiding logic for much of the rest of the book.

In later chapters we will apply the framework to other, more complex, situations, such as the global strategic dilemmas facing Boeing and Airbus.

Impact, Effectiveness, and Efficiency Applied to Talent

We built the talent decision framework earlier on the three anchor points of impact, effectiveness, and efficiency. We call these "anchor points" because they are like the supports for a suspension bridge. Chapter 2 showed that these three ideas are also part of decision sciences in other professions. Figure 3-1 reviews how they apply to talent and organization decisions.

Efficiency captures how investments affect programs and practices. Effectiveness captures how programs and practices affect talent and organization pools. Impact captures how talent and organization pools affect sustainable strategic success. All the anchor points are necessary and work together, and they must all be considered when making talent and organization decisions. Yet, as useful as these anchor points are, we can go deeper to describe a set of logical linking elements that show the details of how each anchor point works. To continue the bridge metaphor, think of the linking elements as the spanning connectors on a suspension bridge between the anchor points.

Figure 3-2 takes this next step. It provides the specific linking elements within each of the three anchor points. As we mentioned earlier, we call

FIGURE 3-1

Applying anchor points to talent and organizational decisions

FIGURE 3-2

HC BRidge framework: Seven key questions

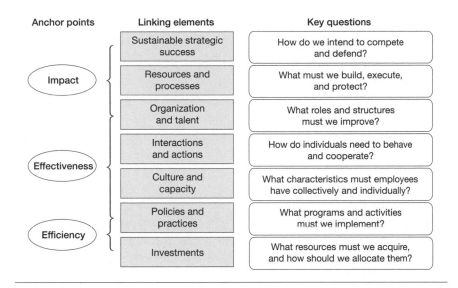

Anchor points	Linking elements	Key questions
Impact	Sustainable strategic success	How do we intend to compete and defend?
	Resources and processes	What must we build, execute, and protect?
	Organization and talent	What roles and structures must we improve?
Effectiveness	Interactions and actions	How do individuals need to behave and cooperate?
	Culture and capacity	What characteristics must employees have collectively and individually?
Efficiency	Policies and practices	What programs and activities must we implement?
	Investments	What resources must we acquire, and how should we allocate them?

this the "HC BRidge framework," and we will describe it in detail in this chapter.

Figure 3-2 depicts the decision framework by translating each of the linking elements into questions. Consider how well the leaders in your organization can answer these questions. As we'll see later, when organizations properly use these questions, they reveal new insights about how to compete for and with talent and about the role and structure of strategic HR management

We will illustrate the HC BRidge framework using the example of a Disney theme park that began this chapter. This example is familiar and straightforward enough to make a good teaching tool. Yet we shall see that even in this relatively uncomplicated and familiar context, the HC BRidge framework reveals insights about talent decisions that defy conventional wisdom and uncovers opportunities for significant and unique competitive advantage. The decision framework in any decision science must provide a tangible approach to defining how the resource can best be aligned to achieve strategy execution. As we will show, when it comes to talent and organization resources, *alignment* requires understanding where differences in the quality or quantity of talent and organization have the greatest strategic effect, *execution* requires knowing what decisions are most pivotal to enhancing those vital talent and organization elements, and *agility* requires having a consistent logic that spans many situations and identifies where change must occur.

Impact Pivot-Points: Where Talent and Organization Most Affect Sustainable Strategic Success

Impact identifies the relationship between improvements in organization and talent performance, and sustainable strategic success. The pivot-point is where differences in performance most affect success. Figure 3-2 shows that this requires digging deeply into organization- or unit-level strategies to unearth specific details about where and how the organization plans to compete and about the supporting elements that will be most vital to achieving that competitive position. These insights identify the areas of organization and talent that make the biggest difference in the strategy's success.

Recall the chapter opening about the Disney theme park. Suppose we ask the question the usual way: "What is the important talent for theme park success?" What would you say? We find there is always a variety of answers, and they always include the characters. Indeed, characters and the talented people inside the Mickey Mouse costumes are very important. A decision science, however, focuses on pivot-points. Consider what happens when we frame the question differently, in terms of impact: "Where would an improvement in the quality of talent and organization make the biggest difference in our strategic success?" Answering that question requires looking further to find the strategy pivot-points that illuminate the talent and organization pivot-points. Figure 3-2 shows that this requires defining strategic success and what most affects it.

Sustainable Strategic Success

The first linking element, sustainable strategic success, asks, "How do we intend to compete and defend our position?" Although this always seems to be a straightforward question, chapter 4 will show that there is usually great value in making it much more specific. This linking element probes deeply into organizational strategies to define the specific competitive or strategic context, the organization's intended position within that context, key competitive differentiators and where the organization will be positioned on them, how it will grow, and how it will be unique and defensible enough to sustain that position.

We say "sustainable strategic success" rather than "competitive advantage" because the principles in this book apply not only to profit-making organizations competing in traditional financial markets but also to mission-driven organizations such as the U.S. Navy, Asian Development Bank, and the United Nations. These principles apply when the objective is to enhance traditional and competitive strategy outcomes and when the objective is sustainability, often referred to as the "triple bottom line."[1]

The Walt Disney Company is a diversified entertainment company with activities as diverse as television, ESPN Zone arcades, retail stores, movies, television, and theme parks.[2] Let's focus on an example from one of the most well-known Disney attractions: Disneyland. What might sustainable strategic success look like for Disneyland? While Disneyland has many competitors, let's compare it to just one: Cedar Point, in Sandusky, Ohio. The Web sites for Disneyland and Cedar Point are instructive. Disneyland's visual imagery shows well-known places, such as Sleeping Beauty's Castle, often with famous characters in the foreground.[3] Cedar Point shows towering steel and wooden roller coasters.[4] Disneyland's motto is "The Happiest Place on Earth," and Cedar Point's is "The Roller Coaster Capital of the World" (or one might say, "The Most Thrilling Place on Earth"). Disneyland emphasizes family fun while Cedar Point emphasizes thrills. Disneyland's Web site provides information on Mickey Mouse, and Cedar Point's Web site provides blogs where patrons can describe their thrilling ride experiences and hold discussions regarding the technical aspects of the rides.

Table 3-1 compares Disneyland and Cedar Point on a common set of differentiators that illuminate the unique competitive position each organization desires and how to make that position valuable and difficult to duplicate. No strategic intent is inherently wrong or right. For example, sports cars are supposed to be noisier than family cars. Creating the

TABLE 3-1

Strategic positioning of Disneyland vs. Cedar Point

	Disneyland	Cedar Point
Key differentiator	Disney characters	Roller coasters
Value proposition	"The Happiest Place on Earth"	"The roller coaster capital of the world"
Brand essence	Fantasy	Thrills
Interesting Web site feature	0% Disney vacation financing option	Blog/discussion page for roller coaster enthusiasts
Discount for seniors	None	75%

Source: Disney Online, http://www.disneyland.disney.go.com; Cedar Point Amusement Park, http://www.cedarpoint.com.

right kind of noise in the engine might be the key to strategic success for a sports car while making the car cab quieter is the key for the family car.

Even in an example as focused as theme parks, we can see there is great richness in the respective strategies. Later chapters will show there is even greater richness in strategies that span multiple products or sectors. Disney's theme park strategic intent is to delight guests with uniquely and surprisingly happy experiences. How does a park do it? This takes us to the next linking element in figure 3-2.

Resources and Processes

The next element of the HC BRidge framework—resources and processes—describes what an organization must create to achieve and defend the strategic position or its mission. Figure 3-2 mentions two important categories. The first is "resources" that must be obtained, deployed, exploited, and protected. For theme parks, resources would include brands, real estate, and relationships with key regulators or local authorities. We'll cover that element in later chapters with other examples.

The second is "processes," which are the transformations that the organization must accomplish to create its unique value. We'll focus on the process of hosting guests in a theme park. This process involves transporting them to the park, orienting them within the park, providing services and experiences while they are on the park grounds, assuring their safety and comfort, and transporting them from the park. The transformation is to make guests happier, more delighted, eager to return and make future purchases of Disney products and services, and so pleased that they will tell stories to their friends and family, creating new Disney guests.

The next challenge in impact analysis is to find the pivot-point in the process where improvement would make the biggest difference to Disney's strategic objective of delighting customers. One way to find the pivot-points in processes is to look for constraints. These are like bottlenecks in a pipeline: if you relieve a constraint, the entire process works better. For a Disney theme park, a key constraint is the number of minutes a guest spends in the park. Disney must maximize the number of "delightful" minutes. Disneyland has eighty-five acres of public areas, many different "lands," and hundreds of small and large attractions. Helping guests navigate, even delighting them as they navigate, defines how Disney deals with this constraint. Notice how this takes the customer delight strategy and makes it much more specific by identifying a pivotal process that supports it.

Organization and Talent

The linking element of organization and talent focuses on what work must be accomplished and how it should be organized. Here we look for talent and organization areas where alignment and performance improvements would make big differences in the strategic pivot-points of processes and resources. Identifying pivotal resources and processes now allows us to see the talent question more clearly. Instead of asking "What talent is important?" the impact question becomes "Where would improvements in talent make the biggest difference in the number of delightful minutes for guests?" Is the answer still "Mickey Mouse and other characters"? Perhaps not, as we shall see.

Figure 3-3 takes the performance yield curve concept and applies it to two talent pools in the Disney theme park: Mickey Mouse and the park sweeper.

Mickey Mouse Is Important but Not Necessarily Pivotal. The top line represents the performance of the talent in the Mickey Mouse role. The curve is very high in the diagram because performance by Mickey Mouse is very valuable. However, the variation in value between the best-performing Mickey Mouse and the worst-performing Mickey Mouse is not that large. In the extreme, if the person in the Mickey Mouse costume engaged in harmful customer interactions, the consequences would be

FIGURE 3-3

Applying yield curves to talent: Disneyland's Mickey Mouse vs. the sweeper

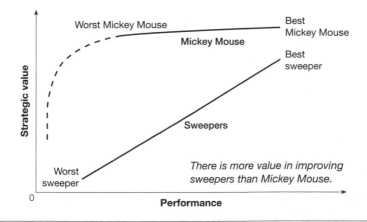

strategically devastating. That is shown by the very steep downward slope at the left. That's why the Mickey Mouse role has been engineered to make such errors virtually impossible. The person in the Mickey Mouse costume is never seen, never talks, and is always accompanied by a supervisor who manages the guest encounters and ensures that Mickey doesn't fall down, get lost, or take an unauthorized break.

Because the position is so well engineered, there is also little payoff to investing in improving the performance of Mickey Mouse. There is great value in investments that ensure Mickey Mouse performance is up to the very high necessary standard, but beyond that standard, differences in talent pool performance are not as crucial. The role of Mickey Mouse is so important that it can't be left to improvising by cast members. If you watch carefully, Mickey Mouse manages to interact with a lot of guests per hour. Each one gets great attention, but the interaction with Mickey doesn't last long. This allows more customers to see Mickey within a short time span, maximizing the number of delighted guests per minute. The Mickey Mouse role is aligned to the process constraint (number of minutes in the theme park) that is pivotal for the unique strategic position (The Happiest Place on Earth).

Finally, Disney characters are known and expected to be excellent, so park guests may be less likely to be delightfully surprised by characters who are friendly, attentive, and so forth. Disney executives report that when guests write letters to share their enjoyable experiences at Disney parks, they often begin with descriptions of unexpected encounters with cast members other than characters. For example, *Eyes and Ears* (the internal publication for cast members at Walt Disney World) publishes "Fan Mail," a column containing letters from guests. One guest wrote about how impressed he was with a hearing-impaired housekeeping cast member who "clearly communicated with our family and was terrific with the kids."[5] That's not to say that guests don't write about the characters, but characters may not be the vital pivot-point for surprise and delight.

Sweepers Are Pivotal Talent at Disneyland. If the talent pivot-point for the guest experience process isn't characters, what is it? When a guest has a problem, folks like park sweepers and store clerks are most likely to be nearby in accessible roles, so guests approach them. People seldom ask Cinderella where to buy a disposable camera, but hundreds a day will ask the street sweeper!

The lower curve in figure 3-3 represents sweepers. The sweeper curve has a much steeper slope than Mickey Mouse because variation in sweeper performance creates a greater change in value. Disney sweepers have the opportunity to make adjustments to the customer service process on the fly, reacting to variations in customer demands, unforeseen circumstances, and changes in the customer experience. These are things that make pivotal differences in the "Happiest Place on Earth" differentiators. To be sure, these pivot-points are embedded in architecture, creative settings, and the brand of Disney magic. Alignment is key. In fact, it is precisely because of this holistic alignment that interacting with guests in the park is a pivotal role, and the sweeper plays a big part in that role. At Disney sweepers are actually frontline customer representatives with brooms in their hands.

Interestingly, interacting with guests encompasses other jobs as well. Store clerks, for example, have similar opportunities to assist guests in surprisingly delightful ways. We hear stories about harried guests who grab several bottles of water from a bin, pay for them, and take them back to their table, only to realize that in their haste they purchased only three bottles of water for their four children. The store clerk comes over to say, "Here's a fourth bottle of water, no charge." When store clerks and sweepers cooperate, the possibilities for delighting customers increase exponentially. For decades at Disney, store clerks have been carefully cast for precisely these moments. Recently, retailers in other industries instituted similar roles by putting greeters at the front of a store or restaurant.

Pivotal and Important Are Different. Again, it's not that Mickey Mouse isn't important: the yield-curve diagram in figure 3-3 shows the Mickey Mouse line is higher than the sweeper line at all points. Even the best sweeper probably creates less value than the lowest-performing Mickey Mouse. In any well-run organization, everyone contributes to the mission in different ways. The key is to understand those differences systematically. The question that reveals these differences is often "What's most pivotal where improving talent and organization matter most?"

Once we understand the talent and organization pivot-points, we are much closer to targeting our talent investments to make a significant strategic difference. We still need to go one level deeper, however, to uncover the specific talent and organization elements and the programs and practices that will optimally affect them. That's the next anchor point in the HC BRidge framework: effectiveness.

Effectiveness Pivot-Points: Where Policies and Practices Most Affect Organization and Talent Performance

Effectiveness defines the relationship between talent and organization performance and the portfolio of policies and practices. How do HR programs and processes affect the capacity and actions of individuals and groups? As figure 3-2 shows, effectiveness is independent of impact because how practices improve performance is independent of the strategic effects of that improved performance. Powerful insights occur when effectiveness and impact are considered together.

Most HR organizations are more adept at effectiveness than impact. HR professional associations affiliate with HR practice areas, such as the American Society for Training & Development or the Employee Benefit Research Institute. The effects of HR practices are the prominent question in research on staffing, compensation, development, performance management, and other HR fields. Most HR textbooks are organized around HR activities (though with increasing attention to how programs integrate with strategy).

Effectiveness is important, but it is often challenging to see how the effects of programs (such as staffing, training, and rewards) on actions and interactions (such as performance ratings, competencies, teamwork, and retention) really affect the business or competitive position. Organizations that ignore impact in favor of effectiveness often produce well-meaning HR programs with great effectiveness on low-impact talent pools. Ignoring effectiveness in favor of impact is equally dangerous, producing situations where opportunities to improve talent could significantly affect sustainable strategic success but with little idea about how to create the capacity to execute on them. Returning to the Disney example, effectiveness identifies the pivotal programs and policies that will most improve the performance of the pivotal talent pool: sweepers. Figure 3-2 shows that this requires asking deeper questions about precisely how the talent pools create their strategic impact through interactions and actions. Let's see how this would work at Disney.

Interactions and Actions

Interactions and actions describe how individuals' behavior and cooperation affects the pivotal roles. What key constituents will be encountered? What will be the key role challenges and aligned responses? What will distinguish effective from ineffective behavior?

Interestingly, in Disney theme parks, the pivotal actions and interactions are probably not improving performance on sweeping! This seems incongruous at first because theme park cleanliness is clearly a fundamental Disney differentiator. No one would deny that park cleanliness is important, but is it pivotal? Disney sweepers and other jobs in the talent pool that interact with customers are pivotal because they affect the constraint of the number of delightful minutes in the park. Our favorite illustration comes from an executive in one of our classes who recalled the time his hot, cranky, and sunburned child was sitting on the sunny curb waiting to watch the parade. A sweeper happened by, noticed the sunburned child, and stopped sweeping. He told the family that there was a shady spot up the hill where they could watch the parade, and he accompanied the family to that spot.

Pivotalness Reveals Distinctions Within Roles. Although a clean park is incredibly important to Disney, the sweeping part of the sweepers' job has a flat slope for maximizing the number of delightful minutes for guests. Meeting the standard of cleanliness is essential for sweepers, but improving cleanliness beyond that standard doesn't surprise or delight guests. For example, there are no radioactive materials or hazardous waste at Disney. So, while a clean park is very important, the level of custodial performance is not as high as might be required by facilities such as operating rooms or nuclear facilities. Creative cleaning is less likely to delight guests than creative customer interaction.

Like the performance of Mickey Mouse, cleanliness is expected by guests, so it may be harder to surprise guests with cleanliness beyond the standard. Like Mickey Mouse, Disney has engineered away most of the variation in the quality of sweeping, through clever park design and even culture (if a sweeper fails to clean something, another Disney cast member will probably catch it before it affects a guest). Sweepers need to meet a very high standard of sweeping, but once they meet that standard, doing more may make only small differences in guest surprise and delight.

Role Challenges and Moments of Truth Reveal Pivotal Actions and Interactions. Pivotal actions and interactions are often revealed through vital role challenges or moments of truth, where interactions and actions make the biggest difference. The pivotal role challenge for Disney sweepers is when a guest needs help or information, and the pivotal aligned action is providing it in a pleasantly surprising, accurate, and appropriate way. Notice that it's not enough to say that sweepers should create delightful guest experiences. The aligned action for sweepers isn't to be entertaining (singing and juggling), even though that would also fit the general description of "delighting guests." Disney has lots of other roles to keep guests entertained, so sweepers can't make as much of a difference there.

More important, sweepers who are busy singing and juggling wouldn't be approached by guests with questions about ride locations, which lines are shortest, and so on. Park guests won't approach Mickey Mouse or Cinderella with those questions either (no one asks Cinderella where to purchase a souvenir). Guests feel more comfortable asking their mundane but very important questions of those in what Disney calls "accessible" roles, and they take advice from such roles more readily. So the people in the sweeper role make the pivotal difference through the quality of guest assistance they offer, and they need to be in the sweeper role to be most effective.

The interactions element of the HC BRidge framework focuses on how individuals cooperate. Interactions can be the formal information sharing or profit and cost allocations between business units, or they can be more subtle, in the form of informal networks, communication patterns, and mutual trust and respect. For example, a pivotal interaction at Disney is the inclusion of sweeper supervisors in planning meetings with park designers. Sweepers are constantly learning things like where the park needs more shady spots to watch the parade, information that is vital to park design. Disney defines the aligned actions of sweeper supervisors to include observing and listening to sweepers talk about their experiences with guests. Sweeper supervisors need to get that information, and designers need to listen to sweeper supervisors. This is cooperation at its most pivotal level. The interactions element of the HC BRidge framework identifies the structures and formal and informal relationships that make those interactions happen. Interactions also reach outside organizational boundaries, as when sweepers interact with guests.

Figure 3-4 shows how the concept of yield applies to the actions of sweeping versus helping guests. The same logic that helped us see more clearly where pivot-points existed in the strategy and what talent pools were pivotal now applies here, revealing pivot-points within the role.

FIGURE 3-4

Yield curves and aligned actions: Sweeping vs. guest relations

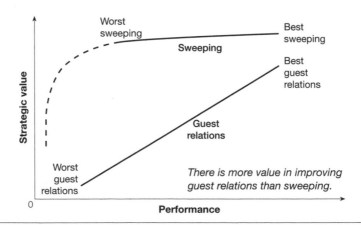

This deep application of similar logic at several different levels is a hall-mark of a mature decision science.

Quality Pivotalness Versus Quantity Pivotalness. What about labor shortages and turnover? Does HC BRidge apply when the significant strategic issue is having or getting enough talent? So far, we have focused on pivotalness of differences in the performance of sweepers or Mickey Mouse. We refer to this as "quality pivotalness." A different kind of piv-otalness focuses on not quality but quantity. "Quantity pivotalness" has a steeply sloped yield curve on the quantity of talent. Quantity-pivotal roles exist where strategic value pivots on finding enough talent, finding it quicker, or reducing turnover.

For Cedar Point, one can imagine that the job of sweeper is mostly quantity pivotal because it primarily reflects the role of sweeping, which is flat sloped. Yet, if Cedar Point runs short on sweepers, its strategy suf-fers. The Cedar Point Web site aggressively encourages kids to apply for summer jobs, many of which are probably quantity pivotal.[6] Disney also needs enough sweepers, but as we have seen, the job at Disney has a sig-nificant role in guest relations. So sweepers are more quality pivotal at Disney than at Cedar Point. At Disney the job of sweeper is *both* quantity and quality pivotal. Talent can be purely quality pivotal (there's plenty available, but differences in quality matter a lot) or purely quantity piv-otal (having more available matters a lot, but differences in quality don't have a large impact), although typically talent is a combination of both quantity and quality pivotalness.

Culture and Capacity

Culture and capacity describes the collective and individual characteristics that employees must have to execute the vital actions and interactions. This element translates the actions and interactions into things like skills, knowledge, engagement, and opportunities. In actual organizations in-sights about culture and capacity often emerge from questions like "What shared values, beliefs, and norms will support or inhibit execution?" and "How will success depend on individual capability, opportunity, and/or motivation?"

Organizational leaders often jump too quickly to one particular solu-tion. Some may like capability ("can employees do it?") and will suggest, "Increase knowledge by giving sweepers ten hours of training on park in-formation." Some may focus on opportunity ("do employees get the chance?"), suggesting, "Let's put sweepers near the ride lines, where all the guests are." Still others may emphasize motivation ("do employees want to do it?"), suggesting, "Let's give a bonus for the number of times sweepers help a guest." These ideas may all be good ones, but a decision science demands a logical way to evaluate and assess them. Careful consideration of which element—capability, opportunity, or motivation—is most pivotal is one way to do that.

Disney provides a good example of a culture that treats all customers as guests and all employees as cast members. Everyone from sweepers to executives goes through an eight-hour training and orientation program called Traditions. Every month *Eyes and Ears* reports on unique examples of guest service, and Disney leaders are often in the park watching for such examples so that they can reward employees. Every Disney cast member knows the four core pillars of the Disney experience: show, safety, courtesy, and efficiency. Disney cast members carry a small card entitled "7 Guest Service Guidelines" (illustrated with pictures of the Seven Dwarfs from *Snow White*):

Be **Happy** . . . make eye contact and smile!

Be like **Sneezy** . . . greet and welcome each guest. Spread the spirit of Hospitality . . . It's contagious!

Don't be **Bashful** . . . seek out Guest contact!

Be like **Doc** . . . provide immediate Service recovery!

Don't be **Grumpy** . . . always display appropriate body language at all times!

Be like **Sleepy** . . . create DREAMS and preserve the "MAGICAL" Guest experience!

Don't be **Dopey** . . . thank each and every Guest!

This makes culture directly relevant to the most pivotal actions and interactions. Often the pivotal moments when individual employee judgment will make big differences occur when no one is there to supervise or direct the employee, and culture helps ensure that the person will make good choices. Disney also provides innovative opportunities for sweepers by designing its park trash collection so that sweepers don't have to walk a long way to discard trash. Even the most capable and motivated sweeper can't do much if he or she spends days walking between the park and the trash receptacles. The key is to balance capability, opportunity, and motivation within a collective culture.

This approach to capacity and culture suggests a different approach to employee engagement. Every Disney employee understands the mission to create "The Happiest Place on Earth" by delighting guests. Virtually any employee action that improves the guest experience might be seen as aligned with this goal. Thousands of times a day, Disney sweepers have to decide whether to sweep or help guests. Truly aligned execution occurs when the sweepers make those decisions correctly. Talentship suggests that engagement should focus on questions like:

- Do sweepers understand the relative pivotalness of sweeping versus helping guests?

- Do sweepers say that they have the capability, opportunity, or motivation to actually stop sweeping and talk to guests?

- Does the culture of customer service enable them to take the initiative to provide the specific service that makes the pivotal difference?

Disneyland accomplishes the daunting task of creating a precisely engineered guest experience largely built on the work of teenagers in their first jobs. To succeed, culture and capacity must seamlessly support the right actions and interactions. Strategy execution also requires decisions about how to make the aligned actions and interactions happen. Next, we will show how to identify the pivot-points where supporting policies and practices must work together to do this.

Policies and Practices

If sweepers are pivotal at Disney for their customer interactions, then should we enhance those actions by rewarding sweepers, by investing more in their training, or both? Figure 3-2 shows that the policies and practices linking element of the HC BRidge decision framework describes the programs and activities that will create the pivotal capacity and culture. Such practices need to work individually, but it's more important that they work as a portfolio. Insights into policies and practices are often revealed by questions such as: How will our practices distinguish us in the talent market? How will our practices work together? What are the conditions for success?

In Florida Disney's sweepers are unionized, which limits Disney's ability to differentiate pay based on individual performance ratings. That doesn't stop Disney from creating a portfolio of programs and practices that enhance sweeper capacity and culture. Performance policies include asking guests to rate or describe something that a sweeper did that delighted them. Disney provides Great Service Fanatic cards for guests to write down the name of a cast member and what that person did that was so special. Great Service Fanatics are eligible for special drawings for prizes; plus they receive a special notation on their employment record.

Sweepers at Disney know that their career path can lead to positions where they will be working with park designers or Imagineers (the engineers and architects that design the rides), a developmental reward that other theme parks may not be able to offer. One Disney executive pointed out that sweepers often want to spend some time in the stores or working with merchandise. Disney can offer them a vast array of experience with merchandise ranging from dolls to CDs to games. Not only is this a reward for the cast member; it builds their product knowledge, which makes them better in their role as a customer ambassador when they return to the sweeper role!

In employee development sweepers receive different training in customer interaction than Mickey Mouse. Sweepers get opportunities to learn from experience that will increase their familiarity with the park and those areas of the park that are most asked about by guests. In fact, while all Disney cast members go through the famous Traditions orientation and training program, there is also a formalized on-the-job training program for Disney sweepers. Trainers include former sweepers, who are selected for their ability to train and their job knowledge and experience. A detailed training outline goes well beyond the custodial basics and includes specific guest service elements. In staffing and sourcing, sweepers are selected not just for their experience or capability at cleaning but for their orientation and passion for providing one-on-one service and for their emotional and verbal capabilities.

Notice how the portfolio of practices is directly connected to the pivotal interactions and actions. Disney would not provide the same customer service training or incentives to everyone. Just as with well-executed marketing or financial decisions, Disney's talent investments are targeted to where they will have the largest effect. Disney is competing with and for its sweeper talent in a way that is very different from competitors, who see the sweeper job solely in terms of sweeping the park or who provide the same kind of customer service training to everyone.

Disney will not only create more of the pivotal capacity and culture; it will also present a unique position in the talent market for the customer-oriented sweeper candidates. For those individuals who are motivated by the opportunity to provide great customer service, Disney becomes a uniquely appropriate place to work. Disney begins to attract the best of the candidate pool because it offers an integrated employment proposition that also exploits its unique business model.

How Alignment Changes the Competitive Game

For Disney's competition, the game has changed. Disney will compete better *with* sweepers, recognizing that sweepers are customer ambassadors with brooms in their hands. Disney will also compete better *for* sweeper talent. It has changed the market for customer-oriented sweepers by identifying, attracting, rewarding, developing, and retaining precisely the kind of customer-focused sweeper it needs.

Before Disney changed the game, other theme parks might have attracted their share of customer-focused sweepers. Now, as applicants learn what Disney wants and that Disney can provide very distinct rewards and development, the company will attract more of the sweeper applicants that want the customer-ambassador role. Disney can further refine the supply by developing tests that reveal which candidates have a passion for customer service, helping it identify characteristics that others miss. When Disney provides training and incentives that further increase the quality of its sweepers as customer ambassadors, it increases the internal supply of such talent. This is how the talentship decision science enhances a widely touted but elusive goal: synergy in talent and organization investments. We will return to this theme later.

As figure 3-2 shows, once we understand precisely how talent pools create pivotal strategic impact, and what programs and practices best prepare them to do that, we turn our attention to investing resources to make those programs and practices happen.

Efficiency Pivot-Points: Where Investments Most Affect the Portfolio of Policies and Practices

Efficiency defines the relationship between the portfolio of policies and practices and the level of investments, identifying where specific resource investments most enhance the portfolio. Efficiency encourages questions such as "What unique resources does your strategy provide that you could leverage in talent management?" and "Where could investing more resources than the industry norm generate unique value in your portfolio of practices?" While every organization must determine a budget for its talent practices, efficiency in talentship focuses on a broader array of resources and on optimizing the investment against the pivot-points. While efficiency focuses on the relationship between investments and policies and practices, there are also specific questions about the investments themselves, including these: What resources will we consider (money, HR staff time, participant time, leadership time)? What will be the resource trade-offs? How much will we invest, and where will we invest it?

Typical efficiency measures in the Disney example might include the cost per hire for sweepers, the cost per training hour delivered to sweepers, the time to fill vacancies, or the average sweeper pay compared to sweepers in other theme parks. HR leaders often diligently benchmark such numbers, attempting to match or exceed the efficiency levels of their competitors. Lacking a framework that includes effectiveness and impact, organizations often maximize cost or time savings by making HR programs more efficient. When efficiency is the sole focus, it can motivate attempts to increase the yield of programs and processes per unit of resource expended. This can lead to trying to "shrink to success."

Disney provides very detailed and intensive on-the-job training for new sweepers. The training lasts forty-six hours (in addition to the eight-hour Traditions program). While Disney doesn't have statistics on the amount of on-the-job training offered by other theme parks, it seems likely that the company probably spends more time and money than competitors to attract, select, and train its sweepers. Disney looks inefficient on benchmarks such as cost per new hire. Of course, the investment is well worth it, as we have seen, because Disney makes the most of that investment.

In fact, when other theme parks focus exclusively on efficiency, it actually lowers Disney's costs! Why? Because the other sweeper employers attract those who meet the minimal standards, who will sweep minimally well. This leaves a wide-open market for Disney to attract and retain sweepers that do great customer care. The sweepers who are less skilled at customer care and are willing to work with less on-the-job training in a job that is defined exclusively in terms of sweeping end up at other theme parks, while those with great customer care potential end up at Disney. Disney doesn't have to get into a bidding war because others are too busy cutting costs to understand the value.

The HC BRidge Framework Applied
from the Bottom Up

Look back at figure 3-2. We have described the Disney example working from the top down, but consider the power of this perspective working from the bottom up. A number of business leaders we've worked with have pointed out that the conversation about talent often begins with a question like "Why do we spend so much more than our competitors to train our people?" Too often, this is taken as a signal to cut training costs! The better approach is to work bottom-up to trace the effects of the investments through the framework to strategic success. By reframing the question this way, the conversation becomes more logical and strategic. Sometimes the answer is indeed to cut or redirect resources being spent on existing programs and practices. Sometimes the answer is to retain the expenditure because it is adding significant value. Regardless of the answer, the quality of the debate is raised.

A fundamental concept of talentship is focusing on talent and organization decisions that most affect sustainable strategic success. As the Disney example illustrated, making talent and organization investments that affect a cascade of pivot-points is the key to attaining the largest total impact. The principle of connected pivot-points is as fundamental to talentship as it is to other disciplines, like finance and marketing. At any stage of the sequence, if there is a non-pivotal connection, the effect of the investment goes to zero. The principle of connected pivot-points demonstrates the importance of looking beyond the particular program or process and beyond whether investments simply work. Many HR investments work in that they create a good effect (such as learning, motivation, or reduced vacancies) in one or more employee populations. The key question is whether the investment is the most pivotal way to create the effect and whether the effect on the talent and organization is pivotal to important organizational outcomes. Working bottom-up is often the best way to gain a new perspective, identifying HR investments that "work" in terms of effectiveness but may not be the most pivotal in terms of impact.

How HC BRidge Aligns All Organization and Talent

The Disney sweeper is a good example, but the HC BRidge framework is useful beyond customer-facing employees. Recall the competitive comparison between Disneyland and Cedar Point. Now consider the job of ride designers, a very different position from sweepers. Designers are highly technical professionals and rarely encounter a park guest. Both Disneyland and Cedar Point employ ride designers who, according to their job descriptions, do very similar things. In both parks they conceive and design rides for the park that are appropriate, safe, and enjoyable. Yet the differences are as strategically important as the similarities.

Ride designers at Disney are part of a team of engineers that are called Imagineers to convey their integral connection to storytelling. Disney needs its ride designers to excel in immersive storytelling, which translates the personalities of Disney characters and stories into rides that engage customers, ranging from very young children to grandparents. It's a triumph that Disneyland's "It's a Small World" ride leaves countless children, parents, and grandparents with the ride's song playing in their heads all day!

An issue of *Eyes and Ears* describes how Disney's "Legend of the Yeti" ride has all the elements of a great adventure story. It is set in a remote mountain village at the foot of the Himalayas, home of the legendary yeti: the Abominable Snowman. Key story elements include: "The fly-by-night tour operator, Himalayan Escapes; the aging 34-passenger industrial railway struggling to reach Mount Everest; cars packed with innocent explorers; a mangled train track that causes the railway to plummet backward; and of course an encounter with the raging yeti."[7]

Yet the magazine also notes that Disney ride designers need to be skilled in technical aspects of the ride: "Creating the 199-foot-tall snow-capped mountain and runaway train adventure . . . required 5,000 tons of steel, 18.7 million pounds of concrete, and 2,000 gallons of stain and paint." Disney ride designers draw on the engineering skills that all ride designers use, but at Disney the pivot-point is how they incorporate immersive storytelling.

In contrast, ride designers at Cedar Point need to be adept at exploring the safe limits of g-forces, the newest construction materials and techniques, and how to pack the greatest thrill into every second of a roller coaster. Disney ride designers seldom have to consider whether the "It's a Small World" ride or the teacup ride generates excessive g-forces, but it was essential that the teacup ride designers understood that runaway teacups played a very significant role in the "Mad Tea Party" vignette of Disney's 1951 animated classic *Alice in Wonderland*.

Eyes and Ears tells of the scouting trip that the creative executive, project coordinator, and architect working on "Legend of the Yeti" took to research the storyline.[8] They traveled to the Himalayas, "learning about its culture, customs, architecture, and horticulture, and investigating the legend of the yeti. Other Imagineers followed later as part of a larger expedition, including scientists." Disney ride designers get paid trips to the Himalayas to help them achieve immersive storytelling. It's unlikely that other theme parks routinely send their ride designers to the Himalayas! It is a reward that only Disney can provide; so it not only reinforces immersive storytelling, but it also offers ride designers something unique to Disney.

Cedar Point would be foolish to send its ride designers to the Himalayas because such deep immersive storytelling is not its pivotal strategic advantage. On the other hand, Cedar Point might well send its ride designers on field trips to an automobile race, to investigate bullet trains, or to the launch of the space shuttle.

This all means that even in a job as technically sophisticated and well defined as "theme park ride engineer," a logical decision science reveals many ways to compete for and with talent differently, depending on the strategy. Talentship applies to both Disneyland and Cedar Point, but the HC BRidge framework produces different conclusions for different talent and organization situations. Even within the same job of ride designers, the performance differences that matter at Disneyland and Cedar Point are marked. If Disneyland or Cedar Point chooses to compete with and for ride designer talent in the same way, the parks will each miss significant opportunities.

Today's organizations have talent and organization decision frameworks that typically treat jobs as equivalents, which is reflected in their decisions about pay, sourcing, and skill requirements. Organizational leaders often strive to benchmark their talent programs and practices with data on the same jobs in similar organizations in the same industry. As we've seen, simply copying programs and practices will lead to wrong conclusions, even for the same job title in the same type of organization and industry.

Conclusion

Table 3-2 provides a detailed summary of the HC BRidge framework. It provides a brief definition and a description of the key concepts for analyzing each linking element. We said earlier that a hallmark of a successful decision science is that its principles become a natural part of the conversations of organizational leaders and decision makers. The last column of table 3-2 shows some of the typical conversation starters that organizations using talentship have used to guide their discussions.

The approach we suggest here is so different from the typical HR approach that organizations often wonder whether they can get there. The rest of this book will explain that, particularly chapter 10. We are hopeful because often without knowing it, many organizations approach one or two jobs or roles this way. The most typical are executives and salespeople. Investments in these jobs are often based on value, rather than solely on cost. Logical connections between performance differences and business outcomes are routinely considered. HR practices—such as staffing, training, and compensation—are often combined to synergistically enhance quality and performance.

In fact, these jobs are often seen as too important to leave to HR, so policies regarding selection, rewards, and development are assigned to decision makers outside the main HR function. We disagree with this kind of approach. Rather than treating pivotal roles as an exception to be managed outside of HR, this logical approach should be applied to most talent and organization decisions, and should be closely connected to the

TABLE 3-2

Detailed summary of the HC BRidge framework

HC BRidge linking element	Definition	Diagnostic questions
Sustainable strategic success	How we intend to compete and defend	What assumptions will be critical to our strategy?
		What unique competitive position do we want to achieve?
		What will make our advantages difficult to duplicate?
Resources and processes	What we must build, execute, and protect	What value chain must we create?
		What tangible and intangible assets will we require?
		Which process or resource constraints must be resolved?
Organization and talent	What roles and structures we must improve	Where would more and/or better people have the greatest effect?
		Where will we most need to make organization boundaries more effective?
		How will management systems need to align?
Interactions and actions	How individuals need to behave and cooperate	What key constituents will be encountered?
		What will be the key role challenges and aligned responses?
		What will distinguish effective from ineffective behavior?
Culture and capacity	What characteristics employees must have collectively and individually	What shared values, beliefs, and norms will support or inhibit execution?
		How will success depend on individual capability, opportunity, and/or motivation (COM)?
Policies and practices	What programs and activities we must implement	How will our practices distinguish us in the talent market?
		How will our practices work together?
		What are the conditions for success?
Investments	What resources we must acquire, and how we should allocate them	What resources will we consider (money, HR staff time, participant time, leadership time)?
		What will be the resource trade-offs?
		How much will we invest, and where will we invest it?

HR function. Executives and salespeople are treated the way they are in part due to decades of experience showing tangible pivotal effects of their quality and quantity. Another irony is that precisely because the talent pools of executives and salespeople have received so much attention, there is greater potential for distinctively competing for and with talent in areas that are less recognized. Executives and sales talent are often high impact but represent only a small subset of the talent where a systematic decision-based approach can contribute to strategic success.

Imagine the competitive advantage if your organization consistently discovered your equivalent of sweepers before others and applied the same integrated and systematic effort to those talent and organization elements as you do your executives and salespeople. Organizations are undoubtedly missing strategic opportunities they could exploit by applying the same systematic and integrated approach to other less obvious, but equally pivotal, talent and organization areas.

A good example of the power of this fundamental paradigm shift is contained in the book *Moneyball: The Art of Winning an Unfair Game*, by Michael Lewis.[9] That book chronicles the success of Billy Beane, who created a championship-level baseball team using a fraction of the pay and other resources of competitors. The key was to define a decision science of baseball that produced insights that no other teams had seen. For example, getting the baseball into the field of play was statistically more significant in scoring than hitting home runs. This redefined the logic of good hitting and thus the logic of selecting productive batters. The same kind of insights are available beyond baseball; however, they require a commitment to approaching talent and organization decisions with unrelenting logic.

This approach is new, so data is limited, but our experience suggests that there are talent alignment opportunities like this throughout organizations, not just where employees face customers. In retail organizations buyers often emerge as pivotal. In the U.S. military soldiers who can appropriately interact with local militias and populations are pivotal. In an air freight company the attorneys who negotiate exclusive rights to airport takeoff slots have emerged as pivotal. As we shall see, technical professionals who can facilitate global teams are pivotal. Like other decision sciences, the logic of the HC BRidge framework remains consistent but reveals different insights depending on the situation.

We invite leaders inside and outside the HR profession to make decisions about talent and organization resources with greater rigor and logic, using the talentship decision science and the HC BRidge decision framework. In the chapters that follow, you will have the opportunity to begin your journey to building and using that kind of logic in your organization. We will take each element of HC BRidge in turn, describing each anchor point in more detail, along with its implications. In chapters 4 and 5 we will describe impact, in chapters 6 and 7 we will focus on effectiveness, and in chapter 8 we will cover efficiency. In chapter 9 we will focus on talent and organization measurement, and we will conclude with chapter 10, offering lessons from our experience in making talentship work in actual organizations. Figure 3-5 provides the map to the book using the HC BRidge framework.

FIGURE 3-5

HC BRidge framework: Chapters

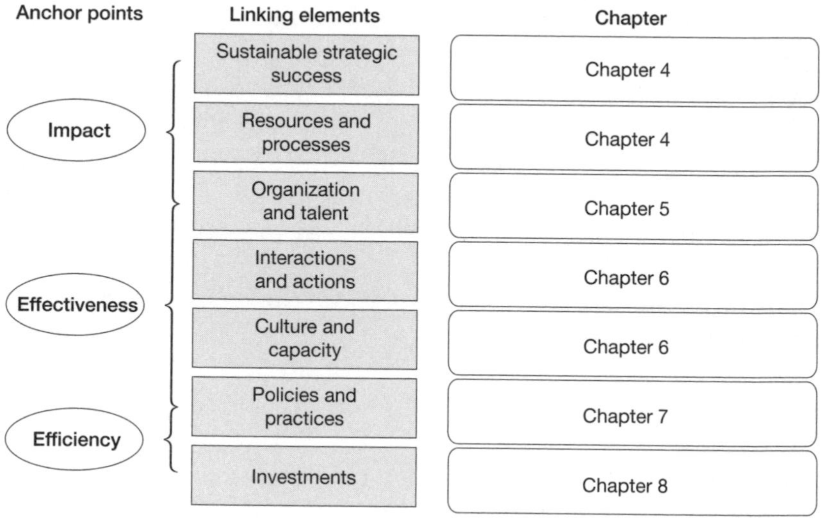

Anchor points	Linking elements	Chapter
Impact	Sustainable strategic success	Chapter 4
	Resources and processes	Chapter 4
	Organization and talent	Chapter 5
Effectiveness	Interactions and actions	Chapter 6
	Culture and capacity	Chapter 6
Efficiency	Policies and practices	Chapter 7
	Investments	Chapter 8

4

Impact in Strategy Analysis

Finding the Strategy Pivot-Points

How concerned would you be if your competitor had a copy of your HR strategy? Too often, the answer we get to that question is "Not very concerned, because ours probably looks a lot like theirs anyway." Indeed, if you compare the HR strategies of two competitors, without indicating the names of the companies, it is often hard to tell which strategy goes with which company. Talent and organization decisions are often based on very broad and generic strategic goals, such as "increase innovation" or "provide world-class customer service." Or they reflect workforce goals that are important but generic, such as "retain more baby-boomer technical talent," "increase diversity," or "build next-generation leadership." These goals undoubtedly fit the organization and its stated strategy, but then they would fit any number of strategies. HR strategies are seldom specific or unique.

Consider this question: "Where does your strategy require talent that is better than your competitors?" Likely, you do not need superior talent throughout the organization; that would not be cost competitive. But you do need superior talent for aspects of your value chain that will enable you to create and sustain a competitive advantage. If you want to establish a competitively distinctive talent strategy, you need a process for determining the strategically important elements.

Impact: Connecting Strategic Success
to Organization and Talent

Impact is the starting point for determining the talent strategy. Impact defines the relationship between sustainable strategic success and the performance of organization and talent. With a deep and logical understanding of these relationships, leaders have the necessary foundation to create truly innovative and distinctive talent strategies and to determine priorities. This chapter will focus on the key issues to consider when analyzing the business strategy to determine the talent implications. This level of analysis often is not done because it requires both line and HR leaders to dig deeper into the business strategy than is commonly done today. Our experience shows, however, that the insight that results from the process is worth the effort, not only for improving the talent strategy, but for implementing the organizational strategy. When there is a deep understanding of the strategy and its talent implications, HR can recommend programs and practices that are tangibly linked to the specific elements of the business strategy.

Figure 4-1 shows that in the HC BRidge framework, impact looks for pivot-points in sustainable strategic success, and then in the resources and processes (and other lenses that we will describe in this chapter) that define that success, and finally impact uncovers the talent pools and or-

FIGURE 4-1

HC BRidge framework: Impact

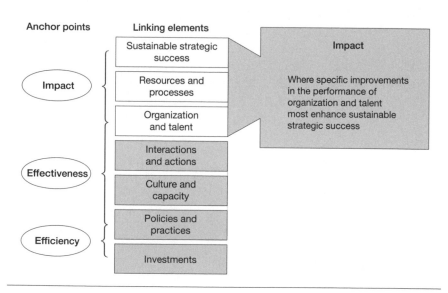

ganization elements that must align with them. We separate the impact analysis into two steps: (1) finding the pivot-points within the strategy and (2) connecting organization and talent performance to these strategy pivot-points. In this chapter we will focus on strategy pivot-points, which are those parts of the strategy whose execution significantly affects the strategy's success. In chapter 5 we will take the strategy pivot-points and determine how organization and talent performance affect them, which will complete our impact analysis.

Strategy Traditionally Emphasizes Mature Decision Sciences

It is important to distinguish strategy formulation from strategy analysis. Most leaders and strategy writing focus on strategy formulation. Strategy formulation is a vital role of leadership within the organization. It typically considers the external environment, customer trends, competitive positioning, and internal strengths and weaknesses. Strategy formulation produces the strategic direction—that is, the plan to compete in the marketplace, which may be quite formal and last over long periods or highly dynamic and adaptive.

Analysis defines the crucial (or pivotal) elements for the strategy's success. Analyzing strategy to reveal talent and organization implications is consistent with an emphasis on strategy execution. With a common understanding of the strategy pivot-points, leaders can help ensure that all resources, including the organization and talent resources, are deployed in relationship to their importance to strategic success.

Existing strategy formulation and analysis processes typically emphasize the decision frameworks of finance and marketing, which are well ingrained in the mental models of leaders and supported by strong analytical staff functions. Because most strategies fully reflect the logic of these more mature decision sciences, connecting finance and marketing decisions to strategy is a relatively straightforward task. As a result, marketing and financial tools are critical, but they differ little from one company to another. They are unlikely to create a competitive advantage precisely because they are so commonly understood.

When organizations analyze impact, they expand the scope of their strategy analysis to include talentship. Talent and organization implications are increasingly important for aligning the organization and achieving the strategic intent. Even a basic strategy in a moderately complex organization requires untold numbers of processes, resources, actions, interactions, and activities to make the organization work, much less thrive in a competitive marketplace. The key to organizational alignment is to find the pivot-points that we described earlier.

Distinguish What's Important from What's Pivotal

Having a more precise knowledge of the pivot-points than your competitors is a source of competitive advantage for executing the strategy. The key is understanding the difference between being important and being pivotal and applying it to the strategy. A good illustration of strategy pivot-points can be found in the 2004 U.S. presidential election between George W. Bush and John Kerry. Both campaigns quickly focused on the pivot-points, known as "swing states," and heavily allocated resources toward them. As a result, Ohio, a key swing state, received more attention than New York and Texas, even though they had more electoral votes.

Similar illustrations of pivot-points often occur in parliamentary elections throughout the world, where small minority parties may hold the key to forming a majority coalition. Germany's September 2005 election was inconclusive in part because neither of the largest parties (the Social Democrats backing former chancellor Gerhard Schroder and the Christian Democrats backing Angela Merkel) won a significant majority. Both parties attempted to build coalitions with the smaller Green Party and Free Democrats without success.[1] The smaller political parties were pivotal.

Leaders often believe they have an intuitive feel for the pivot-points in their strategy. However, particularly in regard to talent, their analysis often is neither rigorous nor systematic. While their hunches might be correct, their mental models can mistake things as pivotal when in fact those things are important but not necessarily pivotal. The lack of a systematic process also significantly jeopardizes the communication of the strategy to all levels of an organization. Strategic intuition is generally better near the top of the organization, where there is more sophistication and much more direct interaction with the strategy. As deployment cascades throughout the organization, the lack of a framework forces lower-level leaders to use their intuition to identify what's pivotal. This is often the very leadership level where competitive advantages are built and leveraged. Using a structured process to cascade the strategy though the analysis pivot-points can help ensure alignment at all levels and a successful implementation of the strategy. Table 4-1 defines *impact* and highlights how it defines pivot-points, the vital decisions it addresses, and offers new questions that we have found valuable in creating improved discussions about strategy pivot-points throughout the organization.

Strategy Seen Through Four Lenses

We find it useful to frame strategy analysis in terms of several lenses, or perspectives, that help determine the strategy pivot-points. Using these

TABLE 4-1

Anchor point: Impact

Definition	Pivot-points	Decisions to make	New talent and organization strategy discussions
• Describes the relationship between sustainable strategic success and the performance of organization and talent	• Where specific improvements in talent and organization performance will most enhance sustainable strategic success	• Where should you target talent and organization performance improvements so they have the biggest effect on sustainable strategic success?	• Where does your strategy require talent that is better than your competitors' for your strategy to win? • What are the untapped pivotal talent and organization elements that your competitors haven't recognized? • When the strategy changes, how should you change your talent and organization? • Where would improving organizational boundaries make you more competitive? • What talent should receive disproportionate investment?

strategy pivot-points, organizations can in turn identify their talent and organization pivot-points. Several strategy analysis lenses have emerged from our work, and we will highlight four of them here: strategic assumptions, competitive positioning, strategic resources, and business processes. Figure 4-2 shows how these lenses fit within the impact anchor point of the HC BRidge framework. In using these four lenses, leaders must dig deeper into their strategy than they typically do to determine the talent implications. At times participants get impatient with the strategy analysis process and want to take a shortcut to the organization and talent implications. However, we have seen that this is one place where time invested up front can pay huge dividends during strategy execution.

Earlier we used an example from the Disney theme parks to illustrate some of talentship's key concepts. In this chapter and the ones that follow, we will provide a more complex strategy situation from the commercial airplane market, one that is more typical of the strategic challenges that face most organizations. The long-standing and continuing competitive dynamics between Boeing and Airbus provide a rich illustration of how applying the strategy lenses results in new organization and talent insights. This case is unique because of the strategic depth, widely available public information, and the tangibility of the product. We will

FIGURE 4-2

Impact analysis process

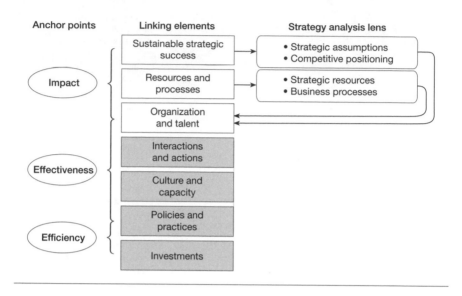

show how each lens identifies pivot-points of the strategy and develop a rich set of implications for organization and talent, effectiveness, and efficiency.

Boeing Versus Airbus: An Introduction

The market for commercial airplanes with the capacity to carry more than a hundred passengers is dominated by Boeing and Airbus. There has been a great deal of competitive intensity between the organizations on several dimensions. Airbus has surprised many industry followers by rising to become the largest provider of commercial jets in the world.[2] Before the emergence of Airbus in 1970, the major commercial aircraft competitors to Boeing were Lockheed (which made its last L-1011 in the 1980s and exited the commercial airplane market after the release of the Lockheed Tristar) and Douglas Aircraft (which was acquired by McDonnell to form McDonnell Douglas, a company that later was acquired by Boeing).[3] Airbus also has a unique organizational history that we describe in more detail in chapter 5, because how it was organized in 1970 still has substantial implications for some of the organizational pivot-points that it faces today.

Airbus's Move to Compete with the 747

In the long-range, jumbo aircraft market, which mainly focuses on international routes, Boeing has held a virtual monopoly with the 747 ever since it was first flown by PanAm in 1970. Since the time of its introduction, the 747 has stood alone as the only aircraft with a passenger capacity of over four hundred seats. In addition, its range significantly exceeded other planes when it was introduced, and it nearly matches all other aircraft today. Well over a thousand 747s have been produced, and it has been one of Boeing's most profitable aircraft. Figure 4-3 shows the position of the 747 relative to existing aircraft (existing aircraft are shown outside of the ovals, and proposed or pre-production aircraft are shown inside the ovals).[4]

In the 1990s, Airbus was a strong competitor to Boeing in the market for planes with one hundred to three hundred seats (the A330 in figure 4-3 shows this), but the super-jumbo market still belonged to Boeing with

FIGURE 4-3

Aircraft positioning map—passengers and range

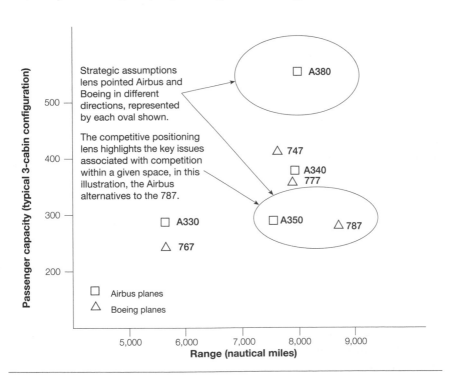

its 747, which typically accommodated 416 seats. In early 1991, Airbus started discussions with major international carriers regarding a super jumbo that would typically accommodate 555 seats. It was widely known that Airbus was exploring the super-jumbo market potential (in 1993 Airbus formally established a team to define the specifications for the A3XX), yet some experts were skeptical. Many senior leaders at Boeing did not expect Airbus to actually launch the program because they did not see a way that Airbus could create a return given the large upfront investment required. In the early 1990s, Boeing had joined the study group of Airbus partners in exploring potential demand for such a plane and determined that there was not sufficient product demand to justify the creation of so large a plane.

To the surprise of many in the industry, and likely some of Boeing's most senior executives, Airbus decided to launch a new super-jumbo program to leapfrog the 747 on its most unique dimension: size. With the launch of the A380 program in December 2000, Airbus asserted its intention to build the largest commercial aircraft in the sky, a distinction previously held by Boeing. With estimated development costs in excess of $13 billion, the first test flight of the A380 occurred with great fanfare in April 2005. Pending flight certification, the first units destined for commercial service were scheduled for delivery to Singapore Airlines in late 2006. Figure 4-3 shows how the introduction of the A380 changed the aircraft competition, with the A380 in the upper-right of the diagram, alone in its capacity of over 500 seats and with a highly-competitive range.

Boeing's Response to the A380 Launch

Boeing might have been expected to try to develop an aircraft to occupy the high-range and high-capacity territory of the A380, but they didn't. Boeing had formally dropped its exploration of the 747X in 1997, when it decided to focus its efforts on planes with less capacity than 555 seats.

Boeing saw a different future in which the combination of increased passenger demand and constrained hubs would cause an industry shift. Hubs would become less central, and there would be a significant increase in the number of direct flights between cities that were not traditional hubs. In Boeing's view, customers would increasingly prefer direct flights, such as nonstop flights from Portland to Brussels or St. Louis to Seoul. However, the demand for seats on flights between such new long-range city pairs would be lower, which meant airlines needed planes that could be efficiently operated at passenger loads of between two-hundred fifty and three-hundred passengers, smaller than the A380 and smaller even than Boeing's 747 or 777. As figure 4-3 shows, Boeing had no aircraft in that class, because its existing 747 and 777 had higher capacities than anticipated as optimum for the new long-range flights. The only aircraft in that capacity range was the Airbus A340. However, while the A340 satisfied the size and range needs, it was an older four-engine aircraft that was not efficient enough to meet the emerging airline requirements that Boeing forecast.

In April, 2004, Boeing formally committed to launching the 787 Dreamliner program (then referred to as the 7E7). At that time, they also signed Al Nippon Airways to be the first customer, with an order of 50 planes, valued at $6 million. Figure 4-3 shows the competitive space that would be occupied by the proposed 787. The 787 Dreamliner was different from existing aircraft because it was to be built with advanced materials (such as composite materials for the shell of the plane) and to include other innovations that would improve fuel efficiency, lower operating costs for airlines, and increase long-haul customer satisfaction with features such as an improved cabin environment and larger windows.

Both Boeing and Airbus had the capital, engineering talent, and other organizational capabilities to build airplanes for either market. Airbus chose to allocate its engineering and production capabilities to build the A380, and if its projections were correct, it would have a market lead that would be difficult to overcome. Even if Boeing ultimately discovered that the demand was for approximately eight hundred of the super-jumbo planes, there still might not be room for Boeing to succeed as a second competitor in the super-jumbo market. Given the time and capital required to build a new airplane, combined with the high breakeven point for such an investment, if the Airbus demand projections were correct it would leave Boeing with few strategic options.

Applying the Strategic Assumptions Lens

The strategic assumptions lens uncovers talent pivot-points in strategy formulation by asking, "Where are we making important assumptions about the future of the industry that are different from our competitors?" These strategy areas represent pivot-points, where pivotal talent pools are associated with the analysis that supports those assumptions or with making the predictions.

Consider the strategic assumptions of Boeing and Airbus. Both companies saw a future with increased demand for air passenger traffic. One of the most significant drivers of the increasing demand was the economic growth of Asia, where there are large distances between many of the economic centers. In addition, general economic growth was increasing demand in all parts of the world. Also, both Boeing and Airbus recognized that the major hubs were significant constraints with limited incremental capacity (such as new runways or gates) available to meet the demand. It was at this point, however, that the companies diverged.

The Airbus market analysis showed that to meet the demands of increased passenger traffic with limited hub capacity, airlines would need to increase the number of passengers that could be carried on each flight. Airbus predicted demand of seven hundred units for the A380 over twenty years, and in some projections potential demand over the life of the plane went as high as eleven hundred or more. The breakeven point for the investment was estimated to be about five hundred units. Boeing accepted different market analysis that projected higher demand for point-to-point routes through less constrained airports, driven in part by increased passenger impatience with the delays and cumbersome procedures necessary to manage growing passenger populations flowing through a fixed hub-city capacity. Figure 4-3 shows that these strategic assumptions led Boeing to choose to design the 787 to compete in the lower oval of the diagram, rather than to compete directly with the A380 in the top-right.

Pivot-Points: Where Strategic Assumptions Differ

The strategy pivot-point from this lens for both organizations is their prediction of the long-term market demand for super-jumbo airplanes. The talent and organization pivot-points are those where performance most affects the accuracy and timeliness of these market predictions. The talent pools include jobs such as market economists, actuaries, statisticians, and data analysts. This is an extreme example, but it illustrates how important a small number of employees can be, often employees who are outside the organization's traditional core competence. In this case well over $20 billion in investment capital—and many times that amount in market impact, reputation, and market capitalization—will be leveraged on the quality of demand analysis made by a relatively small percentage of employees in each organization.

The second application of this lens is to ask, "What can be done to help ensure our strategic assumptions are correct?" Both Boeing and Airbus have invested heavily in public relations and other activities to help persuade airlines and passengers alike that their vision of the aircraft industry's future is correct. With potential clients and in the press, they are competing as fiercely for their view of the future as they are for their respective products and offerings. These strategies require careful attention to the talent implications required to execute them well.

Questions to Uncover Insight in Strategic Assumptions

Several key questions can yield insight from the strategic assumptions lens. They include:

- What strategic assumptions about the future does your strategy depend on?

- Which of these assumptions are the most uncertain? What impact would they have on your strategy if they changed?

- Where are you making assumptions about the future that are different than your competitors?

Applying the Competitive Positioning Lens

Strategy pivot-points related to competitive positioning help focus organizational resources on the elements that are most vital to successfully achieving and sustaining a chosen market position. As Michael Porter noted, "A company can outperform rivals only if it can establish a difference that it can preserve."[5] The competitive positioning lens focuses on the elements that are unique within strategic positioning and translates them into pivot-points that should receive incremental attention during strategy execution.

Why Generic Strategy Categories Alone Do Not Work

It is difficult to uncover the competitive dynamics or implications of strategy if you're using general strategic positioning concepts, such as "differentiated" or "low cost." Even dimensions such as "customer intimate," "product leadership," or "operational efficiency" don't reveal the pivot-points. They are useful concepts, but they are not specific enough to identify strategy pivot-points that reveal talent and organization implications. Yet organizational leaders often attempt to connect precise talent and organization decisions to these broad concepts. Consider the service organization that wants to focus on being customer intimate and provides customer service training to everyone, even those in talent pools that do not, by design, interact with the customer.

One reason these concepts are inadequate is that several competitors are typically classified into the same strategic category. For example, Merck, Bristol Myers-Squibb, and Pfizer all have product leadership strategies and operate within the same industry. Should they have identical talent strategies? Given that the essence of strategy is to operate differently from others, additional insight is required through the competitive positioning lens to uncover pivot-points in the strategy that can reveal organization and talent implications of the relative competitive position.

When we refer to "competitive positioning," we are speaking of the unique value proposition that is delivered to the marketplace. We think of this in terms of what differentiates a company's offering from the other available alternatives. If an offering is undifferentiated, then you can expect to have a low-margin business, because customers can simply compare similar offerings from different providers and shop exclusively based on price. As the 2006 television commercials from IBM asked, "What makes you special?" The answer to that question is the essence of competitive positioning.

Questions to Uncover Insight in Competitive Positioning

When considering a strategy's pivot-points, it is important to understand the intended competitive advantages. We find the following questions to be helpful in applying the competitive positioning lens:

- Where does the strategy require sustained differentiation from competitors?

- Where does it require a competitor's differentiator to be neutralized?

- Where does it acknowledge a competitor's differentiator but seeks other strategies to minimize that differentiator's impact on targeted market segments?

For differentiators to create value, they must be valued by the customer, produced in scale, and difficult for competitors to duplicate.

The competitive positioning lens can be illustrated using the Boeing-Airbus example. We saw earlier that Boeing's first decision was not to try to compete with an aircraft challenging the A380 seat capacity, but to go with the smaller 787. Figure 4-3 shows that the competitive positioning lens addresses how Boeing would differentiate the 787 from the planes that were competitive alternatives, in seating capacity class of between 250 and 300 passengers.

Boeing's 787 Versus Airbus's Alternatives

When Boeing initially launched the 787, it was called the 7E7. The E indicated that the clear value proposition was efficiency. The idea was that even at the lower passenger loads of point-to-point routes, the 787 could be operated efficiently enough to provide airlines with attractive total profits. The 787 was a direct competitor to Airbus' established product, the A330, with the 787 offering longer flight range (nine thousand nautical miles for the 787 vs. six thousand for the A330) and improved fuel efficiency. Airbus acknowledged the longer range of the 7E7 but doubted that there was significant demand for it. Airbus publicly asserted that the proposed 7E7 was too small (the A330 held about 10 percent more passengers) and that this would offset the improved fuel efficiency because the 7E7 passenger capacity was too low to offer sufficient revenues, considering total operating costs, even assuming lower fuel costs per passenger. For these reasons, Airbus initially claimed that it did not see the offering as a threat to its larger-capacity market leading A330, which could also hold 250 to 300 passengers, and could offer greater revenues per flight, albeit with a shorter flight range. However, Boeing quickly succeeded in articulating the incremental value of the 7E7 over the A330, and the renamed 787 attracted orders at a brisk rate as customers were focused on operating costs and found the 787's value proposition highly attractive.

Airbus's Response with the A350

In late 2004 Airbus effectively acknowledged that the 787 was a viable competitor to the A330 when Airbus announced its intention to build a new airplane, the A350, to compete directly with the 787.

The proposed A350 differed from the A330 in at least three significant ways:

- Used new engines (the same fuel-efficient types as the 787)

- Extended the range to effectively match the 787

- Increased the use of advanced materials to reduce overall weight

As a result, two years before the first 787 was scheduled to enter service, the A350 proposal had neutralized two of Boeing 787's most important differentiators over the A330: new engines and extended range. Boeing still strongly defended the other competitive advantages of its 787 offering, including:

- Lower overall cost of operation

- Better passenger experience

- Earlier production and a reliable delivery schedule, based on Boeing's history

This analysis of specific aircraft offerings provides a good example of the deeper strategy insights that provide the basis for much deeper talent strategies. The contrast between the 787 and its competing aircraft re-veals differentiators and how they must be valued by customers, deliv-ered in scale, and protected from competitors. We use a graphical tool, called a differentiator map, to summarize such differentiators. The differ-entiator map for this example is shown in figure 4-4, specifically compar-ing the 787 to the A330 and the proposed A350.

The Differentiator Map

Each row in figure 4-4 is a dimension of differentiation. Each dimension is scaled, with the more strategically positive attributes or features on the right-hand end of the scale. For example, the top row shows small pas-senger capacity on the left and large passenger capacity on the right. Looking at figure 4-4, it is apparent that the proposed A350 brought Air-bus into parity with the Boeing 787 in many key dimensions, particularly several where the A330 had a disadvantage. However, the bottom row of the figure reveals a significant disadvantage of the A350 over the 787 and the established A330. The A350 would not be available as soon as the 787 (the A330 was an established aircraft, available immediately). The differ-entiator map in figure 4-4 also shows that while the A350 brought Airbus to parity on many of the differentiators where the 787 had advantages over the A330, the A350 would not create any significant advantages over the 787 on any dimension. The A350 did not bring any significant new differentiators into the market. As we will discuss later in this chapter, the

FIGURE 4-4

Differentiator map: Boeing 787 vs. Airbus A330 and proposed A350

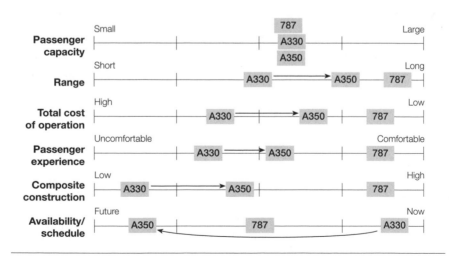

A350 concept was eventually dropped in favor of an entirely new aircraft design, the A350 XWB.

How Competitive Positioning Shapes Talent Strategy

Using the competitive positioning lens to inform organization and talent decisions involves ensuring that the talent strategies are based on a shared understanding of the unique value that the business intends to create. For example, it is vital that engineers working on the Boeing 787 understand that delivering a uniquely comfortable flying experience, not just a lower cost, is a critical strategy element. If there is not a common understanding, each team may work toward valid goals, but collectively they will not align to support a unique value proposition.

We have frequently observed talent strategies that are aligned with the offering's value proposition but lack a sufficient focus on what is *unique* about the positioning. This would happen, for example, if Boeing based talent strategies on its airplanes' safety. While safety is clearly an important goal, it is not a sufficient basis for a distinctive talent strategy. Although it is a necessary condition for success, it is not differentiated from the Airbus offering on that dimension. We believe that this is one of the reasons that so many competitors' talent strategies are so similar. Without a shared understanding among the leadership team of the distinctive elements of the strategy, it is difficult, if not impossible, to develop and sustain a unique talent strategy. In contrast, when the deep and distinctive strategy elements are uncovered, very unique and aligned talent strategies emerge, as later chapters will show.

Resource and Process Lenses

The second linking element in impact is resources and processes. As figure 4-2 shows, there are two strategy lenses that arise from this linking element. To create sustainable value, strategic positions must not only be unique but be difficult for competitors to duplicate. The key is to find the differentiators that can be protected from competitive attack for a period that is long enough to obtain the required return.

Research suggests two primary ways that unique competitive positions can be difficult to duplicate. One way is to build a strategy on resources that are valuable, rare, and hard to imitate or substitute.[6] For example, drug companies have patents. Pepsi has more than sixteen brands that have sales over $1 billion annually.[7] Drug patents and brands are strategic resources because they are valuable and difficult for competitors to duplicate.

Can Your Business Strategy Support a True Talent Strategy?

Talentship connects organization and talent decisions to the organization's strategy. Strategy formulation is different from strategy analysis, but often questions arise during strategy analysis that reveal areas where the strategy itself is not sufficiently well defined.

We often find that organizations have a list of goals (raise revenues, lower cost, improve quality) and compare themselves to others on these specific goals (e.g., through benchmarking), yet they fail to define many vital and necessary strategy elements. We find that there is often very detailed information about the organization's action plans but relatively little about the strategic position and likely competitive responses that the strategy will generate. When HR leaders start applying the talentship strategy analysis tools we've offered here, asking deeper strategy questions puts them in an uncomfortable situation. Their colleagues who are line managers or strategic planners often can't answer questions such as these: What are the key differentiators? How do we intend to protect our strategic advantage from competitive attack? What resources are we building that provide the platform for future strategies? Those colleagues often become defensive if HR leaders press too aggressively.

Michael Porter made this point well when he said that operational effectiveness is not a strategy and noted that a company can outperform rivals only if it can establish a difference that it can preserve. He has gone as far as saying that Japanese companies rarely have strategies. Donald Hambrick and James Fredrickson define five questions that we have found useful for helping organizations assess their strategy and identify possible gaps:

The second way strategies can be difficult to duplicate is when they are built on networks of business processes that are difficult to duplicate on the whole. This could be a particular business process (such as a proprietary method of manufacturing), but often it is a network of processes that work together.[8] As an example, Michael Porter notes that while any one part of Southwest Airlines' operations can be copied, the entire series of business processes focused on a specific low-cost market position has been very difficult to duplicate—even by established carriers that have substantial resources and expertise in running airlines.

Often strategic resources and business processes work in combination to support the sustainability of a strategy. The lenses we describe here can

- *Arenas:* Where will we be active?

- *Vehicles:* How will we get there?

- *Differentiators:* How will we win in the marketplace?

- *Staging:* What will be our speed and sequence of moves?

- *Economic logic:* How will we obtain our returns?

Yet a large number of organizations are highly successful even though they lack one or more of the strategy elements recommended by Porter, Hambrick, Fredrickson, and others. So a fully developed strategy is not a requirement for success.[a] Nor is a fully defined strategy necessary to uncover useful organization and talent insights. Such insights can be revealed by applying the other lenses we'll describe below to analyze organization goals, initiatives, and processes—even if those goals, initiatives, and processes are not necessarily grounded in a fully developed strategy.

Still, talentship undoubtedly is even more effective as strategies become more complete and well developed. In fact, it can be a catalyst for strategy improvement. When leaders use the talentship strategy lenses carefully and avoid defensiveness, the process encourages discussions about where the organization should improve the strategy, how it can improve its strategy formulation and analysis processes, and where it might invest in enhancing the strategic competence of its leaders.

a. See Michael E. Porter, "What Is Strategy?" *Harvard Business Review*, November–December 1996, 61–78; and Donald C. Hambrick and James W. Fredrickson, "Are You Sure You Have a Strategy?" *Academy of Management Executive* 19, no. 4 (2005): 51–62.

be applied independently, but there are many important interactions between them, which is why they are combined into a single element—impact—in the HC BRidge decision framework shown in figure 4-2.

Applying the Strategic Resources Lens

Resources are things that an organization can create, acquire, grow, and protect to support sustainable strategic advantage. Resources can be tangible (such as legal rights in an oil field lease) or intangible (such as a brand). Resources are considered strategic when they form the basis for a valuable differentiator that is difficult for a competitor to duplicate. Identifying strategic pivot-points related to resources requires a consideration of how organizations compete in markets for the vital factors of production and services.[9] As you will see, one of the key strategic resources for Boeing is the organizational capabilities (including patents) that are associated with composite technology, a key differentiator for the 787.

Consider the Boeing advantages for the 787—those that it wanted to protect over time and certainly those against the launch of the rival A350. Two of Boeing's differentiators, next-generation engine and longer range, were eliminated with the announcement of the A350. If the Airbus program proved successful, Boeing's earlier-launch advantage would also be temporary. Boeing needed to carefully consider how it would use resources and processes to establish and protect a competitive advantage long enough to pay off the investment.

Keep in mind that at the time Airbus had considerable flexibility because its plane was "still on paper"; it could redesign its plane to adapt to what it learned from the marketplace or from what it observed as Boeing developed the 787. Two of the key differentiators that Boeing was working to protect included total efficiency for the airline operator (lower total cost of operation per passenger mile over the plane's lifetime) and higher comfort for passengers. What allowed these advantages to be protected? One of the key drivers behind each advantage was the greater use of composites in the aircraft body.

Strategic Resources Associated with Composite Capabilities

The 787 will make more use of carbon composites than any other aircraft ever made. While both the Airbus A350 and the 787 will have carbon composite wings, the 787 will also have a composite fuselage. The use of composites decreases an aircraft's weight, which improves efficiency and provides additional passenger comforts. Boeing's message is clear: a plane made of composites can have larger windows (because composites are stronger than metal), higher levels of humidity (because composites don't corrode), and increased pressurization that allows the plane to maintain a lower effective altitude (because composites can handle greater pressure changes in more cycles without deteriorating). One of the tangible benefits is that passengers will experience less fatigue and less ear stress over the long flights the plane is specifically designed for.

We find that the following questions help apply the strategic resources lens:

- Considering your resources, what makes your competitive advantages difficult to duplicate?

- What resources (tangible and intangible) do you have that your competitors would most like to have?

The greater use of composite construction on the plane is a significant difference between Boeing and Airbus. It is directly linked to the 787's unique value proposition. Based on the designs Airbus had presented, it is not one that the organization intended to duplicate directly with the proposed A350. What makes Boeing's advantages difficult to duplicate? One of the strategic resources for Boeing is certainly its intellectual property related to composite technology.

Boeing has significant intellectual property (IP) regarding composite technology applied to airplanes in general and airplane bodies in particular. A recent scan of U.S. patents and applications yielded over 150 patents on the search "Boeing + composite + structure." Boeing has built unique and important IP in areas as varied as modeling and repairing cracks in the body (a vital difference between composites and aluminum) and in devices that can support the nondestructive inspections of composite structures.

Analysis of the Strategic Resources Pivot-Points at Boeing

Strategy pivot-points are based on the critical issues associated with the strategic resource. Key follow-up questions that will help you identify the pivot-points associated with the strategic resource include:

- What can your competitor do to emulate your strategic resource?
- What can your competitor do to reduce the value of your strategic resource?
- What substitution options are available to (or are being pursued by) a competitor that could neutralize your advantage?

Regarding possible emulation of the strategic resource, Boeing will ensure that it has patents and other protections in place to avoid allowing Airbus or other potential competitors to use critical elements of the composite IP. This safeguard is more important with regard to composites than other IP because they are linked to so many of Boeing's key differentiators. Considering that Boeing has thousands of patents, the ones that are most important to protecting the strategic resource are the pivot-point.

Airbus's Response: Advanced Aluminum as the Alternative to Composites

During this time Airbus tried to reduce the value of composites as a strategic resource with public relations messages that raised questions about the technology's safety. The company had openly questioned the soundness of the Boeing decision to build so much of the plane with the technology, and indeed, Boeing encountered some challenges related to safety in the early implementation of the new technology.

Airbus's primary strategy, however, was to advance the state of the art of traditional aluminum technology. It has invested in new alloys and other processes to further reduce aircraft weight and to improve the structural properties of advanced aluminum. It referred to the composite as "nothing more than black aluminum," indicating that it did not think much differentiation would result with the new technology, compared to its advances in more traditional approaches. The Airbus strategy was to substitute advanced aluminum technologies as an alternative to Boeing's proposed composite advantage.

What must be done to turn the resources into a source of differentiation? What must be done to protect them from competitors' attacks? Questions like these identify important strategy pivot-points that are vital to both strategy execution and to the organization and talent decisions that will follow.

Applying the Business Processes Lens

The final lens that we will use to look at strategy pivot-points is business processes. Processes are transformations that create new value; the results of a process have outputs that are more valuable than the inputs. For example, at the macrolevel, raw materials, labor, and capital go into a car factory and out comes a car.

The previous two lenses (competitive positioning and strategic resources) require comparing the organization to competitors, either in the markets for the ultimate offering or in the markets for the resources that are required to produce the offerings. In contrast, the business processes lens more typically applies an internal perspective. Questions for applying the business processes lens include:

- Where does the performance of a business process limit the organization's success?

- Where does a business process require the most significant change to implement the strategy?

- What are the most important business process interfaces, either internally or with external organizations, such as suppliers or customers?

Linking Strategy Analysis and Quality Initiatives

An important motivator of process analysis has been the increased focus on quality and continuous improvement. Another major driver has been enterprise information systems. All of them produce very detailed process maps that are often used to cut costs or increase speed. Such process maps can also be used to find constraints, which often reveal key strategic pivot-points. Constraints exist where the capacity and/or quality of some process limits the entire system's performance. Constraints are a familiar concept in engineering and operations management. It is a well-known principle that when a process is limited by one particular element, or bottleneck, removing that bottleneck improves performance overall. Operations engineering calculates "shadow prices" (the value of getting one more unit of performance from a constrained process or one more unit of a constrained resource) and has even proposed a theory of constraints as a key to improving manufacturing performance.[10]

Boeing's Heritage of Constraints in Manufacturing Processes

Let's apply the constraint principle of the business processes lens to the Boeing/Airbus example. At the end of 2005, Boeing had orders for 291 of its 787s from twenty-three different customers, a record for a new aircraft. As a result, all available delivery slots for the new plane were filled until 2012, well after Airbus's A350 was anticipated to be in production. Unless Boeing could produce more aircraft before the A350 was available, it would exhaust its advantage in being first to market with the planes already sold. There were more customers that wanted this kind of aircraft, and if Boeing could produce more of them before the Airbus plane premiered, it wouldn't have to compete with Airbus's new aircraft. Yet increasing the speed or rate of production could be risky. Boeing had been hurt badly in results and reputation when it attempted to quickly increase aircraft production in the late 1990s, which eventually resulted in a virtual shut down of its production lines, missing significant customer delivery commitments and writing off over $1 billion.

Changes in Business Processes as Pivot-Points

In addition to applying the business processes lens from a constraint perspective, it is also important to apply it from a change perspective. When looking at business processes, key pivot-points include those that require the greatest change. At Boeing one of the most significant changes was its relationship with its suppliers. The new 787 was different from past planes in the amount of systems integration that occurred outside the Boeing organization. While the majority of parts typically are made by suppliers to Boeing, the 787 design required that large amounts of parts integration, including much of the systems integration, be done by outside suppliers that would then deliver major sections of the plane. Finally, these suppliers were distributed throughout the world since global sourcing is a critical issue for many governments, which play a critical role in the selection of commercial aircraft.

At the same time, the economics required that Boeing achieve unprecedented levels of productivity in the entire supply chain to produce an attractive return on the plane. The organization planned to do the plane's final assembly in less than one week at the Boeing site in Everett, Washington. Given the urgency of the production supply chain and the significant size of the integrated sections that had to be assembled, the company chose to use air freight to ship the major sections from the suppliers to Everett. This required creating a special type of 747 freighter, one that could handle very large sections of the new 787. The 747 LCF (large cargo freighter) is a specially modified 747-400 that opens up 90 degrees from just behind the wing so that the large sections of the 787 can be loaded into its body and flown to Washington. This modified 747 required certification and was expected to be in service in early 2007, just in time to meet the production ramp-up for the 787.

Finally, production demands were so significant that Boeing planned to begin larger-scale production of the plane even before it was fully approved by the governmental authorities as fit to fly. This will result in an inventory of planes that sit on the ramp while the first one to fly completes the rigorous set of tests required of any new airplane design. One pivot-point here is whether significant issues are found during the certification phase. Given the highly integrated design required to achieve the performance standards for the 787, even minor redesigns required by certification testing could be both costly and a vital constraint in the supply chain. If there are required changes for planes that have already been produced, the costs could indeed be significant.

It is clear that Boeing had potential competitive advantages, but to realize them, the organization needed to systematically address the changes required and the potential constraints within the new business processes. Because Boeing's advantages in large part would be based on its first-mover advantages with the 787, the speed with which it can execute the strategy has a direct impact on the final outcome. Boeing failed when it tried to ramp up production in the late 1990s. To experience success with the 787, it would need to execute well on the pivot-points that the business processes lens has identified.

Integrating the Strategy Pivot-Points

The four lenses combine to provide a picture of the pivot-points for the 787 strategy, as shown in table 4-2. These pivot-points are much clearer and more specific than typical high-level strategic statements such as "launch and market the new aircraft." Our experience has shown that organizations need to analyze strategy this thoroughly if they hope to identify talent and organization pivot-points. An advantage of such deep analysis is that the strategy itself will be improved. It is not unusual for line leaders to remark that their HR counterparts are asking very good questions when those HR leaders analyze strategy in this way. In fact, we increasingly find that these strategy analysis techniques and strategic lenses become a valued part of the strategy process. We will return to this in chapter 10 when we discuss how to implement talentship.

TABLE 4-2

Key strategy pivot-points for the Boeing 787

Strategic analysis lens	Pivot-points
Industry analysis	Increasing the perceived value of point-to-point routes in the mind of: • The flying public • The industry • Investors • Vital government and regulatory stakeholders
Competitive positioning	Critical Boeing 787 differentiators: • Lower total cost per passenger mile • Greater passenger comfort • Earlier production
Strategic resources	• Intellectual property protection related to composites • Ensuring all intellectual property can be used in commercial aircraft designs
Business processes	• Fast production ramp-up to capture high initial demand • Using more global suppliers in an integrated way • Global logistics

Strategy Pivot-Points and Strategy Dynamics

One of the questions leaders frequently ask is "What do we do when the strategy changes?" The need for agility actually makes talentship even more valuable. In our work with organizations we find that the ability to quickly dissect and understand pivot-points actually allows the organization to respond more quickly to changes and to align resources to the changing competitive dynamics.

Even as authors, we have experienced just such rapid strategic changes. When we first drafted this chapter, the primary competition was between the 7E7 and the A330. As Airbus realized that the A330 was not competitive, it announced plans for the new A350, so we revised our original analysis based on that announcement and the actions that followed, and that is the version that is reflected in this chapter. By July 2006 Boeing had booked orders for more than four hundred 787s. Airbus realized that its strategy to upgrade the A330 to the A350 was not working and announced the new A350-XWB. The A350 was a derivative of the A330, but the A350-XWB is an entirely new plane, with estimated development costs in the range of $10 billion. The decision meant that the 350-XWB, which would compete with the 787, would not be available until at least 2012. At about the same time that Airbus announced the decision to switch to the A350-XWB design, it also announced that the A380 would not hit its original delivery schedule, causing some to wonder whether 2012 was a realistic date. Boeing could also offer a delivery date of 2012, but in view of Airbus's failure to meet its A380 schedule and concern that Airbus was spreading its resources too thinly across too many new projects, Boeing's perceived greater likelihood of meeting promised dates was now an even greater pivotal potential competitive advantage.

How does this change the pivot-points? A full analysis is not possible yet, but one of the differences is that the A350-XWB will be much more like the 787 in its use of composites to create a wider body. So Boeing will no longer be uniquely positioned on the advantages of composite over advanced aluminum, since Airbus now intends to match the 787 on these factors, just as it emulated the engines and range earlier. On-time delivery will remain one of the biggest pivot-points. Even if Airbus meets its 2012 target for the A350-XWB, Boeing will now have a near monopoly in this segment between the years 2008–2012, with demand well in excess of its planned delivery capacity. So increasing production capacity will become an even more significant pivot-point of the Boeing strategy for the next several years. These strategic developments also make protecting Boeing's composite technology more pivotal as Airbus moves to use more composites. So, the talent pools pivotal to such protection (such as international patent attorneys and composite process design engineers) will emerge as even more strategic.

Notice how the detailed resolution of strategic issues provided by the lenses allows us to see more precisely where Boeing and Airbus need to change. *Agility* becomes more than a watchword; it is translated into specific pivot-points that have clearer talent and organization implications.

Conclusion

The impact anchor point of the HC BRidge framework provides one of the most challenging and one of the most potentially significant changes in how organizations approach their talent and organization decisions. We introduced these ideas a decade ago, and since then we have worked with many organizations to implement them.[11] Recognizing the importance of impact and using it to delve more deeply into strategies for insights about organization and talent resources has profound implications for several aspects of leadership and HR management. In our work with organizations, we encourage HR leaders that support business units or vital business function (often called business partners or generalists) to embrace impact and apply lenses to find the pivot-points in the strategy. The result is that these HR leaders facilitate very different conversations about strategy and how it is achieved and maintained.

But the strategy pivot-points have implications beyond HR. They are often useful for other functions, such as information technology, which also needs to understand the strategy pivot-points to determine where decisions can make significant differences. By posing the questions we have described in this chapter, leaders inside and outside the HR function develop a deep and shared language to produce more unique and specific functional strategies. One result is that the strategies about organization and talent decisions become much more specific, unique, and competitive, as we will see in chapter 5.

5

Impact in Organization
and Talent

Linking Strategy Pivot-Points
to Structures and Roles

Consider the distinctions between two of the most successful organizations in the world: Berkshire Hathaway and GE. Both pursue strategies that require that they offer shareholders value through their ability to create value across a diverse set of businesses in vastly different competitive markets. Yet they could not be more different in their choices about how to organize. Berkshire Hathaway is organized as a holding company of businesses that largely operate separately.[1] GE creates distinctive value by leveraging its management systems across its diverse business portfolio.[2] Whereas Berkshire Hathaway seldom shares leadership talent across its divisions, GE is world renowned for building leaders that move quickly and effectively across its businesses, providing synergy and consistency and leveraging common management systems. Both companies are building valuable and strategic top management and leaders, and both companies have built organizations that deploy that talent strategically. The strategic meaning of these talent pools and how they are organized are very different. Indeed, GE and Berkshire Hathaway are successful precisely because they understand, more completely than most companies, how the organization and quality of leadership and top management talent contribute to their unique strategic value. GE doesn't need the same talent approach as Berkshire Hathaway, and vice versa. In this chapter we describe the elements of talentship that inform decisions about how talent is organized, as well as the differential contributions of talent pools within the organization. This chapter also deals with how organizations can tell when their talent pivot-points are different from others, as is the case with leaders at GE and Berkshire Hathaway.

Chapter 4 described the first stage of the impact analysis, which is finding the pivot-points within the strategy to attain sustainable strategic success through the use of strategy lenses, including processes and resources. In this chapter, we complete the impact analysis by linking the strategic pivot-points to the organization and talent implications. Figure 5-1 shows this graphically, within the HC BRidge framework. The organization and talent linking element translates the strategy analysis into its implications for organization boundaries, management system, and the quality of the people. This element also serves as the connection to the linking elements that define strategy execution through effectiveness and efficiency.

We will use the concept of performance yield curves and highlight the strategic options revealed through understanding the connection between sustainable strategic success and the performance of organization and talent. Organization and talent pivot-points arise at three levels:

- Organizational pivot-points

- Pivotalness between talent pools (talent pool segmentation)

- Pivotalness within talent pools

FIGURE 5-1

HC BRidge framework: Organization and talent

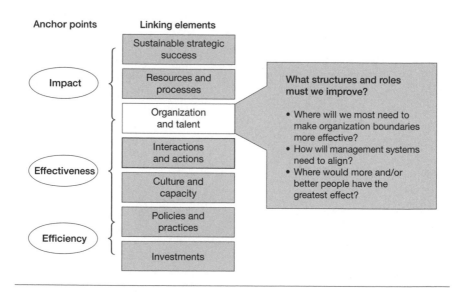

This chapter describes the first two levels from that list, as well as some organization and talent pool decisions that exploit these insights. It also introduces the third type of talent pivotalness (the elements within pools and roles); chapters 6 and 7, which address effectiveness, more thoroughly examine that type of pivotalness and how program and practices support it.

Organizational Pivot-Points

Pivot-points at the organization level involve formal and informal relationships inside and outside the organization, such as formal organization structures, reporting relationships, hierarchy, and management systems, as well as informal social networks and communications. Every theory and framework of organizational design includes alignment with the strategy, but few describe how to analyze the strategy thoroughly enough to reveal the organizing implications. Chapter 4 showed how strategy lenses reveal deep insights, which we will now connect to organization elements.

Linking Organizational Design to Enterprise Portfolio Strategy

Why does your organization have the business units that it has? How do those units create more value together than they do apart? How do the answers to these questions reflect how your enterprise is organized?

While those are seemingly basic questions, we find that many organizational structures are not directly linked back to the fundamental theory of the organization that drives the portfolio. Berkshire Hathaway is clearly driven by a value-based investment philosophy, not unique value added by the integration of its business units. What are the implications? A very small home office and little focus on either common management systems or integrating talent across the organizational units. For example, leaders at Dairy Queen do not typically experience rotational assignment through NetJets or Geico as part of a career path to develop future enterprise leaders for Berkshire Hathaway. The situation at GE, however, is quite different.

A major part of GE's enterprise strategy is to develop and implement state-of-the-art management systems across diverse business units. As a result, leaders are routinely moved between diverse divisions not only to bring new thinking on the management systems to new divisions but also to develop a deep bench of leaders to support new business opportunities, including mergers and acquisitions.

The portfolio strategies for Boeing and Airbus are also quite different.[3] For Boeing the primary portfolio strategy includes significant investments

in both military and commercial projects. One of the goals is to share innovation and know-how across divisions. When Boeing complains about
the European government subsidies that Airbus receives, Airbus is quick
to counter that Boeing receives significant benefits from U.S. government
investment, largely through military contracts. The desire to share know-
how across the organization was one of the major reasons that Boeing
invested in its state-of-the-art leadership center on more than fifty acres
just outside St. Louis. One of the major goals was to create a place where
leaders from across the diverse Boeing enterprise could experience learning together.

At the same time investments that European governments have made
in the European Aeronautic Defense and Space Company (EADS, Airbus's
corporate parent) also have organizational implications. One of the most
challenging dynamics is the need to allocate production and relatively
high-paying aerospace jobs across the countries that provide support to
EADS. The Airbus production process must be organized in part to reflect
the theory of the EADS portfolio, which in large part was driven by a desire to create a sustainable aerospace industry within Europe.

Linking Organizational Design to the Value Chain

When considering the organizational pivot-points of the strategy analysis, one of the first areas to consider is how the value chain (i.e., the supply chain) is organized to deliver the unique strategic position. How does
the organizational design support the delivery of the unique value proposition? Continuing with the Boeing illustration, this is clearly a critical
issue for the 787 offering. One of the most profound pivot-points at the
organization level is the supplier partner network required to produce the
787. This plane is different because Boeing suppliers will preassemble large
segments. One of the primary organizational pivot-points is that a larger
segment of the supply chain extends outside Boeing, including more input
from the suppliers on key elements of component design. To achieve cost
efficiencies and rapid scaling across this supply chain, Boeing must coordinate with suppliers at a much higher level than its usual approach. Traditionally, Boeing did much more of the integration in-house and had
suppliers provide components at a much more basic level of assembly.
Now Boeing must create a more boundaryless manufacturing supply
chain across a much more diverse range of suppliers.

The issues associated with protecting strategic advantages also have
implications for the organization. Any supply chain design must consider
the potential transfer of market power from Boeing to its suppliers. IBM
learned this lesson the hard way. When it decided to make PCs in 1981, it

lent credibility to a novel new product. Unfortunately for IBM, there was far more long-term value creation for two of its suppliers, Intel and Microsoft, than there was for IBM.

Boeing will need to carefully define not only how it intends to work with the network of suppliers but also how it plans to protect itself from competitive attacks from these same suppliers in later contracts. Boeing pursued a strategy of higher-value systems integration, meaning larger blocks of work would be done by outside suppliers, encompassing larger domains of the processes Boeing had historically done in-house. Boeing's organizational challenge is to create large-scale systems integration without creating future competitors at the same time.

This will not be easy. Important parts of the plane will be assembled by organizations in China and Japan. These countries clearly intend to build their capabilities in the commercial-aircraft-manufacturing industry. They are also potential future suppliers to Airbus and, therefore, potential future competitors to Boeing. At the same time, selling planes in Asia is vital, and without significant production within those countries, political barriers will likely result. Boeing intends to successfully use this international group of suppliers in part through a highly integrated information network to manage the engineering, manufacturing, and supply chain across all suppliers. This is just one example of the many types of systems integrations that Boeing believes will provide unique competitive advantage.

Both Boeing and Airbus obviously need to manage their suppliers, as does any organization. However, the talentship strategy lenses look deeper, making the implications for Boeing's talent and organization much more specific and clear. If Boeing is to achieve successful production and increase its early production to capture demand before Airbus is ready, it must be uniquely world class at managing suppliers in a very specific way that is different from Airbus. It needs to be world class at managing the coordination interfaces that make composite-based manufacturing work and at protecting the intellectual capital that suppliers will be creating.

Strategic Organization Challenges for Airbus

Airbus has its own challenges in organizing its value chain and production processes due to its unique organizational structure and history. Airbus was initially formed in 1970 with French and German ownership, followed shortly thereafter by British and Spanish involvement. In 2000 all the interests (other than the British) were consolidated into the newly formed EADS, and in October 2006 EADS purchased the 20 percent stake owned by BAE Systems to become the sole owner of Airbus.

This ownership structure, with its unique political dynamics, has proved challenging from an operational perspective. Several international newspapers and others noted that economic logic is often in conflict with the political logic that is important in shaping behavior within Airbus and among its executives.[4] The *Wall Street Journal* expressed similar sentiments when it said, "The structure of Airbus—created in 1970 by technocrats in France, Germany, Britain, and Spain—is rooted in its origins as a consortium and has long proved more effective at spreading jobs and tapping subsidies than generating profits." Some believe that the challenges present within Airbus are shared by other European corporations that focus on balancing national interests as a significant part of their capital structure, including Royal Dutch/Shell, ABB, and Unilever.[5]

Delays and cost overruns mounted throughout 2006 with the A380 project, costing Airbus a great deal economically and from a public relations perspective. The organization's CEO, Christian Streiff, resigned after just three months on the job. It is widely believed that a major factor in his resignation was the inability to achieve the restructuring that he felt was necessary for Airbus to be competitive. In large part this appears to be a result of the economic logic for the restructuring plan not aligning with the corporate and political structure that was the foundation of EADS.

Organizing Around Strategic Resources

Another pivot-point in organizing is the coordination of strategic resources. Recall that strategic resources are those that provide the foundation for competitive advantage because of the unique value they can create and because they are difficult for competitors to emulate. When building, leveraging, and deploying strategic resources spans organizational boundaries (internal or external), resources are an organizing pivot-point. This is a common challenge in complex organizations where multiple business units share common strategic resources.

When it comes to coordinating strategic resources across both internal and external boundaries, Disney is considered world class.[6] Its formal organizational structures and processes ensure that as a creative concept is developed and released, the strategic resources it generates are leveraged across multiple divisions. If a new character is created through a movie (such as Belle in *Beauty and the Beast*), it will also be a character in the theme parks. Stories about the development of the movie will be shown on the "commercial-free" Disney Channel. The character's outfit will be available in Disney retail outlets. A traveling Broadway show, figure skating show, and permanent show at Disney World will further leverage the concept. Disney's organizing pivot-point focuses on leveraging its primary strategic resources of new creative content across multiple platforms.

For Boeing one of the critical resources that must be coordinated across business units is organizational competency in composite technologies. The key is to collect and make available the relevant expertise and capabilities in composite design and manufacturing. This is complicated by the fact that Boeing has received a great deal of U.S. government funding and much of that has been through Department of Defense appropriations. Boeing must ensure that none of the technology involved is subject to export controls. An airplane that cannot be sold outside the United States would be a disaster, since the fastest-growing markets are overseas. The organizational units that accept Department of Defense funding must manage the resources embodied in their discoveries, realizing that those discoveries may be needed for nonmilitary applications in other parts of Boeing. Talentship emphasizes these deep logical connections between strategy pivot-points, such as strategic resources, and the unique organizational pivot-points that they imply.

Organizational Implications of Business Process Constraints

A third area of insight arises by connecting organization pivot-points with the constraint analysis using the business processes lens. We have noted that constraints commonly lie across internal or external organizational boundaries. The source of the constraint is not the relative capabilities themselves but the challenges that occur at the boundaries. For example, we worked with a service company where the critical challenge was sharing customer information across business units that wanted to reach the same customers while still managing the customers in separate product line silos. Other challenges can include lack of trust, misaligned goals, and a poor understanding of perspectives on each side of the boundaries.

Limitations imposed by the constraint hurt the entire organization, but because the constraint isn't fully within any one unit, it is often not strictly the responsibility of any particular manager or leader. Working effectively across such boundaries is the pivot-point. We have found that focusing on the organizational boundaries where a constraint is affecting the organization can make substantial improvements in the execution of a strategy and improve results.

Relative Pivotalness Between Talent Pools

The next level of analysis focuses on comparing different talent pools. The idea is to segment groups of jobs, roles, and actions according to how much changes in their quantity and quality create changes in vital strategy elements. We noted earlier that pivotalness is different from average value. Comparing talent pools based on pivotalness often reveals very different insights than the more typical comparisons of importance or overall value. For example, Kaplan and Norton describe strategic job families as those where "learning and growth" competencies "have the biggest impact on enhancing the organization's critical processes," using an illustration from our presentation with John Bronson, then of Williams-Sonoma.[7] Yet the importance of learning and growth is different from where it is most pivotal. Organizations often mistakenly believe they have adequately identified their vital talent pools when they distinguish those pools according to average strategic value. Talentship shows that comparing talent pools based on pivotalness will often produce different insights.

There are potentially many pivotal talent pools for Boeing in the execution of the 787 strategy, but we will focus on only two in this chapter: public relations and supplier relations management. In the following chapters we will explore some of the implications for the changing role of engineering within the Boeing strategy.

Public Relations at Boeing

The talent pool of public relations and communication at Boeing becomes much more pivotal in light of the organization's strategy with the 787. While communications has always been important, Boeing now faces a nearly daily battle with Airbus to convince stakeholders that Boeing's vision of the future of the airline industry is correct and that its claims about the 787 are more accurate than the proposed A350.

To help address this issue, Boeing has appointed a talented executive, Randy Bassler, as a key executive in their external communications. Bassler is a highly qualified leader; Boeing might have chosen to deploy his talents to any number of important projects or processes. It chose, however, to allocate his talent in large part to communications because effectively getting the messages out to a wide range of constituents inside and outside the organization is more critical than the same role in other Boeing programs. The company has even given him a blog on the corporate Web site, making him the only Boeing employee to have a direct link from the corporate Web site, where he is listed by first name![8] While the focus is on Randy Bassler, he is just the personification of a highly coordinated public relations effort, one that is clearly pivotal to the Boeing strategy.

Supplier Relationship Management at Boeing

Another talent pool pivot-point is the management of supplier relationships. As noted earlier, many of the pivot-points associated with the strategy are at the boundary between Boeing and its suppliers. While this has organizational implications, it also raises the importance of roles associated with supplier management. The new strategy will make these roles more pivotal than before because the consequences of performance will likely have a disproportionate impact on the program's ultimate success. Such roles are one of the potential "sweepers" within this strategy.

These talent pools are pivotal not only because the performance variance will dramatically impact the long-term success of the 787 program but also because they have to operate in a way that is very different from previous supplier relationship management roles. This will create substantial change within Boeing and will also require that the leaders within supplier relationship management build and deploy a team that can create changes within the suppliers themselves. Chapter 6 will describe these implications in terms of pivotal actions and interactions.

Relative Pivotalness Within Talent Pools

We have described how to identify pivotalness in the design of the organization and how to use pivotalness to segment and compare different talent pools. The third level of talent pool analysis considers which elements *inside* a particular job or role are pivotal. This is different from comparing entire roles, jobs, and talent pools. Within-role pivotalness builds on the suggestion of putting A players in A positions, revealing a deeper level of insight. Huselid, Beatty, and Becker note that A positions are those that have important effects on strategy and have "wide variability in the quality of the work displayed among the employees in the position."[9] This is similar to our conclusions that organizations should identify how variations in talent quality affect critical constraints, that decisions about talent should focus where there is the greatest employee variability, and that talent segmentation should be as rigorous as segmentation in finance or marketing.[10] Thus, it's a good idea to consider A positions, which in our framework is akin to segmentation that compares whole talent pools.

Yet, talentship can also provide insights by looking at pivotalness within the position. Pivotal aspects of the position often are not obvious from traditional descriptions or the typical distinctions between A positions and others. For example, Huselid and his coauthors note that Nordstrom emphasizes personalized service as a differentiator and so has more frontline sales associates providing customer advice than Costco, which emphasizes low prices and product availability and relies more on purchasing managers for its success.[11] This is the relative pivotalness of two different jobs. Yet consider the differences within these positions. Purchasing managers are critical to Nordstrom, just as they are to Costco, but the pivotal actions they must execute are very different. Similarly, frontline sales associates at Costco may be as strategic as those at Nordstrom, but their contribution hinges on very different elements of the position.

Analyzing the pivotal elements within roles and connecting them to specific elements of human capacity, organizational culture, and programs and practices is the next major element of talentship (the effectiveness anchor point in the HC BRidge framework), which we will discuss in chapters 6 and 7. In those chapters we will use the talent pool of aircraft design engineers at Boeing (certainly an A position by any analysis) to show how strategic impact is much clearer when you examine pivotalness within the role. No one level of analysis is more or less useful, and organizations that use all three will see synergies that any one level could miss.

Applying Quantity and Quality Pivotalness to Talent Pools

Recall the distinction, made earlier, between quantity and quality pivotalness. Something is quality pivotal when changing its performance makes a difference in the desired outcome. Something is quantity pivotal when changing the amount makes a difference in the desired outcome. Leadership talent pools offer a good example. Many organizations find that the leadership role is both quantity and quality pivotal. It is quality pivotal because performance variance among leaders has significant impact on the organization's strategic success. At the same time, if organizations do not have a sufficient quantity of individuals to fill the leadership roles they need to execute their future strategies, the leadership role becomes quantity pivotal.

For example, one publicly held company had identified that the leadership talent pool was quality pivotal and asked us to identify where to focus its leadership development. The company felt that it had an adequate number of leaders in current jobs, and in the pipeline feeding those jobs, to address expected retirements and potential turnover. It wanted to build the skills of that group of current and future leaders.

The impact analysis revealed an unseen talent implication of the organization's strategy. This company was a market leader in a mature industry that was not growing. Its strategy was to use the cash flow from its strong position to both lead the consolidation of the industry and to identify new growth opportunities through diversification and through mergers and acquisitions (M&A). As a result, it had done significant strategic and financial planning regarding its potential M&A targets and the required financial capital to complete the M&A. One key element of the financial strategy was to acquire organizations that were undervalued and could benefit from the more advanced manufacturing management capabilities of the acquiring company. The company identified potential targets both inside and outside the industry that fit this criterion.

Integrating the target companies would require leadership transfers from the acquiring parent company to quickly deploy the more advanced manufacturing capabilities. Leaders from the acquiring company would also likely be required to close the anticipated leadership gaps in the target companies because underperforming organizations typically would not have adequate leadership. Many were family-held businesses, where the sale would likely result in family members liquidating their investment and leaving the business, meaning that the acquiring company would need to replace them from its own cadre of leaders. In the end the parent company realized that leaders were both quantity and quality pivotal and represented a significant risk and opportunity. The company had not adequately planned for future leadership infusions into acquired companies. It had recognized the need to increase the quality of its leadership, but without a significant increase in the quantity of leaders, it simply could not pursue its growth strategy.

Competing Better with Insights About Organization and Talent

Impact analysis reveals relative pivotalness at the organization level, between talent pools, and within talent pools. Many of the implications are revealed when organizations apply this analysis internally to the pivot-points in their own strategy. Some of the most powerful insights, however, emerge when the tools are applied to how the organization will achieve a distinctive and unique position in the talent market itself. Few organizations use talent strategy as a source of competitive advantage, but the insights about talent and organization pivot-points reveal several approaches that can create an advantage compared with competitors who follow a more traditional talent market decision model. We will highlight a few of these opportunities next.

Is the Term *HR Generalist* About to Become Obsolete?

The power of impact analysis to guide deeper conversations about where talent and organization decisions are pivotal to strategic success has profound implications for one of the most common HR roles in organizations: the HR generalist. Indeed, the term *HR generalist* may become obsolete as talentship evolves.

Try this exercise in your organization. Ask a group of your HR leaders to write down the job description of an HR generalist. When we do this exercise, we get statements that describe everything from a trusted and essential talent strategy facilitator, to a business partner who is at the table to discuss implications of strategy for HR decisions, to a general contractor who oversees all the different HR programs for the business unit, to a coach and confidante for the general manager, to a protector from corporate HR programs. The last one really does come up. In fact, in an extreme case one of our participants, a general manager outside of HR, noted that his HR generalist could contribute most strategically by actually completing the annual performance assessments for the general manager's subordinates, freeing up the manager to "run the business."

The term *HR generalist* seems to have emerged from the idea that business units needed a dedicated HR executive who could provide a buffer and a connection point to expertise housed in a centralized HR function and who could construct a coherent portfolio of HR practices that reflect the business unit's specific needs. The analogy is often made to a general contractor on a construction project, who chooses and coordinates the work of many construction specialists.

While this is an important role, we believe that when it is the sole purpose of a business-unit HR leader, great opportunities are missed, and a good deal of unnecessary confusion occurs about authority and accountability. The HR leader for a business unit often identifies more strongly with the business unit than with the HR function. Indeed, some business-unit HR leaders report to their business-unit manager rather than to the head of the organization's HR function. So the boundaries between HR leaders within the business units and those in the centers of expertise (COEs) such as compensation, staffing, labor relations and training are often strained. Both roles are strategic, but they are strategic in different ways. The talentship paradigm offers fresh ways to look at this long-standing challenge. In chapter 7 we will discuss how talentship suggests that the question of integrating HR practices should be shared between HR leaders in business units and a redefined cadre of HR leaders in COEs, who are subject matter experts in the principles of program success and synergy.

We believe that the role of the HR leader in the business unit will increasingly emphasize facilitating the kind of deep and logical analysis of connections between strategy and talent that we have described. This is a natural consequence of the essential evolution that extends the paradigm toward decisions. It means that HR leaders in the business units will no longer be judged solely on their influence with business-unit leaders, nor solely for their role in crafting a set of HR practices for the business unit.

Instead, those generalists will more frequently be held accountable for the quality of the logic that the business uses to find its talent pivot-points. They will work closely with their HR counterparts who focus on programs, but their role will not be a protector or a broker. They will focus those programs and their key parameters on the talent and organization pivot-points where they will make the biggest difference. Increasingly, the HR leader in a business unit will be a talent strategy facilitator who succeeds when business leaders have much deeper and more logical discussions about where, and why, talent and organization make a difference.

This new role for the business-unit HR leader will also require that COEs design programs and practices that can more readily be adapted to the various situations that are found in the business. COEs will no longer be allowed to require compliance with a corporate standard solely for reasons of consistency. The decision about whether to allow business units to deviate from the standard increasingly will be made based on logical and strategic considerations, grounded in a common framework that is shared and understood by both the COEs and business-unit HR leaders. Everyone knows that neither slavish adherence to an organizational standard nor complete discretion among organizational units is the right answer. What's missing is a framework for finding the right middle ground.

Interestingly, the traditional HR career path of getting experience in a wide variety of HR functional areas, which made sense for the HR generalist as a general contractor, is probably not the best way to create these new talent strategy facilitators, who use the tools of impact analysis adeptly. Today's organizations struggle with how to inject more business thinking into HR, often hiring MBAs and placing business leaders with financial or operational experience in the top HR positions. These are good ideas, but they often don't reflect a clear understanding of what businesslike HR would really look like. We believe that leaders with HR and non-HR training can serve as talent strategy facilitators. The development experiences they need, however, will be very different from the common professional HR career path of today.

For the HR profession, this solves the dilemma about who is in charge of the business-unit HR programs. Because service delivery is the dominant paradigm today, there is often tension between the HR leaders in the business units and the HR leaders who are functional specialists when it comes to who decides what HR programs the business unit will adopt. This is actually the wrong discussion. When organizations clearly understand the difference between impact and effectiveness, it is easier to see the complementary role of the HR leader in the business unit facilitating strategy analysis through a talent perspective and the HR leader in the COE who designs programs to achieve the requirements such analysis reveals

In several organizations we have worked with, the HR planning process was changed. Rather than beginning with a discussion about what HR programs and practices to implement, the process started with the HR leaders in each business unit describing the insights about talent and organization alignment that they generated using impact analysis tools that incorporated the principles of the strategy lenses. The resulting patterns of pivot-points and alignment opportunities across the different business units often reveal organization-spanning opportunities that logically justify a centralized or standardized approach to HR programs. At the same time, they reveal logical places where business-unit needs are so unique and important that the effort to customize or decentralize some program elements is worth the cost.

There is exciting work in the HR organization we envision being built to reflect talentship. HR leaders in corporate centers, business units, COEs, and HR operations will make strategic contributions. What has been lacking is a decision science to distinguish their unique contributions.

Use Pivotalness to Guide and Explain
Differential Talent Pool Investments

Organizations should improve talent pool performance (quality, quantity, or both) where the slope is steep and the potential payoff is high. If there is a higher potential value from investment in one talent pool over another, it only makes sense to allocate resources (time, attention, money, etc.) accordingly. Yet most organizations fail to do this as reliably or as accurately as possible. There is a strong natural bias to focus on talent pools that have high average value because they are so important and, some assume, also pivotal. Roles with high average value, however, can also be flat sloped (such as Mickey Mouse), and making heavy investments in flat-sloped but high-value positions is often not optimal.

One reason for this bias against segmentation is that it is traditionally very hard to explain to employees why those in some roles get different treatment from those in other roles. HR's roots come in part from fields such as employment law, civil service, and labor relations—many of which were intended to protect workers from inappropriate segmentation leading to discrimination. It is essential that the HR field maintain its staunch defense against inappropriate discrimination, but that does not require equal treatment across diverse talent pools. We have shown that competitiveness will increasingly require more effective segmentation of both employees and roles. Equal treatment is a useful rule of thumb in the absence of such a framework, but the future will demand a more nuanced approach to achieving differentiation without inappropriate discrimination. The difference between such legitimate segmentation and inappropriate discrimination is in part the decision framework for segmentation.

It is important to recognize that increased segmentation of talent pools is an organizational change. It is a change that can produce significant benefits but requires change management. One key is making the pivotal analysis more transparent so that the logic (or the "why") behind the segmentation is clear. Organizations share information about revenues and costs with the management team, using a common framework. As a result, there is a broad base of understanding of the financial concepts. This common understanding provides a platform to make important decisions in an aligned way. Managers may not like it when their unit gets less capital than another unit, but they understand that investments must flow to the units that are most financially pivotal. By contrast, most organizations do not routinely present talent and organization decisions in a way that makes the value connection clear.

Such changes were historically difficult in other disciplines as well. Consider again the application of revenue management from marketing, which we discussed earlier. There has been a radical shift in the pricing of airline seats over the past thirty years. Originally, there were basically two prices: coach and first class. Now, through sophisticated revenue management processes, airlines use sophisticated algorithms and processes to optimize not only each airline seat but the fares as well.[12] Implementing this level of pricing differentiation was not easy. While the economics of the pricing were well known, many feared a customer backlash. What would customers say when they found out that two passengers seated next to each other paid dramatically different fares for the same flight? How could you upset the (highly valuable) business traveler by having vacation travelers on the same flight at a fraction of the price?

Of course, over time the economic efficiency of the yield management system won the day. Now it is impossible to quote airline fares without knowing a variety of factors, and the range of fares that result are so detailed and dynamic that it literally takes massive online databases just to manage the process. Airlines that were early adopters of the new technology (such as American Airlines) achieved significant competitive advantage over the others in the market. Today anyone who tried to compete with the old pricing models would fail, and it is widely understood that such a strategy could not be effective.

The situation regarding the pivotalness of organization and talent resources is similar today. As we have seen, talent pools can vary widely in pivotalness, yet most companies use traditional talent investment decision frameworks that don't capture those variations. When organizations better understand talent pool yield curves and encourage open discussions about their implications, more optimal organization and talent decisions will result, just as happened with financial, customer, and product assets in previous eras. Today decisions about talent and organization are similar to decisions about pricing before revenue management was well accepted, when equity and equality were the prominent decision frameworks. Organizations that understand talent segmentation will have an advantage not only because they can make better decisions but because they will be able to better explain to their employees why decisions that direct investments to where they are most beneficial are actually fair, even though they may not be equal.[13]

Reduce Pivotalness to Mitigate Risk

Our analysis so far has emphasized finding high-sloped organization elements and talent pools and investing in them. Where variance matters most, it makes sense to improve the quality or quantity of the talent pool. However, it is often as effective to find the areas where variation in performance poses a significant risk and to change the relationship between talent and the strategy so that it is less sensitive to performance differences. Areas where there is significant downside risk due to poor individual performance are particularly fertile ground for this kind of analysis. Organizations often spend considerable time and effort to increase the performance of individuals, particularly when poor performance carries significant downside risks. An even more effective strategy is to take the slope out of the pool and make it *less* pivotal.

One way to do this is to minimize the negative consequences of poor performance. Another way is to minimize the probability of poor performance. Either of these is often more effective than trying to raise the performance of poor-performing individuals. Reducing pivotalness on the downside slope often means flattening the upside. So the trick is to understand the trade-offs. Let's look at a few examples.

Team-Based Work. One way that slope can often be reduced is to have key roles worked in teams. Mickey Mouse never goes into the park without a handler. Pilots work in teams in the cockpit of passenger airlines to reduce slope in a different way. A single pilot might forget a checklist element, incorrectly hear an instruction from the tower, or enter an incorrect number in the navigation system. Such errors are less likely to happen with two pilots in the cockpit because the second pilot will usually correct the mistake before it can do any harm. These are both examples of reducing slope in a quality-pivotal yield curve, as shown in figure 5-2.

The slope associated with quantity pivotalness can also be reduced with a team-based approach. A large Midwest bank put its commercial lending activities on a team approach.[14] The bank significantly reduced the pivotalness of quantity by reducing the consequences of turnover in this role. If customers are served by a single banker and that person leaves to go to a new bank, then customers must be introduced to a new banker at a difficult time. In the worst case, they may just decide to switch banks to stay with the familiar banker. When a team of bankers serves a customer and one of the bankers leaves, the customers already have other people they know, and who know them, which greatly lowers the likelihood of losing the account.

FIGURE 5-2

Reducing slope in a quality-pivotal yield curve

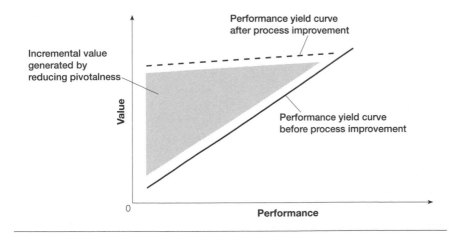

Quality Improvement Programs. The quality and lean movements have been major factors in systematically increasing value by reducing roles' pivotalness. Such approaches use data-based analysis of the system to find opportunities for sustained improvement. When the organization finds a talent pivot-point—a place where performance variation has a significant impact on the business—one of the recommendations we commonly make is to apply quality improvement or lean analysis frameworks.

The cockpit of commercial planes again illustrates how to mitigate risk by removing performance slope. Over the past several years there has been a significant emphasis on improving pilot training, combined with significant focus on improving both the systems within the cockpit and the teaming processes used by pilots. The combination creates a significantly safer airline system through systematically reducing the pivotalness of the pilot role. Pilots remain extremely important, and their role justifies significant investment. That investment is often targeted, however, at ensuring that pilots are up to a very high standard and that they don't deviate from that standard.

Notice again how this approach provides deeper insights than the typical job analysis, strategic position mapping, or even the admonition to put A players in A positions (those with high performance variability). Here talentship reveals uncharted strategic opportunities in taking performance variability out of such positions—in essence, competing better by making A positions into B positions.

Consider Development Pivotalness, Not Only Performance Pivotalness

An interesting feature of roles with a flat slope on performance is that they may offer less risky opportunities for development. Much research suggests that skill development occurs through experience. Often the most potent development experiences occur in high-profile positions that also have very steep performance slopes. Individuals placed in those positions usually face the daunting task of maximizing their performance and their development at the same time. Because performance is so closely monitored, the usual response is to emphasize performance, often to the detriment of learning and development. The role of CFO provides a good example of this dilemma and the opportunities it presents.

What if an organization purposely reduces the pivotalness of performance in a role to increase pivotal development? Boeing and Northrop Grumman assigned the role of CFO to two senior executives, Mike Sears at Boeing, who had no prior experience in accounting, and Wes Bush at Northrop Grumman, who had no prior experience in finance.[15] Both had degrees in engineering and had spent the vast majority of their careers in line roles.

Didn't this risk having those leaders make serious mistakes? Why did financial analysts (or the boards) accept this and not clamor for more finance and accounting experience? We think that investors and analysts saw the situation as a developmental opportunity and a good succession-planning move. There were stable financial systems in place and more than adequate cash. Financial structure decisions would never be made by the CFO alone, and innovative financial structuring was not key to strategic success. Any such decisions would be well supported by the finance team, including external advisers.

All these conditions lowered the pivotalness of performance in traditional areas requiring finance and accounting expertise in the CFO role. Yet, precisely because performance was relatively flat sloped in these elements, allowing these executives to serve as CFO gave them a uniquely effective chance to learn the complexities of the finance system, to get a broad perspective on how the portfolio of businesses worked together, and to apply their unique leadership skills and experiences to a wider range of business units within the organization. For most companies of such size and scope, there are very few opportunities for executives to learn through direct experience with the complex interactions required to manage a portfolio business. As a result, for Boeing and Northrop Grumman, there was more slope in the role of CFO for development of future CEOs than in its traditional performance elements. Such a move would not be appropriate in the hub-and-spoke airline industry, where the very future of the organization depends on complicated financial restructuring, making the CFO role far more pivotal.

It has been suggested that the flat-sloped positions are C positions (not C-level positions, but "C" in terms of the A, B, and C grading system), where rewards and development are less strategically critical, except perhaps to avoid significant mistakes. Again, the talentship perspective provides the framework to look beyond a simple focus on existing performance variability. It suggests a much more nuanced and integrated view that accounts for the hidden and obvious capacities of talent and organization elements. By understanding the hidden development potential of roles with flat-sloped performance yield curves, organizations can vastly enhance their ability to find unique sources of competitive and strategic success.

Enhance Flexibility Regarding the Talent Requirements

Talent pools often face a shortage of quality candidates because the role's performance yield curve is steeply sloped and requires a very high level of applicant quality to mitigate the risk of poor performance. What if we alter the role so that we produce high value from a wider range of available talent?

Such strategies have often been applied to other vital resources. One example is the source of sweetener for soft drinks. For years the exclusive source was sugar. Prices shot up during the sugar shortages of World War I, and without a sugar alternative, Pepsi was forced into bankruptcy.[16] However, corn emerged as a sweetener, and soft drink companies adjusted their processes. Now production plants can easily switch between sugar and corn syrup, based on the relative prices available in the market at any time.

The same strategy can be applied to talent sources. The key question to ask is "Can we change our production function (business processes) to get greater value from a more readily available talent pool?" One significant example of this is the massive use of call centers in lower-cost labor markets with lower-skilled worker populations. By reengineering the call-center processes to make them more standardized and using technology to reduce the risk of mistakes, organizations can employ individuals who might otherwise have been poor performers under a less controlled system. Once again, flattening the performance yield curve produces a strategic advantage.

Even in the U.S. labor market, companies such as JetBlue airlines have changed their reservation system so that people—mostly women with families—can work as reservations agents from home instead of a centralized call center. Again, using technology and other tools, the role was redesigned so that a remote labor pool could perform at an adequately high level. This change allowed a large potential employee population to consider the role, when the use of a traditional customer service call-center model would have prevented many of them from doing so.

Whole new business models have been based on underleveraged talent pools. One example is Tupperware. A truly creative part of that business was the creation of the "home party" concept, which allowed large numbers of people outside the traditional workforce to become Tupperware entrepreneurs.[17] (Organizations such as Amway and Mary Kay followed a similar multilevel marketing model.)[18] Tupperware was designed to capture value from an underdeployed resource in the talent market. By creating a system where housewives could be reliably expected to put on a great party, Tupperware tapped into a labor supply very different from the talent market for experienced traditional salespeople.

Compete in Labor Markets Based on Pivotalness

Where does your strategy require talent that is better than your competitor's talent for your strategy to work? Not only does pivotalness help you understand the relative impact of talent within particular talent pools, the relative pivotalness of talent pools between opportunities reveals often-overlooked ways to compete in talent markets.

For example, the sales role in a new company usually has a much steeper-sloped performance yield curve than a sales role in a more established organization with a known reputation, brand, and product lines. The more established organization relies less on sales to carry its product message, reach its customers, and so forth. As a general rule, the stronger the relative market offering, the lower the prominence and the flatter the slope for sales professionals. It's not that they are less important in established organizations, but variability in their performance creates less variation in organizational results.

The rules change when organizations compete for the same talent pool, but that talent pool is differentially pivotal in different organizations. Organizations where the talent pool has a steep slope should invest more heavily to attract and retain the high-quality candidates. Organizations that have a flatter slope shouldn't be lulled into matching the pay levels, staffing processes, or retention rewards of their high-sloped competitors. Yet, because talent markets are often heavily based on simple job titles or generic job descriptions, such mistakes are common. Today traditional labor market analysis is based on job titles, not pivotalness. Pivotalness, however, is often the key to competing appropriately. We will return to this point when we discuss effectiveness in chapters 6 and 7, which explore how to find pivotalness within the job or role.

This logic is better understood in more mature markets. For example, retailers routinely distinguish customer segments by their pivotalness to the strategy. Wal-Mart does not expect to compete for the customers that prefer Nordstrom. It does not devote lots of resources to attracting those customers, even though based on generic benchmarking, they are very lucrative retail customers. Wal-Mart realizes that the payoff from trying to attract such customers in a Wal-Mart store just isn't very high, based on its value model. On the other hand, Wal-Mart competes very diligently for upper-middle-income and middle-income customers who believe Target or Sears offers better value at a low price.[19]

A talent decision science applies this logic to the talent market. There are some interesting implications for the common practice of establishing pay levels by surveying what competitors are paying for jobs with similar titles and requirements. In such surveys it is common to benchmark pay and reward levels based on the entire group of competitors. Yet this will combine competitors for which the job is differently pivotal. Thus, salary surveys will reflect pay levels that combine some high-sloped competitors with lower-sloped competitors.

To return to our example, salary surveys would generally not distinguish sales pay levels of organizations with new products from the pay levels of those with well-established brands and images. Paying at the fiftieth percentile of the survey ignores these differences. Yet more established organizations can actually afford to pay less and allow some of the better salespeople to go to the competition because their established products don't require such high performance in the sales role.

Organizations are often averse to wasting money by overstaffing because it increases labor costs without gaining much productivity. But organizations routinely stockpile or lock up other resources that have high value in the market to create a barrier to competitors. This is common with oil-drilling rights and landing rights at key airport hubs. The same principle can apply to talent. As counterintuitive as it seems, it may make lots of sense to offer higher pay and greater retention incentives for talent in highly pivotal roles as a way to attract and keep talent away from competitors. Recall the discussion of Corning in chapter 1, where locking up talent might delay competitors for years.

Conclusion

Impact unearths strategy pivot-points and uses them to uncover the performance yield curves for organization elements and talent pools. This provides significant opportunities for untapped strategic advantage through logical, systematic decisions about competing in the talent marketplace. We call the examples examined in this chapter "talent pool strategies." Just as organizations have specific strategies for their financial resources or product line management, talent pool strategies are emerging as a new domain of competition. However, many companies develop these strategies either by benchmarking against their competitors (which rarely creates strategic distinctiveness) or with their own hunches about what is pivotal, without doing systematic analysis. Neither approach reliably leads to decisions that are consistently better than the competition's.

Talent and organization are vital resources, so those with the best information and the processes to systematically use the information to create innovative strategies will have a vital competitive advantage. The power of pivotalness in organizing talent pools and between talent pools foreshadows how pivotalness can provide equally important insights about the elements within jobs, roles, and talent pools, and how to connect those to the investments in policies and practices to enhance organization and talent. That's the subject of effectiveness, which we will turn to next.

6

Effectiveness in Performance and Potential

Aligning Pivotal Interactions and Actions Through Culture and Capacity

Recall our observation from chapter 1 that between 2001 and 2003, organizations spanning a vast array of sizes, industries, and maturities simultaneously adopted a performance management system that required leaders to rate their employees so that 20 percent were rated top performers, 70 percent were rated middle performers, and 10 percent were rated bottom performers. The reason? Jack Welch's book (*Jack: Straight From the Gut*) appeared on the best-seller lists in 2001. Welch credited GE's success to its "20-70-10" system. CEOs, board members, or heads of a division said to their HR leaders, "This performance management system worked for GE. Why don't we have one?" Few realized that the same performance management system was also applied at Enron! Would your organization be among such fad followers, or do you have a decision framework to systematically identify the unique culture, capacities, and programs and practices that best support your unique competitive strategy?

This chapter begins our exploration of the effectiveness anchor point in the HC BRidge framework. Where does your strategy require distinctive culture, talent capacity, and policies and practices that create a unique position in the talent market? Too often, decisions about talent and organization practices are made by simply following the leaders, adopting the same practices as financially successful competitors, or doing the same thing for every employee. As we shall see, talentship suggests a more distinctive and specific approach.

Effectiveness describes the relationship between talent and organization performance and the portfolio of policies and practices that create and support that performance. Effectiveness guides organizations to go beyond simply doing the same thing for everyone or the same thing that industry leaders are doing. Effectiveness is essential to strategy execution because it reveals where organizations can change the game by enacting programs and practices that uniquely reflect strategic pivot-points.

Figure 6-1 shows that in the HC BRidge framework, effectiveness looks for pivot-points in the interactions and actions and then in the collective culture (values, norms, etc.) and individual human capacity (capability, opportunity, and motivation) that enable those actions and interactions. Finally, effectiveness uncovers the programs and practices that create the needed culture and capacity. This chapter focuses on the actions and interactions and the culture and capacity anchor points, and chapter 7 takes up the policies and practices anchor point.

Before we delve into these specific linking elements, consider the role of effectiveness in the decision framework. Like impact and efficiency, effectiveness describes a pivot-point, which reveals the vital decisions and provides a script for new and much deeper talent and organization strategy discussions. Table 6-1 describes how effectiveness does this.

FIGURE 6-1

HC BRidge framework: Effectiveness

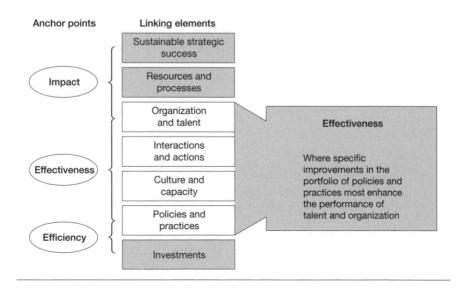

TABLE 6-1

Anchor point: Effectiveness

Definition	Pivot-points	Decisions to make	New talent and organization strategy discussions
• Describes the relationship between organization and talent performance and the portfolio of policies and practices	• Where specific improvements in the portfolio of policies and practices most enhance the performance of talent and organization	• Where should you target policy and practice portfolio improvements so they have the biggest effect on talent and organization performance?	• Where could your strategy enable distinctive policies and practices that give you a unique position in the talent market? • What apparent and overlooked characteristics of your employees and culture could support or inhibit execution? • Where do your policies and practices align (or misalign) with the strategy and with each other? • What distinguishes effective and ineffective programs and practices in your strategic context?

Now let's see how applying decision science principles to actions and interactions reveals even deeper strategic insights.

Actions and Interactions Reveal How to Play the Roles

Chapters 4 and 5 showed how impact analysis uncovers the pivotalness of different talent pools and structures (such as sweepers versus Mickey Mouse at Disney or coordination between internal teams and external suppliers at Boeing). Chapter 5 noted that there is a third level of analysis— the pivotalness of different behaviors *within* a talent pool. Here, we focus on this third level. We show how organizations can look within roles and organizational structures to find the actions and interactions that make those roles pivotal and aligned with strategic success.

As shown in figure 6-2, the interactions and actions element of HC BRidge focuses on the question, "How do individuals need to behave and cooperate?"

Actions are pivot-points that involve individuals behaving independently, and interactions are pivot-points where two or more individuals act

FIGURE 6-2

HC BRidge framework: Interactions and actions

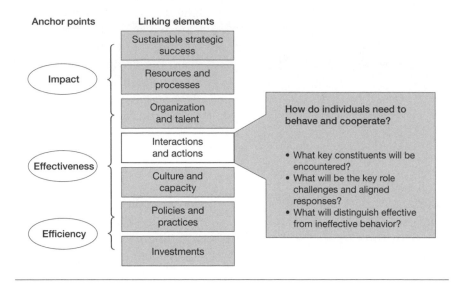

cooperatively. Pivotal interactions occur between employees within the organization and also between employees and constituents outside the organization. Let's continue with the Boeing/Airbus example to see how this works.

Pivotal Actions and Interactions at Boeing

Pivotal actions and interactions are found by identifying the vital role challenges where the quality of a response makes the biggest difference. Writers who describe the "service-value-profit chain" often describe such challenges as "moments of truth" because they epitomize the difference between good and great service. For example, in a retail clothing store, getting customers into the fitting rooms makes a big difference in how much they buy, so a moment of truth is when retail associates have the chance to guide the customer into the fitting room.

The pivotal role challenges for Boeing engineers changed dramatically with the 787. Historically, Boeing had followed a build-to-print model where engineers designed every component in detail and outside partners came in only at the last stage, fabricating the part to meet Boeing's very detailed internal specifications. With the 787, partners were brought in four and a half years earlier to participate in the early design work and provide their manufacturing expertise. Recall from earlier chapters that

Boeing's strategic challenge was to reduce the risk of missing the target delivery date and cut the costs of development and manufacturing. Boeing reduced the risk by engaging its partners early, and it cut costs by having partners pay a portion of the development costs in exchange for a bigger share of the eventual profits.[1] Boeing worked with partners in countries as diverse as France, Italy, Japan, Korea, and China in part because countries where Boeing places significant production capacity also purchase more Boeing aircraft (Chinese airlines had already ordered sixty of the new jets as of January 2006). The job of an engineer used to be to do the design. Now the job includes facilitating and coordinating global partner relationships.

What are the pivotal aligned actions and interactions here? Boeing's history of aircraft engineering likely makes traditional engineering actions and interactions flat sloped, albeit at a very high standard (like sweeping at Disney). Airbus is also very good at traditional engineering, so it is likely to be very difficult to create a competitive differentiator there. Instead, within the engineering job, the pivotal aligned actions and interactions increasingly will be found in the role challenges of coordination, integration, and facilitation across different cultures and boundaries.

The Yield Curve for Boeing Engineers

Figure 6-3 shows this example in terms of our yield curve metaphor. Notice that the top line, "engineering design," is high because it is extremely

FIGURE 6-3

Yield curves for aligned actions/interactions: Engineered design vs. engineering coordination

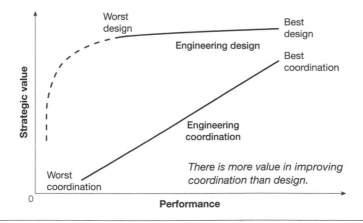

The Pitfalls of Adopting Policies and Practices That Correlate with Financial Performance

Many organizations will say, "We achieve effectiveness and impact in one step! We subscribe to a consulting service that surveys our peer companies, determines what HR practices each company uses, and correlates the practices with financial performance. We just adopt the practices that most strongly relate to financial performance." Adopting the practices of financially successful organizations may enhance organizational performance, but optimizing decisions to unique talent needs and talent market opportunities is harder than that.

Consider if your advertising department adopted this approach. We noted earlier that NASCAR advertising works for products such as automobile parts and beverages. The practice of NASCAR advertising correlates with (and very likely causes) increased sales. Yet not every organization should advertise with NASCAR just because it works for other companies. The marketing decision science guides organizations to advertise on NASCAR based on a specific context, so organizations that do so are also most likely to benefit. In talentship effectiveness combined with impact provides this kind of a framework to identify the vital context for decisions about talent policies and practices.

important and valuable. Yet it is also flat because Boeing and other aircraft companies have honed the job of designer for decades; once an engineer is hired and fully experienced, the difference in value between a top designer and a medium-quality designer is not large among experienced engineers. It is not uncommon for organizations like Boeing, with a long history of engineering prowess, to have large manuals describing product or manufacturing process design and engineers who never need to use those manuals. The left side of the top line indicates the consequences of performance levels below the accepted standard of quality. If design goes bad, it is very, very bad for Boeing, which is why the line is flat for most of the range. Boeing has engineered out that risk.

The lower line in the diagram, "engineering coordination," is below design because coordination is important but perhaps not as fundamentally necessary as design. The bottom line is also much more steeply sloped because the variation in the performance of engineers on the actions and

We see the same logical inconsistency when HR organizations take broad strategy statement goals—such as "speed," "quality," or "service"—and try to translate them too directly into practices. Several years ago one of us worked with a top HR manager in a global multiproduct company. After hearing the talentship perspective on strategy analysis, the manager said, "You're going to get a kick out of our recent HR strategy document."[a] He pulled up documents noting the prominence of digitization in the organization's strategic objectives. The company was committed to making its information and services more digitally accessible to its customers. The manager then showed the HR strategy. It indicated plans to digitize as much HR information as possible, moving it from paper to electronic form and putting it onto Web portals. Digitizing information about pay, benefits, and turnover might be useful, but it is not necessarily connected to the talent and organization pivot-points that would most improve the company's digitized information and services in the competitive marketplace.

Our work with organizations shows that leaders inside and outside the HR function seem uniformly tempted to look for answers that let them jump directly from broad strategy goals to talent and organization policies and practices. Leaders need to be patient enough to do the deeper analysis of effectiveness, and that begins with a careful consideration of aligned actions and interactions and the culture and capacity required to make them happen.

a. Interview with manager by John Boudreau, June 2001.

interactions affecting coordination is much higher than the variation in design and because differences in this performance are increasingly connected to Boeing's strategic success. This is not to say engineers don't care about coordination. But, because engineers have traditionally been hired, trained, rewarded, and managed to standards that mostly reflect their design performance, the opportunities for improvement in coordination are greater. As coordination has become more important, those differences imply greater changes in value, shown on the vertical axis in figure 6-3.

A New Kind of Pivotal Engineer at Boeing

Imagine what might happen if Boeing engineers continued to work in the traditional ways when the success of the 787 requires that Boeing suppliers of key components must now do much more of the design and quality control than before. If Boeing were to unilaterally change engineering designs on the 787, it is likely suppliers would rebel or retaliate in other ways. Bad feelings and delays would likely result. In fact, several news stories had descriptions of just such problems.

Simply put, Boeing wins if its engineers perform better on the actions and interactions that avoid coordination gaffes with engineers from other countries. Improving the performance of Boeing's engineers in this arena also enhances the aligned actions of engineers that work for Boeing's partners. If supplier engineers are treated with respect and encouragement by their Boeing counterparts, they will be more likely to offer ideas to cut costs, size, etc., which translates into less weight, fewer parts, and lower costs.

Frequently, the pivotal role challenge for Boeing engineers will be to come up with solutions neither they nor their suppliers would develop on their own. For example, Boeing must work closely with Japanese engineers. There are many cases in other industries of such relationships proving rocky not because the engineers don't have the engineering skill, but because the accepted work culture of American engineers is very different from that of Japanese engineers. If the American tendency toward informality and open debate offends Japanese sensibilities because they see it as disrespectful or aggressive, essential collaborative solutions are not likely to result. The pivotal interaction is for engineering specialists from Seattle and Japan to cooperate.

Chapter 2 noted that an important pillar of any decision science is optimization. More is not always better. Unlimited cooperation is not optimal for Boeing, and its talent strategy must reflect the limitations of cooperation and collaboration. Boeing must still work to retain the core knowledge that will distinguish it from competitors. Recall the many patents Boeing owns with regard to working with composite wing structures. Boeing's engineers and designers may well need to work much more effectively with intellectual property experts to be sure they understand precisely what intellectual property is pivotal and how to build and protect it, all the while maintaining open and collaborative relationships with partners. A deep understanding of aligned actions and interactions is the key to uncovering these opportunities.

Uncharted Opportunities Beyond Traditional Job Descriptions

Finding unique and valuable opportunities in aligned actions and interactions often requires looking beyond the traditional job descriptions and structures. Organizations create jobs to combine common duties or tasks, as well as the knowledge, skills, abilities, and other characteristics required to perform them. Job analysis reveals required tools and technologies, typical working conditions, and so on. Rewards, development, staffing, and a host of other HR practices are based on those job descriptions. Recent writers advocating more strategic HR still refer to "A *positions*" and "strategic *job* families."[2] This is useful, but it still relies on the traditional idea of a job. Job descriptions typically reflect the current state, and they focus on how the typical individual spends his or her time, or on what elements of the job are most important on average. For example, the Position Analysis Questionnaire is one of the most extensively used and studied methods for analyzing jobs and uses the following scales: extent of use, importance to this job, amount of time, possibility of occurrence, and applicability.

Pivotalness Beyond Typical Tasks or Relationships

This traditional focus on what's true today for collective job holders means the job definitions will often miss pivotal and emerging role challenges and aligned actions and interactions. They will often reflect task groupings that are quite logical descriptions of what individuals do, but they may miss essential combinations of actions across jobs that produce collectively pivotal talent pools. For example, at Disney, people in the jobs of sweeper and store clerk each have a part of their job that involves helping park guests in unexpected ways. There is no single job or position that contains all these actions. Rather, parts of the two jobs form the talent pool that defines customer interaction, though the sweepers and the clerks also have other important parts to their jobs. Job descriptions are not designed to reveal pivotalness, yet pivotalness is often the key to improved decisions.

The insight that Boeing's engineers are pivotal not just for design but for global coordination is unique partly because it required thinking outside the traditional job description of an engineer. The traditional engineer job description would likely be based on the tasks that engineers do in many companies and industries. It might reveal that engineers interact with other engineers inside and outside the company, but because its validity is often based on reflecting what engineers do in many industries and on average, it typically won't reveal that global coordination actions are pivotally aligned or the unique nature of those interactions that make them pivotal for Boeing.

Stable job descriptions are important because they support systems that must operate in the long term, such as setting average pay levels and designing basic training, selection, and staffing systems. Certainly, such job descriptions are useful for the broad decisions that must be made about how to group tasks and how to construct systems that maintain and support those tasks over time. Without a decision science, this often means that job descriptions are not changed even when their relationship to the strategy changes. Traditional engineering job descriptions focus on solving technical problems and applying technical knowledge. At Boeing such job descriptions could miss the fact that the company's decision to pursue the 787 increased the pivotalness of actions affecting the global coordination of teams. The old DNA of the job of a design engineer wouldn't reflect the new pivot-points.

We see this frequently with regard to sales jobs that were originally designed when the sales task involved in-depth and specific knowledge of one product. When the mission shifted from selling one product or service to selling solutions based on an integrated array of products and services, the old job description no longer reflected the new pivot-points. Yet many organizations continued to reward and track traditional behaviors designed to sell individual products (computers, financial services, insurance policies) even as the new pivot-point changed to understanding the customer's complete needs and designing solutions to address them.

In another example, from the pharmaceutical industry, the sales role traditionally had a pivotal aligned action based on how much time the salesperson spent with physicians in positions to make large purchases. Today television ads that describe an array of symptoms end with "Ask your doctor about . . ." Often it's difficult to tell what the product actually cures! Such ads get patients to ask their doctor about specific pharmaceutical products in part because doctors have less and less time to spend with salespeople. At the same time, the Internet makes it possible for physicians to bypass the salesperson completely. The new strategically pivotal aligned action for salespeople may now be to ensure that physicians have a large stock of samples when patients inquire about a certain drug or to be certain that the company Web site is easily accessed by the staff in the doctor's office or hospital, not just by the doctor.

The book *The New American Workplace* notes that increasing flexibility and agility requires something more than a traditional job description:

The traditional notion of "a job" is changing, if not disappearing. Until recently, organizations depended upon formal job descriptions as a way to manage and control the behavior of workers . . . American businesses are decreasingly using jobs and job descriptions as the basic molecules of the way they organize and manage tasks; instead, they use flexible work assignment descriptions, such as the titles of the projects an individual is working on, the deliverables of those projects, and how the individual's contributions to those will be measured. These dynamic descriptions change on an irregular basis as projects are completed and employees are given new responsibilities and assignments.[3]

For example, a 2006 article in *Fortune* notes that organizations with increasingly "broken business models" are opting for radical flexibility: "The most extreme example of meeting chaos with chaos is probably Semco, the celebrated Brazilian outfit where there are virtually no job titles, a few executives trade the CEO role every six months, and workers set their own hours and choose their managers by vote."[4] In times of fluid and flexible role descriptions, the logic of impact and effectiveness are essential to avoid chaos.

The Implications for Future Work Analysis

One implication of effectiveness is that organizations must become more adept at identifying how to conceive and manage these new roles, which will be constantly changing and not easily captured in traditional job descriptions. This requires more than a flexible work analysis system. It requires a system that uses a decision science to construct the new roles based on a clear, logical connection to strategy. The principles of aligning talent and organization to strategic pivot-points, and identifying the vital aligned actions and interactions, provide an economic logic to guide flexible work definitions so that they are strategically meaningful. Thus, a maturing talent decision science will undoubtedly mean more pressure for flexibility in traditional job descriptions. Organizations must be constantly vigilant to the need to change their conception of pivotal roles to reflect new alignments with emerging strategic and organizational processes, resources, and differentiators.

Does talentship require organizations to completely abandon their job-based structures and systems in favor of completely new systems that focus on actions, interactions, roles, and talent pools? No. Organizations can improve their decisions without dismantling job-based systems that work well for the majority of tasks. No one has done the scientific study, but we suspect that this issue will follow the familiar 80-20 rule in which 20 percent of decisions drive 80 percent of the significant value. For example, 80 percent of sales are often driven by 20 percent of product inventory. Still, organizations manage *all* their inventory. They pay more attention to the vital 20 percent, but they don't ignore the rest. We suspect that this rule may reveal that some minority of jobs (perhaps 20 percent) will require significant changes in the traditional job system to capture and exploit their pivotalness, but organizations that consistently recognize the 20 percent first and apply a more decision-based and flexible approach will compete better.

Just as with inventory, organizations must still manage all their jobs, not just the 20 percent where pivotalness requires profound changes. You can't pay, train, and staff only the pivotal aligned actions. Talentship calls for organizations to be more systematically vigilant for opportunities to operate in the white space between traditional job descriptions; it also reveals when the traditional job descriptions are adequate. The difference is that without a well-developed decision science, jobs where change is pivotal remain unexamined and unchanged, or jobs go through costly changes when there is no strategic reason.

In practice, organizations in the early stages of using the HC BRidge framework often discover a good deal of low-hanging fruit, where significant talent decision improvements can be made, even within the existing job structure. This first step often involves looking for aligned actions and interactions within existing job structures, defining as "pivotal jobs" those that contain the aligned actions/interactions, and defining as "pivotal talent pools" combinations of existing jobs.

As organizations become more sophisticated, however, talentship will eventually reveal profound differences between the way actions and interactions are grouped in the job structure versus what is needed to exploit strategic opportunities. The right response will be to break through the job description inertia. As hard as it is, organizations will sometimes have to redefine the "sweeper" job to be "customer ambassadors who sweep" or the "engineering design" job to be "global coordinators who design." That will mean difficult changes in all the systems that affect those jobs. It will mean teaching the organization to think very differently about the contribution of people who were formerly considered just sweepers or designers. Indeed, the fact that such changes are difficult is often why they are so unique and protectable!

Culture and Capacity

The next part of the HC BRidge framework is the culture and capacity linking element, which translates pivotal actions and interactions into the individual and collective culture and capacity required to make them possible. Again, the key is to take the pivot-points at one level and translate them into pivot-points at the next level. This linking element describes what collective and individual characteristics employees must have, as shown in figure 6-4.

FIGURE 6-4

HC BRidge framework: Culture and capacity

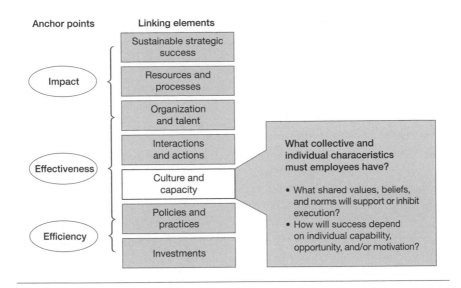

Decades of behavioral science suggest that the capacity to act is a function of three essential elements. They go by various names, but we will use *COM* to stand for capability, opportunity, and motivation. Capability asks, "Does someone have the ability?" Opportunity asks, "Does someone get the chance?" And motivation asks, "Does someone have the desire?" Any one or all of the COM elements can produce a high yield of aligned actions, but the high-yield COM elements are not always the same, nor is it always important to improve all of them. In the same way, if any one of the elements goes to zero, then the level of the other two doesn't affect overall capacity. Thus, the challenge is to create an environment where these COM elements are in balance and at high levels.

Capability, opportunity, and motivation are individual factors. At the organization or group level, the parallel concept is culture. *Culture* has many meanings and is often associated with groups, teams, organizations, and even nations. Schein described culture as "taken-for-granted, shared, tacit ways of perceiving, thinking, and reacting," noting that culture is "one of the most powerful and stable forces operating in organizations."[5] Here we use the word *culture* to mean the pattern of values, beliefs, and norms shared by a group that new members learn as the accepted way the group relates. Culture evolves over time, and it manifests itself when more than one person interacts. Thus, in the HC BRidge framework, culture is an organizational counterpart to the capacity of the individual.

Culture and Capacity Applied to Boeing

Considering the significant changes in the pivot-points for engineers and designers that we described earlier, what are the COM and culture challenges that Boeing faces? Boeing's challenge is to nurture world-class technical professionals who meet a very high standard as engineers or designers and who can create and nurture the emerging global relationships that make or break Boeing's productivity and innovation.

Aircraft design is important at Boeing, but for Boeing's engineers, the more pivotal capability is different. If Boeing can successfully create a unique capability to work with an extended base of external partners, it will be a formidable competitive advantage. For Boeing, success in creating the COM necessary to manage an extended partner base is as important, and perhaps more pivotal, than the COM to do aircraft engineering.

In terms of culture Boeing's values, norms, and assumptions have been honed through decades of building planes in-house with arm's-length partner relationships. The new cultural pivot-point is different. Boeing must think more deeply and precisely about the broad concept of culture. It is not enough simply to create a culture of globalization or one that is boundaryless. It is important that Boeing develops and holds its leaders accountable for very specific norms and values that include listening and encouraging partners to provide their best ideas and then respecting and using those ideas effectively and quickly.

Boeing engineers and designers must be measured on capabilities such as knowledge of the norms of specific international partners, opportunities such as the chance to work as employees of partner companies, and motivations such as a passion for like individual engineering achievement and for new motivations like a passion for being the invisible glue that holds together diverse teams inside and outside the company's boundary.

Culture and Capacity Beyond Boeing's Organizational Boundary

Earlier we emphasized that the talent resource often lies in the potential value of those outside the organization. One of the most pivotal talent pools for Boeing lies completely outside its organizational boundary. A good example is a Mitsubishi-employed engineer in Japan. From the *Los Angeles Times*, we learn:

Toyohiro Nagase has quietly led a strengths/weaknesses analysis technique team of more than 100 Mitsubishi engineers at Boeing's famed design center in Everett, Washington, to fashion the blueprint for the 787's wing. He first worked with Boeing in the late 1970s on the 767 when Mitsubishi was given a contract to make a small section of the fuselage. A decade later, he was named leader of a group that spent a year in the United States learning from Boeing engineers how to make part of the fuselage for the 777. "Working with Boeing is nothing new to me," said Nagase, 52, who has spent about one quarter of his career with Boeing in Seattle. "Our responsibilities have been growing, and this is the first time they've asked us to do the wing box."[6]

Certainly, Nagase must be a good engineer, but his more pivotal role will be to bring his understanding of Boeing to create productive and efficient working relationships between Boeing and Mitsubishi analysis teams. Having spent a quarter of his career with Boeing, he has the unique capability and motivation to provide precisely this kind of social glue. With the 787 project, he was given the opportunity.

Think how much more precisely Boeing's leaders could chart the future of the company on the "soft" human capital elements by analyzing them with this level of precision. While the Nagase story is inspiring, in many organizations such stories are merely isolated examples with no common language or framework to interpret them or to reliably replicate them. It's like having stories about great investments or great marketing campaigns without portfolio theory or customer segmentation theory to tie them together and isolate the important considerations. By understanding how COM and culture support aligned actions and interactions that are pivotal to strategic resources and processes, such stories become teaching tools that help leaders incorporate the talent decision framework into their mental models.

Integrating and Balancing COM and Culture

Capability, opportunity, motivation, and culture must work together and be in balance. If any one of them goes to zero, then human capacity will go to zero. Lacking a systematic decision framework, many business leaders get in the habit of thinking of only one of the elements as the way to fix problems they see in actions and interactions. Typically, they seize on capability building (such as training) or motivation building (such as stronger monetary incentives) to the exclusion of culture and opportunity. Yet opportunity and culture can be powerful when leaders have a framework to understand where they are pivotal.

The other lesson from HC BRidge is to align culture and capacity with the actions and interactions that support the strategic pivot-points. Too often, organizations assert general beliefs in COM elements such as "life-long learning"; "engaged alignment"; "performance-based motivation"; or cultural elements such as "innovativeness," "speed," or "customer focus." As we have seen, these are all valuable but not in the same way in all roles. For example, retail organizations such as Limited Brands, Nordstrom, and Wal-Mart prize information about customers. The insights that associates on the store floor should gather, however, are very different from the insights that market researchers gather in the merchandising organization. Store associates don't need the capacity to figure out which fashions will be popular next year or what color will be in, but they do need the capacity and culture to pay careful attention to the way customers shop, what store processes seem to lead them to buy more, and what seems to cause them to stay in the store longer.

Understanding the aligned action and interaction pivot-points allows a much deeper analysis of precisely what sort of culture and capacity are most vital and where they make the biggest difference. Organizations that compete effectively will find more opportunities to create unique relationships between capacity, culture, and their strategy pivot-points, avoiding today's tendency to treat them more generically.

Competencies in HC BRidge

Today organizations frequently organize their talent systems around competencies. The word *competencies* has no single accepted definition. It is used to mean everything from broad individual traits to specific skills and a well-defined set of capabilities with behaviors and behavioral standards associated with them. Sometimes competencies are developed as very unique to the business model of organizations or the specific requirements for a given role, and sometimes they are general traits or behaviors that apply to a broad class of roles. Thus, competencies often incorporate elements of capability, motivation, and aligned actions in HC BRidge.

Even when competencies are derived from a careful analysis of the tasks people do and the roles they are expected to play, competency systems often reflect either generic traits or focus on skills and knowledge, ignoring opportunity, motivation, and behavior. Such systems often add significant value to organizations, but as the talent decision science matures, it requires careful distinctions between the linking elements of culture, capacity, actions, and interactions. It also requires a search for pivot-points and their logical connections up and down the model. Competency models like this are often useful organizing frameworks but not decision frameworks.

To make competencies a more precise definition of position requirements, some organizations have extended the competency model into a performance model, incorporating information about specific role responsibilities and challenges, including both general and role-specific technical competencies. Another innovation is integration around common competency definitions, platforms, or architectures, applied throughout the organization, that have greater ability to develop future talent through transitions between roles, using a common framework.

Thus, competency models run the gamut from general organizing frameworks to more job- or role-specific performance models. Whatever their sophistication, they can be more useful if their information is embedded in a decision framework like HC BRidge that logically connects competencies to specific strategy pivot-points and creates synergy among policies and practices. At a minimum the application of any framework should consider the appropriate weighting of the competencies, based on the pivot-points. In a more mature environment, the performance models themselves would reflect the specific pivot-points within the role, given the strategic context.

Engagement and Alignment in HC BRidge

Organizations are appropriately concerned with whether employees are engaged and aligned with strategic organizational goals. While *alignment* and *engagement* are defined in many different ways, in most cases the definition of *alignment* is the degree to which employees understand how their individual behaviors contribute to the broader organizational goals and which of their actions are most vital to those goals. In HC BRidge actions and interactions describe the elements of alignment. Capability elements of capacity and culture include whether individuals know and understand which of their actions and interactions are pivotal, which are important, and the difference between the pivotal ones and the important ones.

Engagement usually refers to how satisfied or motivated employees are in their work or how much they view the organization's goals as important personal goals for themselves. This concept is a component of motivation in the HC BRidge framework. Too often, *alignment* and *engagement* are defined based on broad and generic strategy statements, such as "provide the best customer service" or "lead the industry in innovation." Such statements are useful, and it is useful to know whether employees understand the organization's broad mission and are motivated to achieve it. This definition of *alignment*, however, provides little guidance to employees regarding which specific actions and interactions contribute most.

For Boeing engineers, both traditional design and global collaboration are important to achieving the broad strategic goal of a successful launch of the 787. Engagement on both is valuable. But, as we have seen, a deeper understanding of the relative value of these actions is needed for engineers to engage properly with the right aligned actions and interactions.

Integrating Interactions and Actions with Capacity and Culture at Williams-Sonoma

The opportunities that are revealed by a deep analysis of actions/interactions and capacity/culture were illustrated in 1999, when we worked with John Bronson, then the senior vice president of HR at Williams-Sonoma, on the talent implications of the company's new Internet strategy.[7] At that time the Internet was booming, and virtually every company was trying to find a way onto the Net. San Francisco–based Williams-Sonoma, already famous for its insightful merchandising and deep understanding of retail customers of home and kitchen goods, was considering an Internet channel in addition to its stores and catalog.

Like so many other companies, Williams-Sonoma was competing in the labor market for the best programmers and Web designers. It was a hot market and not an easy one in which to compete. Moreover, Williams-Sonoma couldn't offer the kinds of groundbreaking projects that were the hallmark of other Silicon Valley companies, such as Cisco and Sun Microsystems. It couldn't offer the kind of astronomical potential stock price growth of start-up companies. It couldn't offer salaries, campuses, and perquisites that other companies could offer, because the profit margins in multiple-location retailing didn't approach those of software and technology companies, who were lavishing everything from concierge services to on-site automobile detailing on their technical professionals.

Needless to say, a traditional approach to HR investments that emphasized working harder at recruitment and sourcing was not the answer. The company would just be chasing the same group of technical Web professionals as everyone else, with some decided disadvantages in its market position. The talentship process encouraged Bronson and his colleagues to consider Williams-Sonoma's strategic pivot-points, align their talent and organization around those pivot-points, think beyond simple position descriptions, and determine the implications for investments.

Williams-Sonoma's position in the retail market was enviable. Patrick Connolly, then executive vice president of the catalog group and now chief marketing officer, told InformationWeek magazine, "We have 19 million names in our customer purchasing-history database, and 75 percent of our customers say they use the Internet. We don't have to spend 40 percent or 60 percent of our revenue to build a brand and bring traffic to our site."[8] What had created such a formidable and loyal group of potential Internet customers? It was Williams-Sonoma's traditional attention to detail, its innovations in product design and merchandising (e.g., searching the world for the very best kitchen knives), its commitment to lead its customers by directing their attention to new innovations and discoveries, and its fundamental core values built around a certain image, look, and feel running through its stores and catalogs.

Considering the aligned actions and interactions within the job of Web designer and programmer at Williams-Sonoma, it became clear that the company actually needed technical professionals who could effectively work with the skilled designers and copywriters that had made the look of the stores and catalog such a success. Designers and copywriters who mastered the art of creating typography, images, and sentences that project the company's unique image in its catalogs would now ensure that its Web pages projected the same brand image. As for the internal organization, many creative people working in the catalog and store areas told us they were interested in moving to the Web. They viewed it as a fascinating way to extend their capabilities.

In terms of the market for technical professionals outside the organization, our interviews with Williams-Sonoma's technical workers revealed some crucial information. Such individuals are often assumed to be motivated primarily by money and the opportunity to improve their technical skills. Yet among Williams-Sonoma's technical professionals, the reasons they joined and stayed with the organization went well beyond money and technical skills. They said things like, "I can produce Web pages anywhere, but this is one of the best places to learn about merchandising or about the logic of retailing." Qualities for which Williams-Sonoma is recognized—image, products, and sophisticated retail skills—were significant and unique attractors for a certain subgroup of the technical population. One technical person said, "If I were working for Cisco, I'd be doing really interesting technical work, but it is all embedded in the programs that run routers. Here my work shows up on the Web page that my parents use, and I feel great when I see a person at a mall with that green bag and know that I had something to do with their purchase."[9]

By identifying its unique strategic pivot-points based on product authority, merchandising, design, and a compelling look and feel, Williams-Sonoma realized that the talent pivot-point for its technical Web professionals was in their actions and interactions related to high-level imagery and coordination with the core processes of retailing, merchandising, and design. Not only did that help the company better target the right population of technical professionals, but it also gave the organization a unique position in the labor market as one of the few places where Web technicians could develop skills in retailing, merchandising, and design. Williams-Sonoma needed Web professionals with technical skills, to be sure, but the key pivot-point beyond the standard technical skills was the capability, opportunity, and motivation to create a Web channel that was culturally and strategically integrated with the company's brand.

When the organization is aligned with the key strategic pivot-points, the actions and interactions of many roles come together. Not only are technical Web professionals better matched to the organization's value proposition, but other roles complement them. The merchants and designers at Williams-Sonoma now have Web professionals they can work with to extend and refine their vision about the brand. Leaders of the catalog and store channels can work with technical Web professionals who also have a passion and an understanding of the importance of Williams-Sonoma's consistent look and feel. One tangible example in 1999 was the fact that text on the Web site was created as graphics, not as font-based text, as was typical of most sites. Why did the design treat text as a graphical element? Because it was the only way to guarantee that the text would appear precisely the same on virtually every computer screen, guaranteeing that every Web customer would have the same visual experience.

Conclusion

In this chapter we've focused on two effectiveness components: actions/interactions and culture/capacity. We've seen how talentship and HC BRidge reveal insights deep within traditional job descriptions to identify more precisely the employee behaviors that make the difference and the necessary individual and collective characteristics that make those behaviors possible. This kind of deep analysis is the key to avoid being shackled by traditional job descriptions, confusing work behaviors that are flat sloped with those that are steeply sloped, or relying too heavily on only one element of human capacity or culture that has been successful in the past.

Clearly, this kind of deep understanding improves decisions about the programs and policies that will make it all happen. This is especially important in fast-changing and mass-customized employment environments. The dilemma has been recognized by researchers, who have noted the need to make employment deals fit increasingly specific work behaviors and subpopulations. Denise Rousseau coined the term *i-deals* to describe idiosyncratic employment arrangements for those with the most strategic value to the firm.[10] This chapter has shown how to identify the specific aligned actions and interactions that describe that strategic value. In chapter 7 we will take up the question of how to construct equally specific and strategically relevant practices that create the deals.

7

Effectiveness in Policies and Practices

Creating the Strategic Portfolio of Talent Programs

Take a close look at where your HR organization spends its time, how it reports its results, and the guiding frameworks for its strategies, contributions, and plans. Very likely, you will find that they all are organized around programs and practices. In organization after organization, we find that leaders inside and outside the HR function gravitate toward programs and practices. It is almost a fixation. Discussions about HR strategies often begin with questions such as these: There is an aging workforce, so what programs are we using to retain our workers or to capture their knowledge before they retire? We need to be technologically up-to-date, so what programs are we implementing to improve our brand with the bright kids coming out of college? We don't have sufficient bench strength, so what succession-planning program can you build?

Sound familiar? We find that when organizations start to incorporate talentship, one of the greatest hurdles is that their leaders are impatient for HR to explain what's going to be done. Lacking a decision science, HR leaders, in the paradigm of client service delivery, are often all too eager (even relieved) to avoid the difficult discussions about impact and effectiveness and to jump right into designing programs. As we have seen, competing for and with talent will increasingly require that organizations embrace those difficult discussions before turning to the more familiar task of designing HR programs and practices. The *essential evolution* means recognizing the importance of policies, practices, and services but requires extending the focus to include the quality of decisions.

Still, policies and practices are a vital and important element of a mature decision science, as the prominence of policy areas such as accounting, advertising, and sales attests. In this chapter we address that element of the HC BRidge framework, connecting policies and processes to the talentship decision science. The policies and practices element of the HC BRidge framework reflects the programs designed to create and support culture and capacity. This includes policies and practices inside and outside the HR function. This is shown in figure 7-1.

Policies and practices are familiar ground for organizations and their HR functions, so we won't attempt to cover the technical delivery of HR policies and practices in detail. There are many professional textbooks and associations devoted to the important work of improving the quality and delivery of practices and policies related to talent and organization. Instead, we'll use this chapter to describe often overlooked decision factors for policies and practices where talentship suggests that organizations can learn a lot from other decision sciences. The questions we address here have proved useful in helping organizations refocus the professional activity of their HR functions toward a more decision-based approach. We focus on the three questions in figure 7-1.

FIGURE 7-1

HC BRidge framework: Policies and practices

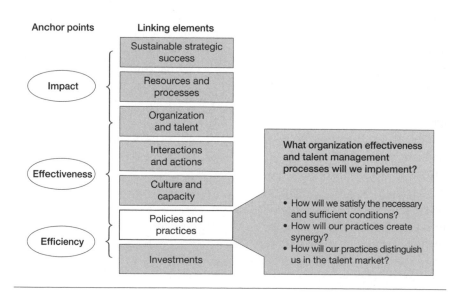

Necessary and Sufficient Conditions

One of the most frequent frustrations we encounter from business leaders is that talent decisions are often presented as choices about whether and how to implement one or more HR practices or techniques. For example, HR strategy is sometimes an array of technologies, such as recruitment advertising, Internet technical training, or a new approach to assessing performance or setting merit-pay levels. These all may be fine programs, and they often are individually valuable. Even in organizations where the connection between HR and strategy is recognized and valued, it is surprising how discussions about programs focus mostly on the program budget (usually how to do the program at a lower cost) and on which programs it will be spent. There is often too little focus on the conditions required for success or on the principles that underpin how the program or practice will achieve its results.

More mature decision sciences approach this differently. For example, finance may automate the process of gathering information for the chart of accounts, but the discussion with business leaders typically focuses less on whether to automate and more on how doing so will help the manager make better decisions. This may be done by using automation to organize financial information so that business leaders get precisely the information they need to understand which accounting factors affect important outcomes such as asset utilization.

When marketing implements customer relationship management programs, it often incorporates the principles of customer relations and ensures that the new program provides leaders with not only the data but also a framework to enhance vital customer relationship decisions. Marketing focuses on the necessary conditions that must exist for the new program to work and on the sufficient conditions that the program must achieve to be successful. For example, the success of a new customer relations database requires that the users understand the principles of effective customer relations and that they be held accountable for achieving specific customer outcomes.

This distinction between the program and the requirements for its success is nicely captured by a mathematical concept known as "necessary and sufficient conditions" that apply to HR.[1] A set of necessary and sufficient (N&S) conditions comprises both the necessary requirements for an outcome and all sufficient conditions to satisfy an outcome. A simple example from plane geometry is the N&S conditions to have a square. You need to know that there are four sides, that each is a straight line of equal length, that they connect at their endpoints, and that one angle of connection is a right angle. No geometric figure other than a square satisfies all these conditions, and you have to know all of them to be certain you have a square. Notice that you don't need to know that the other three angles are ninety degrees because that condition is satisfied by the others.

This idea is also quite common in engineering. There is only one necessary condition for an object to fly. The net lift (from whatever source) must exceed the weight. There are many different ways this N&S condition can be created. With a blimp the lift comes from gas that is lighter than air and uses gravity as the lifting force. Birds use flapping wings. Airplanes use differential air pressure created by the difference in speed between the air flows above and below a wing surface. The key here is that you can define the N&S conditions independently of the techniques used to create the conditions.

We find that when organizations begin to frame their conversations about talent programs and practices in terms of N&S success conditions, they uncover ways to be far more logical, productive, and systematic than when the conversations are primarily about techniques. For example, when considering investments in employee staffing, it is not unusual for organizations to frame the debate in terms of whether one technique or another is worth the investment. Examples include whether to purchase a selection test that more validly predicts job performance or to tap a recruitment source that may provide more applicants.

Yet, without a shared idea about the N&S conditions, there is little basis on which to make decisions. How much is greater test validity worth? Is this a situation where greater validity makes a difference? Is the increased validity worth a possible reduction in the quantity of applicants who won't put up with the test? Is it possible that the better applicants might not accept our offers? Such questions are often lost in the debate over whether the technique is more valid or whether the recruitment source taps better applicants. Too often, the logic is something like "We are not getting enough high-quality employees, so we need to do something. Recruiting from sources that have more high-quality applicants sounds like a good thing, so let's do that." Yet it's quite possible that the problem isn't having enough good applicants but getting the good ones you do have to accept your offer! It's like debating whether to implement a program to reduce the costs of ordering more raw materials inventory before you know whether the ordering costs are too high. It may be that you're just holding on to too much inventory or not pricing appropriately.

N&S Conditions Applied to Talent Acquisition

Talent acquisition provides a good example of the distinction and its power to improve decisions. We find it very useful to see the talent acquisition process through the metaphor of a supply chain for any important resource. Talent acquisition's goal is to have the appropriate quantity and quality of employees. Various staffing techniques can increase prediction validity, the number of applicants, and the percentage of accepted offers. Every one of these things can be helpful, but they are not always helpful, and they are not equally helpful. For example, if you can't get good applicants to accept your offers, then tapping recruitment sources with better-quality applicants doesn't help you much. This is an example where the decision science principle of optimization applies once again.

Figure 7-2 depicts the staffing process as a series of stages through which talent flows and that ultimately define the conditions that must be met. Like a filter, each stage eliminates an additional subset of the original group. In the diagram the talent flows in the top row show the results of the filtering process, beginning with a potential labor pool that is winnowed through recruitment and selection down to a group that receives offers and then is winnowed further as some accept offers and remain with the organization. The staffing processes in the lower row show the activities that accomplish the filtering.

Notice how the diagram is similar to standard supply chain diagrams that show the stages through which a key raw material must move (such as extraction, transport, storage, etc.). The N&S conditions of the staffing supply chain are the quality and quantity of talent that is optimal at each stage. HR organizations often develop diagrams like this, called "staffing process maps," through HR processes or Six Sigma analysis. Usually, these analyses are used only for reducing the costs or speed of each process stage. This is a lost opportunity, because these very same maps can help analyze a process for its N&S conditions, with very significant insights. Let's look at each stage of the staffing process to illustrate this.

Building and Planning. The first process, building and planning, influences the number and quality of individuals who might potentially become qualified candidates. It includes forecasting labor force trends and talent demands, as well as direct intervention to increase the population qualified for future talent needs. For example, the American Business Collaboration, a corporate partnership, produces middle school science and technology camps that serve five hundred kids at ten camps in cities in the United States and overseas. The program is funded by IBM, Texas Instruments, and Exxon Mobil. Boeing is exploring possible expansion of a popular summer science camp for first- through twelfth-graders near Huntington Beach, California. AT&T backs three science and math camps in Detroit and Chicago, and Intel sponsors three science camps in Colorado and Oregon. As the *Wall Street Journal* reported, year-round mentoring for

FIGURE 7-2

Staffing as a supply chain

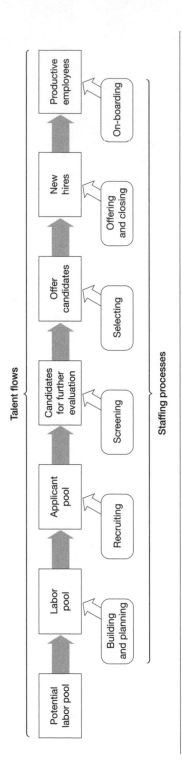

campers reinforces lessons learned: "With pink-streaked hair and body piercings, IBM software engineer Janel Barfield fit right in at the Austin, Texas, middle school cafeteria she visited last year to see the technology camper she was mentoring. When the girl confided that a relative had laughed at her dream of becoming an astronaut, Ms. Barfield said: 'Girl, he doesn't know what he's talking about. . . . You'd make a great astronaut.'"[2] There's no guarantee that every student in these camps will apply to one of the sponsoring organizations. At this stage of the pipeline, the goal is to increase the population of those that might.

Recruiting. The second process, recruiting, gets individuals in the labor pool to apply to the organization. It includes recruitment advertising, job fairs, and online job posting, and it increasingly encompasses less direct activities, such as company product or service advertisements that create an attractive image for job candidates. Recruiting should strive for optimal quantity and quality rather than the largest number of applicants or the highest qualifications.[3] The most effective applicant pools may be smaller (if a high percentage of them take the offers) and may even be less qualified than others (if the organization can train them after they are hired). For example, one of the biggest challenges in online recruiting is that online ads that generate a large quantity of applicants may require much higher costs of resume screening.[4] The key is to optimize the higher quantity against the organization's ability to use that higher quantity, based on its own unique requirements and integrated with its other programs.

Screening. The screening process decides which applicants should be rejected or hired immediately. Often screening is seen as weeding out the unqualified, but when labor is in short supply, screening can identify high-quality candidates who can bypass the selection process and receive immediate offers. So optimal screening must balance the benefits of quick hires and low cost against the long-term costs of making a poor hiring decision through too-low standards or missing "diamonds in the rough" with standards that are too high. These are subtle and important considerations, yet screening activities are often measured only with regard to cost and time or by the number of candidates who survive the initial screen. An interesting variant is to screen using temporary work. In India, which is facing an increasingly acute shortage of professionals, temping becomes a means to screen candidates and in effect becomes a fast-track apprentice program.[5]

Selecting. The next process, selecting, determines which of the pre-screened applicants will receive offers. Is it always worthwhile to increase the validity, or the relationship between selection techniques and per-formance? When selection is seen in the context of the talent acquisition pipeline, high validity is a necessary condition only if there are enough applicants and if the applicant pool varies enough in quality to make it important to find the good ones. For example, consider the situation when an organization recruits college graduates from regional campuses where the quality or fit varies a great deal but applicants have strong regional ties and are likely to accept an employment offer in the area. A highly valid test of management skills can be very important in finding the stars. On the other hand, when recruiting at a top business program, there is little to be learned from a such a test; increasing the rate of acceptances, how-ever, may be very pivotal.

Offering and Closing. The process of offering and closing defines and makes the offer. The focus is often only on whether a high proportion of offers are accepted (i.e., the yield rate). The pipeline approach described here suggests that a more complete perspective would also examine whether the highest-quality applicants accept or reject offers and whether the or-ganization is forced to make offers to candidates who are marginally qualified because of severe shortages. The offering and closing process often begins long before the final offer is presented. When striving for racial and ethnic diversity, it is interesting to examine whether the signals about organizational diversity that candidates encounter during their site visit may affect their later willingness to accept employment offers.[6]

On-Boarding. The final process, on-boarding, establishes new hires in their position and retains them. On-boarding is often evaluated by whether it removes barriers, such as a new hire not having all the equip-ment he/she needs to do their job, or if new hires received necessary in-formation such as pay and benefit policies. The pipeline framework reveals that the N&S conditions should reflect retention and productiv-ity: How long must employees stay to justify the investment in getting them to join? Can we optimize by reducing some investments early in the pipeline and making up for them at this later stage through training or motivation?

N&S Conditions for Development

The principles of optimization and N&S conditions also apply when con-sidering outcomes in the realm of individual capacity. For example, consider how decisions about development are often approached. It is not unusual for such decisions to focus on learning or training techniques. In fact, many textbooks on training divide the training process into "doing the needs analysis," "implementing the learning experience," and "evaluating results." This is a useful way to organize the decision to invest in one or another development program.

That approach can be enhanced, however, by incorporating the N&S conditions that must be created in the learner. One such framework was created by David Peterson and Mary Dee Hicks of Personnel Decisions International.[7] Their framework divides these characteristics into five conditions, as displayed in table 7-1.

Consider how differently the logic and decisions about learning occur under the two different approaches. In a traditional model, if learning outcomes don't materialize, the focus is often on whether HR failed to do a thorough needs analysis, provided a poor learning experience, or didn't evaluate results correctly. In contrast, using the decision framework in table 7-1, an organization could measure and compare business units on their performance on each of the learning elements and then determine which units are high or low on each of the five necessary conditions. Suppose certain learning outcomes didn't occur in one particular unit but were achieved in other units. Suppose further that in the unit that did not achieve the outcomes, employees were equally prepared (insight and motivation) but reported fewer opportunities and rewards for using their learning in their work (real-world practice and accountability).

The HR organization has some influence over the opportunity for real-world practice and accountability, but these are typically much more influenced by leaders within the business units. The N&S approach enables

TABLE 7-1

Necessary and sufficient conditions for individual development

Development condition (in learners)	Learners must . . .
Insight	Know what they need to develop
Motivation	Be willing to invest the time and energy required to develop themselves
New knowledge	Know how to acquire the new capabilities required
Real-world practice	Receive and use opportunities to try their new skills at work
Accountability	Internalize their new capabilities to improve performance and results

Source: Mary Dee Hicks and David B. Peterson, "The Development Pipeline," *Knowledge Management Review* July–August 1999.

a richer conversation that first examines learning based on logical and scientific principles and then frames the solution in terms of the decisions and actions that are affected both inside and outside the HR function.

N&S Conditions as a Decision Foundation

N&S conditions aren't only useful for the talent acquisition pipeline and the development pipeline. We have found that N&S conditions exist for virtually all talent and organization processes such as succession planning and compensation. In organizations we have worked with that have adopted the N&S approach to their processes, we see a marked change in conversations about key policies and practice—from an exclusive concern with new techniques (tests, recruitment ads, etc.) to a greater emphasis on the conditions that each policy and practice must meet.

When such conditions are articulated in each of the functional areas of HR, opportunities for stronger synergy emerge. For example, if an analysis using the talent pipeline reveals the managers that are good at predicting new hires' future value, then an organization could consider altering the rewards program to allow those managers to earn the right to make special hiring offers (e.g., an unusually big signing bonus or a salary offer beyond the usual range for this type of job) for candidates they consider particularly worthy. The N&S conditions for a reward system now integrate with those for the staffing system.

This approach is akin to more mature decision sciences. For example, the finance function first determines a set of N&S conditions and principles that define a well-managed business unit in terms of money, such as cash flow and asset management. Financial management discussions occur within those frameworks, and accountability rests where decision making makes the biggest difference. For example, a manager may not like the results of the cash-flow analysis, but he or she would seldom consider blaming the finance department for poor cash-flow results. Rather, the finance function is accountable for the decision principles and frameworks and for assisting managers to make better decisions. We foresee a future in which decisions about talent and organization programs and practices are approached with similar rigor.

A Portfolio Based on Synergy

Earlier we showed that human capacity requires capability, opportunity, and motivation to be in a synergistic balance. Similarly, policies and practices require synergy and balance. Research suggests that integrated combinations of HR practices are often key to creating culture and capacity.[8]

This is often called "internal fit" or "internal alignment." Yet it is amazing how often we see this principle violated in organizations. Classic examples of overlooking fit include pairing individual performance incentives with organizational design and training that emphasize teamwork and coordination. Individual incentives can discourage cooperation if they motivate internal competition. Why invest in team-based designs and training only to discourage those effects with too much emphasis on individual rewards? When policies and practices are developed in the HR functional silos and considered only individually, optimization across policies and practices is difficult.

Focusing on Optimization, Not Just Maximization

A decision framework emphasizes optimization, not just maximization. Too often, organizations strive to maximize the returns from each program separately. A large number of approaches exist to calculate the ROI on programs such as training, compensation, staffing, and work-life balance.[9] These approaches provide a useful logic, but too often they consider only one program or practice at a time. A mature decision framework shows when more is *not* better, even when it comes to the ROI from individual HR practices. The key to success is often in combining practices so that the total return is maximized, rather than pushing only one program to its fullest capacity. Investors achieve maximum returns by emphasizing the synergy of a portfolio of investments, not by trying to achieve goals through only one type of investment. In the same way, organizations need to carefully combine different programs and practices to balance their respective advantages and disadvantages. Synergy matters.

This means that measuring and tracking the effects of investments in talent and organization programs and practices becomes more complicated. Reporting the ROI of one program at a time will generally miss important synergies. Emerging research is developing statistical methods that can capture the effect of configurations, or sets of practices.[10] One conclusion from this research is that the logic for creating the sets must be much more rigorous, which is why a decision science is so important. Once again, we see that it is often a lack of clear logic that prevents better measurement and decision making, not a lack of measures.

Improving Benchmarking

Understanding synergy between HR programs and practices and their alignment with strategic pivot-points is essential to avoiding some of the most common mistakes that occur in benchmarking. HR practices are often adopted because they resemble the practices of industry or business leaders.[11] One of our favorite examples is the extraordinary simultaneous decision by organizations in virtually every industry, competitive environment, and global region to implement a forced-distribution performance management system. Not only did they all simultaneously decide to require that employees be given performance ratings that distributed employees across the performance range, but they even required leaders to rank subordinates so that 10 percent fell in the bottom category (i.e., employees who needed to improve or be managed out), 70 percent in the middle (i.e., satisfactory employees), and 20 percent in the top (i.e., high-performing employees, those with high potential).

Imagine if such a phenomenon had occurred in the discipline of finance and such a large variety of organizations had decided to adopt a debt and equity structure based on 70 percent stock, 10 percent debt, and 20 percent cash! The motivation for such a widespread decision would have to be groundbreaking research and insights about capital markets and the organizations' performance.

In HR the reason was not that every organization had done a deep strategic analysis of how the forced-distribution performance management system fit their strategic goals. Rather, their business leaders had read the book *Jack: Straight from the Gut*, by Jack Welch.[12] That book vividly describes Welch's conclusion that the 20-70-10 system helped transform GE in the 1990s. What is often missed, however, is that at the same time GE was using this system, so too was Enron, as recounted in the book *The Smartest Guys in the Room*.[13] Were organizations that adopted this approach benchmarking GE or Enron?

The answer lies in synergy. GE had decades of history and experience building leaders who were highly skilled and motivated at assessing their talent. The company had a long history of performance-based rewards, coaching, and feedback and had developed deep organizational processes for both formal and informal communication about performance and values. GE devoted a great deal of time and energy to those processes at all levels of the organization for many years before introducing the 20-70-10 system. With such a history, the 20-70-10 system had a supporting array of other talent practices that complemented it and made it effective. Many organizations have, to their regret, learned this lesson the hard way—by implementing the 20-70-10 system without such supporting processes—and found that it did more harm than good.

The talentship perspective suggests that by carefully analyzing where the pivot-points are and what specific capacity and aligned actions and interactions are necessary, organizations can capitalize on the power of a synergistic and integrated portfolio of HR practices. More important, rather than simply adopting certain combinations (such as high-commitment work practices) because they have proved to be generally effective, organizations can potentially develop very specific practices that reflect their own unique competitive position in the market for their offerings, as well as in the market for talent.

Policy and Practice Synergy at Boeing

We have seen how talentship and HC BRidge reveal opportunities for more sophisticated and targeted talent policies and practices at Boeing. An interesting example of synergy is how Boeing's practices reach beyond its traditional boundaries.[14] Recall Nagase, the Mitsubishi designer whose pivotal role was to understand Boeing and help the company integrate Mitsubishi's intellectual and technical contributions into wing design and production. He spent 25 percent of his career as a Mitsubishi employee, located at Boeing's plants in Seattle. Thus, Boeing's programs and practices—such as career planning, training, and development opportunities—created a synergistic effect on his development, career path, and motivation. We often think of talent and organization policies and practices as they apply to those employees within the organization's boundary, yet here is an example of a synergistic career plan for a Mitsubishi engineer that created precisely the kind of boundary spanner that Boeing needed.

Such talent outcomes often occur by chance. Talentship encourages more systematically identifying this kind of sophisticated human capital development. How many other potential Nagases exist within Boeing or its partners? How good is Boeing at identifying them and then creating the array of programs and practices that will systematically nurture them? Is Boeing doing this quicker and more precisely than its competition? Answers to those questions for Boeing, and similar questions for your organization, mean the difference between competitive success and failure and will increasingly characterize how leaders approach talent and organization decisions.

Competitive Advantage: Where Talent Supply Complements Talent Demand

Talentship reveals sophisticated opportunities to integrate talent supply and demand, just as portfolio theory and market segmentation revealed sophisticated opportunities to integrate supply and demand for financial and marketing resources. Classic supply-demand principles predict that

Are High-Commitment or Financially Correlated Work Practices the Answer to Synergy?

Certain combinations of HR practices have been labeled "high-commitment" work practices because they emphasize employee involvement and commitment rather than a more traditional approach that defines performance very strictly. High-commitment work practices include pay that is contingent on performance (often at the group level), careful recruitment and selection, training that is designed to support more high-involvement work, and employee participation systems (suggestion systems, high-performance teams, extensive selection testing, etc.).[a] Studies have found that the combination of such practices yields higher overall productivity and lower labor costs as a proportion of productivity. Yet this is unlikely to be the only pattern that works, and it probably doesn't work everywhere. There is no definitive answer regarding precisely which HR practices complement each other, though it seems reasonable to conclude that HR practices can either reinforce or work against each other and that if they reinforce each other, better results are likely to occur.[b]

Another intriguing finding of the 1980s was a correlation between the frequency of HR practices and financial performance. Mark Huselid, Brian Becker, and others showed that when HR leaders are asked to describe whether they use any of a series of HR practices (such as valid selection tests, performance-based pay, training focused on job-related skills, team-based work design, etc.), their answers were correlated with financial indicators (such as return on assets).[c]

This spawned consulting products and many articles and marketing presentations reporting that firms with stronger financial performance report doing more of certain HR practices. Such research has proved extremely valuable in reframing the discussion about the value of HR toward explicitly including the organization's strategic outcomes. Business leaders often mistakenly conclude, however, that these findings suggest that implementing such practices will raise their financial performance. The pattern of results does not necessarily mean that adopting such practices will actually increase financial performance.[d]

Writers have also noted that this research often focuses on generic HR practices that are applied organizationwide rather than in particular talent pools where aligned actions and interactions are likely to be pivotal to specific business and organizational strategy elements. The practices are often compared with organization-level financial or accounting outcomes and less often with the intermediate processes and resources that earlier chapters showed are vital to understanding the unique strategic connections. Again, the research that established these connections is very valuable. If business leaders try to achieve sustainable strategic success by matching generic practices of high-performing organizations, however, they may act against the admonitions of Michael Porter, Jay Barney, and other scholars who have repeatedly noted that strategic success is achieved by attaining specific and unique differentiated positions in the markets for resources and products.[e]

For example, performance-based pay may well lead to higher performance and ultimately to improved financial performance—unless it is applied in flat-sloped positions where performance variation is low or where variation in performance doesn't matter. Many organizations set their pay levels for jobs at the fiftieth percentile of labor markets defined by generic job descriptions and what a wide array of other employers are paying for those jobs. For example, it may make sense for Boeing to break the rule of the fiftieth percentile and pay more for engineers who can facilitate global teams—but only if Boeing can find those engineers and leverage the additional pay to produce a strategically higher-quality workforce. Simply paying more because "engineers are important" or because "we have an engineering shortage" is not a sufficiently sophisticated decision approach.

Research that shows HR practices correlate with financial outcomes or that a particular combination of such practices increases manufacturing performance is undeniably an important breakthrough. Demonstrating that programs and practices make a difference, however, is not the same as making strategic decisions. Such findings, as important as they are, do not absolve organizational leaders from the hard work of articulating their unique strategic pivot-points, the supporting processes and resources, and how unique programs and practices can create the talent and organization effects that will enhance those pivot-points.

a. John Paul MacDuffie, "Human Resource Bundles and Manufacturing Performance," *Industrial and Labor Relations Review* 48, no. 2 (1995): 197–221.

b. Brian Becker and Barry Gerhart, "The Impact of Human Resource Management on Organizational Performance: Progress and Prospects," *Academy of Management Journal* 39, no. 4 (1996): 779–801.

c. Brian E. Becker and Mark A. Huselid, "High-Performance Work Systems and Firm Performance: A Synthesis of Research and Managerial Implications," *Research in Personnel and Human Resources Management* 16 (1998): 53–101.

d. Patrick Wright et al., "The Relationship Between HR Practices and Firm Performance: Examining Causal Order," *Personnel Psychology* 58 (2005): 409–446.

e. See, for instance, Michael E. Porter, "What Is Strategy?" *Harvard Business Review*, November–December 1996, 61–78; Jay B. Barney, "Integrating Organizational Behavior and Strategy Formulation Research: A Resource-Based Analysis," *Advances in Strategic Management* 8 (1992): 39–61.

markets set prices where suppliers charge what buyers will pay. Supply
goes up as the price increases (witness the scramble to build or bring on
line refining capacity as oil prices rise), and vice versa. Demand goes up as
the price drops, and vice versa. Supply and demand curves are typically
thought of as lines that intersect at one price. In real markets the supply
and demand curves are thick, rather than thin, lines. So the intersection
of supply and demand may actually be a range of prices, providing room
for organizations to strike unique bargains.

Disney faced this kind of market for land in Florida. For decades the
land had been bought and sold with one purpose—growing citrus fruit.
Disney arrived in the market with special organizational resources that
could make Florida land much more valuable—not as citrus groves, but as
resorts and theme parks. Disney's demand curve for Florida was higher
than the demand curve for citrus growers because Disney could generate
more value from the land. Disney understood its demand for land, so it
could purchase Florida land at or near citrus grove prices and create value
using it as a theme park.

A logical understanding of demand reveals opportunities to affect the
supply of a resource in ways that often are hard for competitors to duplicate. In the 1960s Disney acquired twenty-eight thousand acres of Florida
land, an area roughly twice the size of Manhattan. Disney wanted to create a buffer zone around planned parks to avoid the traffic congestion
and development that had quickly surrounded Disneyland, in Anaheim,
California. Disney also realized the land might someday be used for a
leisure-based community. Because Disney had such a clear and (in the
1960s) unique strategic demand for the land, the company secured
arrangements for the supply of land that were uniquely valuable. In 1985
the *Wall Street Journal* reported that:

> In 1967, the Florida legislature, in a series of five acts, obligingly en-
> dowed Disney with powers normally reserved for county governments.
> Through the new, but unpopulated, municipalities of Bay Lake and
> Lake Buena Vista, and through the specially established Reedy Creek
> Improvement District, the company was authorized to float tax-exempt
> bonds, to establish its own zoning and to exercise police and eminent-
> domain powers. The legislature also gave the district specific authority,
> so far unexploited, to build an airport and even to generate power by
> nuclear fission.[15]

Such land-supply arrangements are of little value to a citrus grower but
essential to a parks developer.

Unique Supply and Demand for Boeing Engineers

Talentship reveals unique ways to integrate talent supply in the Boeing example. As Boeing aligns its talent and organization resources to the strategic pivot-points of global collaboration, it dramatically redefines its demand for engineers, as we saw earlier. The traditional engineering role emphasizes technical engineering, but Boeing, more than other competitors, requires that engineers facilitate cooperative relationships with global partners.

This insight allows Boeing's programs and practices to uniquely affect its supply. Boeing might go to universities to encourage engineering students to take courses in facilitation and negotiation or offer bonuses to engineering applicants who have these skills. Boeing's selection systems might include interviews, assessments, or tests that probe not only technical engineering skill but also the ability to work with and for global partners and to facilitate cooperation and trust. Performance management systems might tap the impressions of Boeing employees as well as those of key global partners. Boeing might add rewards and recognition based on the quality of engineering designs and on the quality of relationships. These practices will increase the supply of engineers who are most motivated and skilled to perform the pivotal aligned actions and interactions.

Boeing's strategy requires it to use suppliers for traditional parts assembly and increasingly for design responsibility for certain subsystems—on a global basis. Boeing can afford to compete more aggressively for engineers that are good global facilitators by offering better rewards and an environment where they get lots of opportunities for such facilitation. So more of the engineers with a passion for global facilitation will start to apply to Boeing, and Boeing will be able to identify them better than competitors.

This also holds for Boeing's internal market for talent. Boeing can provide internal career opportunities for its existing engineers to develop such skills. Boeing will now have a unique career path that creates engineers who are uniquely adept at collaboration and facilitation. Such development opportunities will in turn attract engineer applicants who are passionate about that role, creating a self-reinforcing cycle.

Traditional selection, development, performance, and reward criteria for aerospace engineers might not emphasize these factors. Boeing will not accomplish the necessary talent changes simply by broad-based investments in generic competencies, such as cooperation, open-mindedness, global mind-set, or coordination. Every Boeing engineer is not in an equally pivotal role, and some should receive much greater investments

Talentship, Synergy, and Choosing the Right Battles in the War for Talent

A great deal has been written about the war for talent. Whether the world will soon face a general labor shortage can be debated, but it seems certain that there will be extreme competition for one or another specific type of talent. The discussion often focuses on broad definitions of talent, such as "leaders," "engineers," "salespeople," or "customer service representatives." It is typical to define a goal like "to become an employer of choice." Organizations commonly implement such missions by tracking overall turnover rates, recruiting yields, and applicant opinions. The problem is that defining the talent war this way gives organizations little choice but to compete for the same talent with the same tools, tactics, and perspectives used by many other organizations.

Talentship asks, "Is it equally important to be an employer of choice for every talent pool and action/interaction?" To be sure, some organizations refine this a bit with statements such as "We want to be an employer of choice for people who are passionate about customer delight" or "We want to attract and retain talent that innovates" or "We want to be the employer of choice for the top people in the field." Yet even this begs the question "Is it equally important to compete for customer-focused, innovative, or high-performing talent across all talent pools?"

As we have seen, the answer is probably no. Impact and effectiveness reveal the aligned actions and interactions within the pivotal talent pools and organization, and the capacity and culture needed to support them. The programs and practices linking element of HC BRidge reveals opportunities to affect the supply of talent in ways that use the deep understanding of talent demand to create unique talent market advantages that are difficult for competitors to duplicate.

The typical way that organizations define their war for talent is like defining the war for customers simply in terms of "potential consumers of our product." Customer segmentation identifies the customer and market segments that are vital to strategy, and it identifies the customer segments most likely to respond to the organization's unique offerings. The future of talent markets will be similarly defined, and organizations that build skills in talent segmentation now will be better prepared to compete in those markets. Talent segmentation allows organizations to compete on a much more precise employment value proposition, much as customer segmentation increased the precision of the customer value proposition.

than others. The only way for Boeing to target those investments where it can have the greatest effect is to develop the capability to have a deep, logical, and analytically rigorous decision framework that reveals precisely where the pivot-points are and how to optimize them.

Building HR Practices from a Foundation of Trust at Starbucks

Trust is a term that is frequently invoked by organizational leaders but rarely well integrated into a true strategic advantage. Yet something as soft as trust is the basis for a sophisticated strategic synergy between talent demand and supply strategies at Starbucks.

Try a Google search on "Starbucks and human resources," and you'll get a raft of stories extolling how the global purveyor of coffee, music, and other products has achieved awards for being a great place to work and how it is unique in providing an array of benefits and high pay to its full-time baristas (the employees in the stores who serve the coffee) and to its part-timers as well.[16] The typical explanation has been described many times by reporters, academics, and consultants: Starbucks depends on good performance from its frontline workers, it needs to attract the best candidates for that work, and it needs a lot of those workers to fuel its massive growth. So Starbucks carefully selects its employees and provides the highest pay and benefits, massive amounts of training in coffee and customer service, and incentives for employees to stay.

This all sounds pretty simple, so why doesn't every multilocation retailer invest like this in frontline talent? The answer is that this model works for Starbucks precisely because of synergy between the company's business model and the way it approaches talent supply and demand. In fact, it might *not* be a good idea for other competitors simply to copy Starbucks. Talentship guides us to see how Starbucks has unique strategic pivot-points that make these investments particularly appropriate, using strategy analysis that goes well beyond the simple logic that frontline employees matter and therefore all companies should attract and retain the best by investing in them.

In location after location, Starbucks remains one of the most attractive employers for the talent pool of potential baristas. Dave Pace, executive vice president, Partner Resources, for Starbucks, expresses a fundamental value: "We don't treat our employees well because we are a successful business; we are a successful business because we treat our employees well." At Starbucks, it's cultural.

Starbucks' Strategy Pivot-Points: Growth and the Experience

For Starbucks, two key strategy pivot-points are essential to understanding why its commitment to fundamental cultural values is so vital: (1) growth and (2) the Starbucks experience. Regarding growth, Starbucks' competitive advantage depends in part on its scale. A core promise to its shareholders is continued price appreciation, and that requires massive growth in new stores as well as in-store sales. Consider the scale of Starbucks in April 2006: "Our total store count now is over eleven thousand on a global basis, and we're opening approximately five stores per day, every day, seven days a week, so it's an unbelievable growth machine that we have to try and feed and keep up with . . . There's over one hundred thirty thousand partners that participate in the business around the world, and we're hiring something above two hundred partners per day, seven days a week as well."[17]

Starbucks also must provide the experience that brings customers back (often over eighteen times a month). Product quality is important, as it is for every coffee retailer, but for Starbucks a key pivot-point is the distinctive and compelling in-store experience. With each passing day, Starbucks creates more products of greater complexity and adds new product types to the array of things that its store employees must know (e.g., music, movies, Wi-Fi, etc.). At the same time, it requires its store employees to understand and maintain an experience for customers that makes them feel valued and trusted. Baristas decide when to redo a customer's order if it's not satisfactory. They are expected to know the names of regular customers. Moreover, they are encouraged to put their own personal style into creating the in-store experience.

Translating Growth and the Experience into Starbucks' Talent Strategy Based on Trust

Putting the pivot-points of growth and a unique experience together requires supporting processes that ensure consistent standards across a far-flung domain of stores, where part-time employees can make or break the value proposition. How do you ensure consistently high standards? Many food retailers do it by standardizing the job to the point where a person can't do it differently no matter how hard they try. For example, fast-food restaurants often have pictures of their items on cash register buttons to help cashiers who may not read English well. Numbering the frequently ordered menu items and combinations also simplifies ordering. In fact, such practices have an interesting effect on customers who can be heard ordering a combination of a hamburger, fries, and a diet drink by saying,

"I'll have a #1 with a large diet, please." McDonald's has taken this concept to a high degree of specialization and geographic reach, as this *New York Times* item shows:

> Like many American teenagers, Julissa Vargas, 17, has a minimum-wage job in the fast-food industry—but hers has an unusual geographic reach. "Would you like your Coke and orange juice medium or large?" Ms. Vargas said into her headset to an unseen woman who was ordering breakfast from a drive-through line. She did not neglect the small details—"You Must Ask for Condiments," a sign next to her computer terminal instructs—and wished the woman a wonderful day. What made the $12.08 transaction remarkable was that the customer was not just outside Ms. Vargas's workplace here on California's central coast. She was at a McDonald's in Honolulu. And within a two-minute span Ms. Vargas had also taken orders from drive-through windows in Gulfport, Miss., and Gillette, Wyo.[18]

This is an example of what we noted earlier, removing variation from a role to reduce the risk. McDonald's removed drive-up order taking from the role of food server in their restaurants. In terms of our performance yield curve, such actions make the food server a flat-sloped talent pool with little downside risk and little upside performance potential. This is not inherently wrong or right. Rather, it is a choice that should be made based on logical strategic considerations.

Starbucks takes a different approach. The baristas are not only pivotal; they become more pivotal every day. And the slope in their yield curve includes some pretty big consequences if they make a mistake. Starbucks' unique business pivot-points require that the company can't standardize this kind of job performance, so it must rely on something less tangible but potentially much more powerful. A culture of trust and employee empowerment.

A core element of Starbucks' value proposition to customers is trust. Customers trust Starbucks to deliver high-quality products and a high-quality experience across a huge array of stores and products. Talentship reveals that this customer value proposition provides a way to achieve Starbucks' key strategic pivot-points: high service standards with explosive growth. The challenge posed by Howard Schultz, the chairman of Starbucks, to Dave Pace is to grow big while staying small.

The vital pivot-point in Starbucks' culture, which most analyses of Starbucks' success overlook, is one that Dave Pace has on the very first slide when he talks about the Starbucks' approach to its human capital. Pace frames his discussion about HR strategy at Starbucks around one concept: trust. Virtually every organization says that trust is important, but what sets Starbucks apart is that the company approaches trust with a deep and precisely logical perspective on how it aligns talent and organization with strategic pivot-points.

It is no accident that the personalities and quirks of Starbucks' baristas are the subject of blogs and human interest stories. The *Cincinnati Enquirer* featured a story about Elizabeth Saunders, a mezzo-soprano opera singer, trained at the University of Southern California and the University of Cincinnati's conservatory of music, who belts out customer orders in operatic form. "Singing orders came out of necessity, she said. The professional opera singer said a year ago when she started working for Starbucks she noticed yelling out orders strained her voice. So she asked the manager if she could sing them. Sure, he said. And so the performances began."[19]

What does trust have to do with this? As Dave Pace puts it:

> I describe this like playing the world's largest telephone game, where one person tells something to the person next to them, they tell the person next to them, they tell the person next to them, and you work your way around the table. Then you see if what comes out at the other end is what was actually said. And there's usually quite a bit of distortion. The challenge for us is, in order to build and sustain the culture that we have in the organization, we have to take somewhat of a similar approach where we tell our existing employees about the culture. They have to tell others, and those others have to tell newer people, and then suddenly the new people are the ones that have to tell other new people.

Tapping the Hidden and Apparent Talents of Starbucks' Baristas

Achieving massive scale while maintaining the experience means allowing frontline employees the freedom to bring their unique talents to the task. It means seeing beyond the standard job descriptions of coffee servers to realize that the talent and organization resource includes a variety of hidden capacities among the baristas that make the Starbucks experience so compelling and so consistent and yet achieved in such different ways.

Frontline employees at Starbucks must have the capability, opportunity, and motivation to understand what the high standards represent and creatively achieve those standards in their own ways. The typical analysis of Starbucks notes that baristas are encouraged to experiment and produce new product ideas. That's certainly an aligned action that goes beyond the standard coffee-server job description. Starbucks takes the idea of creativity to a new level, however, when it shows that even operatic singing is a valued and legitimate way for its frontline employees to contribute.

Aligning Starbucks' Programs and Practices to Create Synergy

Dave Pace notes the importance of recovery in maintaining trust: "We used to have pockets on our aprons, so our conclusion was that people were sliding money into those pockets. The reality was it involved a very small number of people. Pockets were removed from the aprons as a solution to this. We sent an unbelievably conflicted message with this to our frontline partners, and we heard about it. About a year and a half ago, we announced that we were bringing back pockets, and you would have thought we had given everybody a $50,000-a-year raise because it was that important for our frontline partners."

Seen through this lens, the logic for the array of programs and practices that Starbucks provides its frontline workers is much clearer. It is also much clearer why this approach works for Starbucks but might not work for others. A fast-food retailer whose business model is built on standardization and process control would probably find a population of opera-singing servers more of a bane than an advantage! Thus, these deep insights about strategy pivot-points and aligned actions have clear implications for the practices and programs designed to create capability, opportunity, motivation, and culture at Starbucks.

For Starbucks, providing health insurance for its frontline workers conveys that the company can be trusted to take care of them if things go wrong. Providing the same pay and benefits to part-timers and full-timers communicates that everyone is a trusted member of the family and should help each other deliver for the customer. Starbucks provides very in-depth training on its products. A story on Tea & Coffee Trade Online describes it in the words of a Starbucks partner who is training another:

> Training initially begins with what I would like to call "Starbucks University." Many were ready to get behind the bar and experience hands-on training immediately. So, when I handed them a large spiral book and told them they had six hours to complete the sections, I often received looks of confusion and concern, much like when a teacher hands his students a pop quiz. Each section of the training manual was divided into sections that provided an in-depth description of the responsibilities required of all baristas. A written test was given after each section was completed to ensure the partner's understanding. Usually, a new partner can take two days just finishing the book before they ever touch a cup![20]

Beyond Strategic Change Agent: The Exciting Future of HR Centers of Expertise

It is a common misconception that if HR professionals do not become strategic business partners and change agents, then they have no future in the HR profession or all other elements of HR will be outsourced and potentially provided by the lowest-cost vendor. A significant majority of the HR professionals we have worked with are justifiably proud of their careers and their unique contributions in HR functional specialties such as compensation, benefits, training, labor relations, staffing, and recruiting. As we noted earlier, the emergence of finance and marketing decision sciences didn't make the services of accounting and sales obsolete. In the same way, we foresee a bright future for HR leaders who make contributions as organizational experts in functional specialties such as motivation, development, talent pipelines, diversity, engagement, and providing employees a voice at work. HR functional specialties will evolve, just as accounting and sales evolved with the emergence of finance and marketing. We see these specialties increasingly adding value as centers of expertise (COEs).

Effectiveness provides a logical connection between the strategy insights of impact and the programs and practices required to translate those insights into unique ways to compete for and with talent. This chapter has shown the implications for a different approach to HR policies and practices. We have noted that these policies and practices will increasingly work together as an integrated portfolio, and that they will increasingly be held accountable not simply for the excellence of their processes and individual programs but for the underlying N&S conditions and the synergy through which such programs affect pivotal talent and organization elements.

A more subtle implication of talentship is that the analogy to marketing and finance is just as informative for the evolution of COEs as it has been for the evolution of strategic talent management. COEs in human resources will likely transform in ways similar to accounting with the emergence of the finance decision science and sales with the emergence of the marketing decision science.

The first implication is that human resource COEs will not become obsolete, nor will they become merely outsourced transactional processes. In fact, HR COE's will have an expanded and very exciting role. Accounting and sales remain vital internal functions, even with the maturity of the finance and marketing decision sciences. Accounting and sales evolved by becoming better aligned with their respective decision sciences. The data that is tracked in accounting and sales, as well as the way that data targets those functions' activities, reflects the evolution of principles such as economic value added in finance and yield management in marketing.

Indeed, it is often through the accounting and sales processes that business leaders actually learn and apply the decision science principles of finance and marketing. The accounting function translates principles of cash flow into processes that help managers execute and learn about better cash management. The sales function translates principles of customer segmentation into processes that help managers execute and learn about better customer relationship management. Thus, in accounting and sales the COEs not only deliver; they translate and teach. Business leaders actually learn some of the principles of the decision science by using the programs and practices that accounting and sales create.

In the same way, there will be exciting work for human resource COEs and the leaders within them. For organizations to fully apply talentship, they need strong and synergistic functional centers. Such COEs won't merely follow the traditional approach of emphasizing individual processes and programs and being accountable for low-cost services that are benchmarked against the best-practice organizations. Rather, COEs will increasingly be the repository for the organization's logical point of view on fundamental talent principles.

Future organizations can hardly expect to succeed if they don't have leaders who share a consistent and logical perspective on questions about motivation, learning, talent development, and organizational design. Talentship is built on great decisions about talent, both inside and outside HR, just as an organization requires good decisions about money and customers outside the finance and marketing functions.

Who will provide the principles and frameworks that business leaders use to understand what motivates, develops, retains, and attracts pivotal talent? We think these principles and frameworks can reside in the new human resource COEs. A fundamental new purpose for human resource COEs will be to teach, not just implement. Careers for HR professionals will include paths that lead to high-level functional expertise, just as many organizations have career paths for other technical professionals that lead to high-level positions, such as fellows in engineering, chemistry, or physics. Such fellows will not only be essential to the effective running of the processes in their area; they will also be responsible for ensuring that the organization's decisions are informed by the appropriate research in human behavior and organizational effectiveness.

Providing in-depth training in product processes and the essentials of the coffee product conveys the message that it is important to understand the vital fundamentals, in part so that frontline employees understand where innovations are consistent with those fundamentals and where they are not (it's important for the opera singer to know that belting out orders is consistent but that making the cappuccino differently from standard is not). Starbucks' performance reviews offer the possibility of careers to progress from the store to the executive offices. The company can do that because of the quality of in-store talent it attracts.

This practice is also essential to the portfolio of practices because with massive growth comes increased demand for another pivotal talent pool: store and regional managers. Starbucks needs thousands of store and regional managers, but not just for the generic manager role. Because of Starbucks' strategic pivot-points of growth, scale, and trust, it must create managers who can effectively nurture the delicate balance between high standards and discretion. There is nothing in the standard job description of a barista that includes opera singing, but it is precisely that capability, and the savvy of the store manager to nurture and feature it, that provides Starbucks with some of its most potent competitive distinctions.

Disney, Williams-Sonoma, and Starbucks are similar in that their culture has been defined by the founder and reinforced from the top. For example, every year Williams-Sonoma has a conference in Arizona where it brings its managers to catch them up on the business's development. At the conference, a highlight is the ceremony for the Catch the Spirit Award given to associates who caught the customer service spirit of founder Chuck Williams. It recognizes the best of the best and provides an implicit challenge of who will be next year's award winner. Award-winning associates wear a Catch the Spirit pin on their apron.[21]

The Starbucks example focuses on culture and trust, but the basic analysis elements are the same as for Disney, Boeing, and Williams-Sonoma. The key to understanding how to invest in programs and practices lies in understanding the vital pivot-points in talent and organization, which are revealed through a logical analysis of the strategic pivot-points that drive sustainable strategic success. When organizations logically connect talent and organization to strategy, they find unique positions where they can compete for and with talent in a way that competitors simply can't duplicate.

Conclusion

Effectiveness extends the logic of the talentship decision framework and the decision science principles of optimization, segmentation, and pivot-points to decisions about policies, practices, and organizational design. Understanding these connections sets a high bar for such choices. It reveals uncharted strategic opportunities that often require big changes in how HR and organizations approach their decisions. It is no longer sufficient merely to design and implement programs and practices in functional isolation. Identifying pivot-points makes it clear that a synergistic combination of policies and practices is required to create the necessary change.

Organizations frequently assert that they have integrated and coordinated HR programs to support their strategies. Too often, what this means is that their investments in programs and practices can *retrospectively* be connected to broad and general strategy statements. In contrast, effectiveness translates insights about specific pivotal roles into the specific pivotal policies and practices that will enhance execution where it matters most. Effectiveness analysis is an antidote to the common practice of spreading HR investments equally among everyone and to the tendency to jump to one element of human capacity (such as capability or motivation) as the answer to all problems.

It also provides a powerful way for organizations to find unique competitive positions in the supply and demand for talent, where the synergies between their business models and their talent requirements reveal powerful unique offerings to attract and retain the talent they need.

Finally, effectiveness reveals an exciting role for functional specialists in the HR organization by extending beyond today's focus on HR processes and programs to take on a role as the teachers and developers of the fundamental decision principles about human behavior and organizational effectiveness.

As organizations get better at applying talentship, we will see far more specificity, logic, and integration between how they analyze and respond to talent and organization questions of supply, demand, and strategy. Much as the quality of advertising and sales depends on a good brand strategy, the quality of talent and organization policies and practices will rely on good strategies that integrate impact with effectiveness. Those strategies will be integrated on principles of necessary and sufficient conditions, synergy, and market uniqueness.

8

Efficiency in Organization and Talent Investments

Acquiring and Deploying Resources to Optimize the Talent Portfolio

Efficiency describes the relationship between the portfolio of policies and practices and the level of investments used to produce them. Efficiency is a familiar perspective on talent and organization activities. In fact, efficiency is often the *predominant* decision framework for talent and organization investment decisions. HR data and benchmarking systems are dominated by efficiency measures, such as cost per hire, time to fill vacancies, the ratio of headcount in the HR function to the organization overall, and the ratio of HR functional costs to total costs.

Pivot-points in efficiency are where specific improvements in resource investments will most enhance the portfolio of policies and practices. Figure 8-1 shows where efficiency fits in the HC BRidge framework. The decisions to make in the efficiency anchor point revolve around questions like "Where should we target resource investment improvements so they have the biggest effect on the policy and practice portfolio?"

It may surprise many HR and non-HR leaders that we have saved the efficiency discussion until the end of the talentship discussion. Making programs and practices more efficient is traditionally the most common path to business relevance for HR. In fact, most of the top HR leaders we work with admit that no matter what else they do, every annual HR strategy must prominently describe how HR will cut some significant percentage from its prior-year budget or headcount. Shouldn't a book on a strategic

FIGURE 8-1

HC BRidge framework: Efficiency

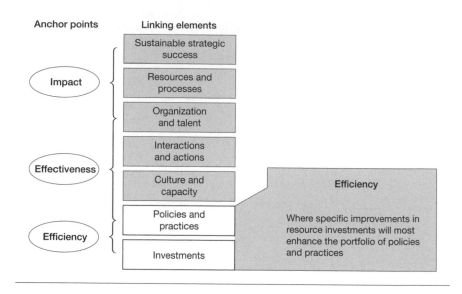

decision science for HR *begin* with the tangible opportunities to contribute to the bottom line through greater efficiency?

Of course, our choice to leave efficiency for last is not accidental. It is precisely because today's approach to talent and organization decisions is so efficiency heavy that it is important to place efficiency in the context of effectiveness and impact. As we'll see in this chapter, and in chapter 9 on measurement, overemphasizing efficiency out of context can lead to dangerously misguided decisions. In contrast, when organizations have the context of impact and effectiveness, their decisions about efficiency become a stronger part of an integrated strategic approach. The efficiency anchor point is a vital consideration in talentship because it describes the investments to make in organization and talent. Those investments cannot and should not be ignored, and as we shall see, they are often subtle and not recorded in standard accounting or budgets. Too often, however, efficiency is treated in isolation, which undermines its potential.

Talentship suggests that it's important to know how much is being spent on policies and practices, but the more appropriate questions focus on the broader opportunity costs of investments and their returns. Table 8-1 shows how the definition of the efficiency anchor point implies vital pivot-points, decisions and new talent and organization discussions.

TABLE 8-1

Anchor point: Efficiency

Definition	Pivot-points	Decisions to make	New talent and organization strategy discussions
• Describes the relationship between the portfolio of policies and practices and the level of investments	• Where specific improvements in resource investments will most enhance the portfolio of policies and practices	• Where should you target resource investment improvements so they have the biggest effect on the policy and practice portfolio?	• What unique resources does your strategy provide that you could leverage in talent management? • Where could investing more resources than the industry norm generate unique value in your portfolio of policies and practices?

Typical conversations about talent and organization investments focus on them as expenditures, such as the level of HR expense, its allocation, how it compares to benchmarks, and whether it meets budgets. Decision makers undeniably need to understand the resources required to implement HR programs and practices. It's important not to waste money and time. Efficiency measures can be used to determine whether the costs of policies and practices are reasonable.

Efficiency is a tempting source of information about HR and talent investments. It provides a formidable vehicle to demonstrate that talent decisions have real economic consequences. Many HR organizations have shown eye-popping cost savings as a result of outsourcing HR activities; implementing self-service or Web-based systems; and reducing turnover, the time to fill vacancies, headcount, and health and pension benefits.

Perhaps efficiency is a bit too tantalizing. For example, the writers of *The New American Workplace* noted a common theme: that organizational leaders see "people as costs."[1] An exclusive focus on the costs of talent is cited as one reason why organizations often fail to invest in work systems that have proved to be associated with business and financial performance. Such investments require resources, and the resource expenditures are often very obvious within the accounting system while the returns to those investments typically are not.

An overemphasis on efficiency is another illustration of the relative historical immaturity of the talent decision science, compared to finance and marketing. For example, organizational leaders would question whether their marketing department was compromising quality if its key goal was getting the industry's cheapest advertising. In fact, they have well-developed frameworks for analyzing the effects of marketing investments to ensure that cost savings are not achieved too aggressively. Yet it is not unusual for those same leaders to measure talent and organization investments *only* in terms of costs and to admonish their HR organizations to achieve benchmark levels of efficiency, often with only cursory attention to how those objectives are met.

Figure 8-2 shows several prominent guiding questions that connect decisions about efficiency to the other elements of the HC BRidge framework. Using these questions, along with the logic shown in table 8-1, provides a more complete picture approach to efficiency.

SAS: Competing Through Inefficiency?

In contrast to the typical approach, consider the case of SAS, a company widely admired for its progressive HR practices and for its consistent and impressive financial performance.[2] The company also has on-site health care. Established in 1984, the SAS health care center (HCC) has grown and evolved along with the company as a whole. The HCC now has fifty-nine employees and completed 48,908 patient visits in 2005. Of course, in 2005 this business model ran against other American companies, most of which were restricting health care expenditures or outsourcing them

FIGURE 8-2

HC BRidge framework: Investments

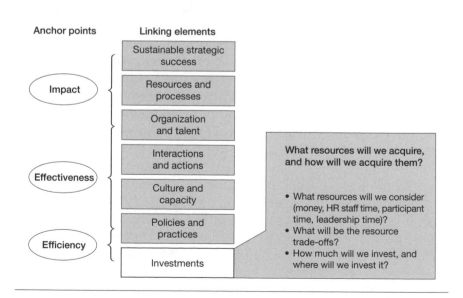

to save money. For most organizations, avoiding on-site health care benefits produces significant savings, both in direct costs as well as administrative costs. These are tempting savings for business leaders and tempting opportunities for HR leaders to deliver tangible bottom-line value through cuts and the resulting cost savings.

Of course, this was all true for SAS! The decision to establish and maintain an on-site HCC undoubtedly committed SAS to significant future investments. Costs will certainly go up. By many efficiency benchmarks, SAS looks worse than others by doing this. Yet Jeff Chambers, vice president of HR at SAS, points out that the decision is perfectly rational when you consider SAS's business model and the role of long-term talent relationships in supporting it.

SAS relies on annual product renewals from its clients, who use its software for deep analysis of their organizational databases. SAS also relies on employees for innovations and services that are tailored to those clients' particular industry requirements and their unique competitive positions in their industries.[3] This means that client relationships with SAS advisers need to be based on a deep shared understanding about industry-specific competition and on long-term trust. This may be more important for SAS than for its competitors, whose business models are based more on software purchases than renewable licenses and whose value proposition is not so deeply dependent on close and deeply informed relationships with clients.

Talent alignment with this strategy extends well beyond those who work directly with software purchasers. SAS software designers and programmers must also be thoroughly familiar with specific industry and client needs, and they must be able to create software designs that can efficiently scale across multiple clients, industries, and competitive situations. Understanding which design elements really need to be unique versus which can borrow from existing elements from other industries may be the difference between a software design that achieves economies of scale and one that doesn't. This means that designers, programmers, and customer-facing talent at SAS must work seamlessly and with a deep common understanding of clients. Clients come to depend on SAS because they have a special relationship with SAS employees, and SAS delivers on its promise of singular practicality and innovation through years of common learning and experimentation.

How does SAS create the capability, opportunity, and motivation to achieve this kind of deep, common, client-focused synergy? In part, the company does it by creating an employment model that attracts and motivates people who join and stay for the long run. This requires SAS to present a distinctive value proposition in the market for programmers, designers, and client advisers. A long-term employment deal is an unusual predisposition in professions where the norm is to move from project to project, often changing employers many times in a few years to find the most interesting work or a higher paycheck (consider the heyday of California's Silicon Valley). SAS, located in North Carolina, provides an array of employment practices (on-site day care and health care, etc.), that attract employees who form a bond with the company and with their colleagues.

Now to the question of efficiency. Compared to its industry counterparts, SAS undoubtedly has higher costs for talent programs and practices. Cutting its unique employee benefits would substantially lower its employment costs and bring the company closer to benchmark levels. Yet seen within its business model, SAS's apparently inefficient decisions make sense. For example, investing in on-site health care means that, compared to competitors, SAS will be more attractive to those who hope to work for SAS until retirement and who want a company they can count on to take care of them and their families. It sends a signal that SAS is different and that those who desire a longer-term relationship with their employer belong there. In turn, SAS creates a workforce on which it can reliably build a business model based on deep insights about clients and on long-term relationships with and between vital SAS talent pools.

The richness of SAS's employee benefits, including on-site health care, contributes to its low annual voluntary turnover rate of less than 5 percent, compared to the software industry average of 18–20 percent. Easy access to health care on the company's Cary, North Carolina, campus translates into employee time savings that in 2005 alone was conservatively estimated at $2.6 million. Because of high employee utilization of the HCC (90 percent at last measure), the value of services delivered has exceeded overhead costs every year for more than a decade—$1.9 million in 2005 alone. While not studied extensively to date, SAS believes its real health care savings have yet to be realized based on early risk identification, appropriate intervention, and a disease prevention model in a very stable employee population. SAS expects to see a lower incidence of chronic preventable diseases and lower morbidity based on its robust programs and coverage for preventive health care and cancer screening.

Efficiency considerations routinely motivate employers to forgo or reduce costly employment practices. If SAS relied on efficiency measures, no matter how tangible, the company would likely suffer negative strategic consequences far exceeding the efficiency improvements. Organizations that choose to limit or forgo such practices are necessarily wrong, but if organizations rely solely on efficiency considerations, they risk missing opportunities to create effectiveness and impact. Efficiency can bring attention to areas where talent programs and practices are very costly and present potential opportunities to improve efficiency by cutting their costs or reducing their scope. When such decisions are made by considering all three elements of the HC BRidge framework, organizations can improve efficiency without compromising more fundamental, if less visible, value.

The rest of this chapter will examine efficiency, revealing that the actual costs of talent and organization investments may actually be much higher than typically realized. Then we will show why efficiency is so important and why it presents such a compelling component of the talentship decision science and the HC BRidge framework. Along the way, we will provide cautionary notes to keep efficiency in perspective.

The Iceberg Below the Surface: Opportunity Costs and Talent Investments

Budgeted costs of talent programs and practices are obvious to every organizational leader and the focus of a great deal of attention. While calculating such costs is often difficult, it is not our purpose to provide a guide to those calculations.[4] Suffice it to say that it is important to accurately account for the cash and other expenses directly associated with talent programs and practices.

Although much attention is directed to reducing the costs that show up in accounting statements or the HR budget, monetary resources are only the tip of the iceberg in efficiency. The full array of resources needed to implement talent and organization programs and practices is actually much broader. Defining this unseen array of investments requires drawing on a decision concept from economics: opportunity costs.

Opportunity costs reflect what must be given up as a result of a decision. They consider the value of what is given up for the best alternative use of that resource. Just as with other resources, for talent and organization programs and practices, opportunity costs provide a perspective on investments that goes well beyond the monetary expenses recorded by the accounting systems or budgets.

The following sections use the opportunity cost concept to describe some talent investments that are often overlooked.

Time of HR Employees and Contractors

The time of employees and contractors in the HR department is an important cost of programs and practices. It is not unusual for organizational leaders to lament the fact that they don't even know how many individuals are employed in their HR organizations, let alone the number of contractors and consultants. They may often complain that no one can explain precisely what all those HR people actually do.

We don't advocate a fixation on such numbers without a solid logic for how they will be used, but a complete decision framework certainly must recognize that talent and organization programs and practices require diverting the talent resources of the HR organization from other tasks. From an opportunity-cost perspective, the appropriate way to consider the cost is to determine the lost value of those other activities. When employee time is accounted for, it is usually determined by multiplying the salary or reward costs for employees by the time they spend on the program. This is often a reasonable approximation of the opportunity cost, but when the needed HR employees must be diverted from particularly essential activities, the hidden cost may be much higher.

For example, opportunity costs are often at the heart of the argument for shifting to employees some administrative tasks traditionally done by HR professionals, such as completing enrollment forms for company training or benefits. The idea is that if HR professionals are engaged in filling out the forms, the time they spend is taken away from more vital tasks, such as strategic planning, executive coaching, or effecting culture change. Because those HR professionals are already employed, the actual salary budget won't change whether they are filling out forms or engaged in strategy, coaching, or culture. They will still receive their pay and benefits. Opportunity costs reveal the true sacrifice of the decision to invest HR professionals' time in activities better done by employees themselves.

Time of Those Outside the HR Department

A frequently overlooked category of opportunity costs is related to the time of those outside the HR department. Perhaps the most obvious example is the time of organizational leaders who serve as presenters or instructors on training programs. Other prominent examples include the time of executives in conducting performance appraisals, selection interviews, exit interviews, and so forth. Such contributions are often essential for ensuring high-quality programs that effectively create strategically relevant capability, opportunity, and motivation. These investments are frequently overlooked as legitimate costs of talent programs and practices.

This is not to say that these individuals shouldn't invest their time and energy in talent programs and practices. In fact, earlier chapters contained several examples showing that such investments can be vitally important for leaders outside the HR function. When strategic logic supports investing time and energy, these leaders would be foolish not to do it.

When investments are requested or required without a clear logical rationale for their contribution to strategic success—or worse, to help the HR organization offload its cost to achieve its internal budget goals—then organizations risk wasting a precious resource and HR organizations risk creating an impression of ill-considered impositions on time and energy that would be better spent elsewhere.

Enlisting the assistance of organizational leaders outside HR is often the most efficient way to gain applicants' and trainees' attention and allow them to benefit from the leaders' unique experiences and perspectives. Prominent examples of such investments include the practice of Microsoft's Bill Gates, who often interviewed key hires himself and even made personal calls to hot recruiting prospects at their homes. Gates maximized the effect of such calls by timing them for when candidates were likely to be with their family (such as dinnertime). Imagine the effect of job candidates telling their spouse or parents, "That was Bill Gates on the phone, personally asking me to consider Microsoft's job offer." Another favorite example is the time that the CEO and top officers of GE spend each year on what they call Session C, assessing the performance and potential of their top cadre of managers.[5] Such stories are often used to motivate top organizational leaders to devote more time to HR programs and practices.

However, asking leaders and other employees to devote time and energy to talent programs and practices just because other leading companies do is seldom a good idea. When such requests are not supported by a thorough grounding in effectiveness and impact, leaders rightfully wonder whether their valuable time is being spent wisely. Is it being invested where it has the greatest effect on the talent and organization areas that matter most? The HC BRidge framework and talentship provide an answer that traces investments from programs and practices to strategic success.

As with the costs of employees inside the HR organization, the opportunity cost is not simply the prorated salary and benefits of outside employees and leaders. It's the lost value of the things they would be doing if they weren't devoting their time to the talent and organization programs and practices. Here the difference between budgeted compensation costs and the true opportunity costs is often abundantly clear. If top organizational leaders can't clearly see the effectiveness and impact of the programs they are asked to be involved in, they are often quite vocal about the value of the other work they could be doing!

It is not uncommon for us to hear from line leaders, "My HR business partner is truly strategic because he protects me from all those time-consuming programs that corporate HR keeps inventing and that keep me away from my real work." By now it's clear that we don't advocate that definition of strategic talent contribution. We have shown that organizations often have significant opportunities to create unique competitive advantage through careful investments of leader time and energy on the talent and organization pivot-points that are most strategically relevant. Our experience is that leaders relish the opportunity to make such contributions—when they can see a clear line of sight between their contribution to HR programs and business value. Too often, the logic is so vague that business leaders often conclude that all such contributions are less important than their other tasks. This is a significant mistake.

Throughout this book we have argued against the common practice of a peanut-butter approach to talent decisions and investments. Such approaches often engender skepticism from business leaders and employees who are asked to invest in programs or activities because HR—or even the CEO—says that everyone must do it. A strategically differentiated approach to talent decisions provides the credibility of asking for such investments where they matter most and forgoing them where they do not make a strategic difference, and it provides the logic to communicate the distinction.

Time of the Participants

Another investment that doesn't show up readily in accounting statements is program participants' time. When employees are participating in training, performance reviews, rotational programs, and other programs, their time is a key investment. Because program participants are already on the payroll, the opportunity cost of their participation is often not explicitly included in investment calculations. When it is included, it is often by prorating their salary or total compensation.

Again, the true opportunity cost of employee involvement is the next-best use of their time or what they would be doing if they were not involved in the program. Just as with the contributions of organizational leaders, program participants are often painfully aware of what they could be doing if they weren't devoting time to the program (BlackBerry devices and other personal digital assistants have only made that more obvious). Again, the peanut-butter approach exacerbates this problem. How many times do we hear employees say, "I don't know why I have to attend that training program, but HR says everyone is required to go through it"?

Providing program participants a clear line of sight to the value of their contributions and the logical connection between the programs and the business and strategic success is essential to ensuring that participant investments are not wasted. Otherwise, program participants may soon conclude that participation in talent and organization programs and practices is simply not worth the effort.

Influence or Political Credits

An often overlooked investment is influence, or "political credits." When the logic connecting talent and organization programs and practices to sustainable strategic success is less tangible, gaining support for such programs often requires drawing on the credits, credibility, or influence that individual HR leaders have with their constituents. This is true for talent decisions much more than decisions in more mature decision sciences such as finance and marketing, where the decision frameworks are more mature and more integrated in leaders' mental models.

We believe this must change, and frameworks like talentship and HC BRidge can contribute to that change. Still, in today's organizations successfully implementing important talent and organization investments means calling in favors, or credits, from key opinion leaders. This approach may be required to gain leaders' contributions in implementing the program, to acquire financial or time resources, or to convince employees to participate. When that's true, such costs are not included in formal accounting, but they are nonetheless very real.

We encourage organizations to aspire to a future in which calling in credits is less necessary because all organizational leaders understand the value of talent investments. That said, a discussion about the necessary investments to achieve talent programs and practices would be incomplete without acknowledging this reality.

What Efficiency Does Well and Avoiding the Pitfalls

With a better idea about the full extent of investments required for talent and organization programs and processes, we can turn our attention to the uses of efficiency-based analysis. Efficiency provides an essential element of a complete decision framework. Without it we don't know our investments, so it is impossible to judge whether they are producing a significant return. Efficiency also has the ability to gain leaders' attention and to connect tangibly to organization reporting systems. In this section we will describe what efficiency does well. Efficiency is so compelling that organizations tend to emphasize it over effectiveness or impact. So as we describe what efficiency does well, we will also provide cautionary notes about the pitfalls to avoid.

Efficiency Ties Tangibly to the Accounting System

The accounting system is essential and effective for guiding decisions about money. It is among the most mature management systems with well-developed and reliable measures, so it is a common perspective through which leaders view organizational success. Efficiency provides a significant path to demonstrate relevance within the accounting system. HR leaders and writers have long sought to connect HR to the bottom line by presenting accounting measures for the HR's department or by applying cost accounting to talent issues such as turnover, absences, and theft. The potential accounting returns are sizable and often very real.

For example, it is not unusual for the cost of processing and replacing a single employee turnover to be one and one-half times the average compensation and benefits in that job.[6] So, if HR can demonstrate that investments in staffing, pay, or employee communication reduce turnover in very high-turnover jobs, the cost savings are often very large. The same sort of analysis can be applied to the cost savings of reducing absences and other costly employee behaviors.[7]

Prominent examples of impressive economic cost savings from efficiency are often found in centralizing HR programs. It is not unusual to calculate millions of dollars in cost savings by centralizing and standardizing HR activities and removing the duplication and waste that results when such activities are done in each business unit, function, or region. If leaders doubt that decisions about talent-related programs and processes affect the economics of the business, saving millions of dollars through program centralization can quickly dispel such doubts.

The fact that these connections to the accounting system are quantifiable and concrete also makes them dangerous. A fixation on talent costs can lead organizations to invoke across-the-board workforce cutbacks as a way to meet cost goals. Yet, as Cascio and others have shown, evidence suggests that long-term financial success is not related to the size of across-the-board cuts but rather to restructuring that is targeted to where cuts make sense in light of the organization's strategic goals.[8] Because efficiency connects so tangibly to the accounting system, an efficiency focus can lead to downsizing directed at the talent pools where costs are highest. It's easier to make your cost-cutting goals if you cut in the high-cost areas, so highly paid or high-cost talent pools are a tempting target. But often they are also the pools where the greatest value is lost through cuts.

Overemphasizing accounting cost savings can lead organizations to chase cost-saving opportunities in talent and organization areas that they would not tolerate in other areas. For example, we have noted that when oil prices are falling, petrochemical companies often cut costs by laying off professionals in the exploration and production areas only to rehire those people when oil prices rise again, often at a much higher expense than if they had just kept their existing talent employed through the downturn. In contrast, petrochemical companies routinely hold leases on oil fields throughout the business cycle on the expectation that prices will rise to a level to make those oil fields economically viable.

Efficiency Is Easily Benchmarked

Efficiency measures are often derived from objective information about the activities, expenditures, and staffing levels of the HR function or HR programs. It is much easier to compare efficiency measures between organizations versus effectiveness or impact measures. The components of efficiency are fairly comparable—including the number of HR employees to total employees, the total HR functional budget to total costs, cost per hire, cost per training hour, or other such measures.

HR and business leaders in search of objective information on how their efforts compare to others often find great value in comparing such numbers to industry standards. In 2006 the standard of a hundred employees for every HR employee was so widely accepted that it was almost a mantra for many business leaders, and many HR organizations were told that their top priority was to achieve this ratio. The availability of benchmarking surveys that report industry and national averages on efficiency ratios provided a compelling opportunity for HR organizations to measure their progress ("we have achieved a lower cost per hire than our peers"). Again, when faced with business leaders and other constituents for whom accounting results are prominent, this kind of evidence is satisfying and compelling.

Relying too heavily on accounting cost savings in designing HR programs or HR organizations, however, tends to promote a "shrink-to-success" perspective that leads to less-than-optimal investment in talent and organization infrastructure. It can lead to arbitrary budget limits on HR and organization programs and practices that may have very significant positive net returns. This phenomenon is often encountered when cost cutting leads to excessive layoffs or early retirement that removes talent that's essential for the future, as happened in companies such as AT&T in the 1990s.[9]

The same thing can occur with regard to HR programs or staff. We have encountered many HR organizations that say, "Investing more in staffing, compensation, or training pays off, but if we invested more, our cost per employee would exceed the benchmark standard. Our leaders expect us to achieve a cost level comparable to the lowest-cost quartile in our industry. We need to meet our cost objectives to have the credibility to make a case for more investment."

Yet, as we have seen, when effectiveness and impact are appropriately considered, spending more on talent often creates value far beyond any costs saved by adhering to industry norms. Recall what would happen if Disney theme parks invested in sweepers at the benchmark levels of competitors who don't realize sweepers' value as customer ambassadors, or if Starbucks invested in baristas at the same level as competitors whose business models are built on standardized processes and minimal customer interaction. Efficiency-based benchmarking is useful for drawing attention to possible overspending, and it certainly demonstrates to non-HR leaders that talent programs can be evaluated objectively. However, it is best used cautiously as a guide to the quality of particular talent decisions.

Efficiency Provides a Tangible Measure of Outsourcing Performance

Perhaps the most dominant use of efficiency is in estimating the effects and tracking the performance of efforts to outsource HR activities. A significant justification for typical HR outsourcing decisions is that they will lower the costs of HR programs. The logic is that by having HR activities (such as payroll, applicant tracking, and employment information management) done by an outside organization, costs can be reduced through economies of scale, centralization, and access to the most efficient infrastructure and systems. It is rare to encounter an outsourcing deal that doesn't include a significant commitment to cut such costs. Indeed, outsourcing contracts often contain key performance indicators that largely reflect savings in time, cost, or other efficiency measures. Because of their objectivity, their relevance to the well-established accounting system, and their obvious connection to the bottom line, efficiency-based cost savings are useful ways to hold outsourcers accountable.

The cautionary note here is probably best summed up in a common observation by many organizations that pursued outsourcing only for its impact on costs: "We ended up with our old mess for less."[10] More thoughtful and successful approaches to HR outsourcing emphasize the importance of first considering how HR programs and processes can be improved and how they relate to the organization's strategy and mission.[11]

There is a paradox in overemphasizing efficiency in outsourcing. The same programs and practices that offer tempting outsourcing savings also may create the largest effectiveness and impact. For example, providing information about employee benefits incurs high costs and offers a tempting outsourcing opportunity. Yet, in many organizations, benefit discussions give employees an opportunity to voice concerns about such things as work-family balance, supervisory problems, and other issues that may be precursors to their departure, sickness, or burnout. If this activity is outsourced in the most low-cost way, accurate information may well be communicated, but there may be no resources to take the time to explore what's behind employee questions or decisions, losing valuable information about how well the organization is competing for and with talent.

Efficiency Provides Tangible Milestones for Process Improvement

Total quality, process improvement, and Six Sigma tools have provided revolutionary advances in organizational efficiency and profitability. It is not surprising that organizations have applied these tools to talent programs and practices. Efficiency offers compelling milestones to demonstrate the effects of such endeavors. It is enormously satisfying to identify ways to remove time and money from processes such as on-boarding, employment testing, and training. Reduced cost per hire, cost per training hour, or time to on-board are frequently cited as evidence of the effectiveness of quality improvement efforts to improve talent and HR management.

The tangibility of efficiency outcomes seems tailor made for Six Sigma approaches. When the Six Sigma black belt asks HR leaders to identify outcomes that can be objectively measured and that are influenced by HR process decisions, a list of efficiency elements is usually fast in coming.

It is easy, however, to ruin great talentship with Six Sigma. The most articulate expression of this cautionary note comes from several quality green-belt Six Sigma consultants who say that when they were doing Six Sigma process improvement for functions like manufacturing, sales, and service, the goal was pretty obvious. For example, one said, "We knew if the lightbulb needed to be brighter, longer lasting, whiter . . . We defined our process improvement goals to those outcomes. In HR we always seem to be taking time and money out of the process, but I worry that we don't know if the faster or cheaper process is still working on the right outcomes. In HR process improvement, no one ever seems to be able to tell me the ultimate objective. It's like improving a lightbulb manufacturing process when we don't know if it should be brighter, longer lasting, or whiter."[12]

Six Sigma tools can do much to improve talent programs and practices, but like so many tools, they can also do much harm. A vital key to the difference is the depth of the logic that governs the decisions. When Six Sigma is embedded within a clear understanding of the connections between programs and business or strategic success, Six Sigma principles can accelerate the process of shifting investments to their most productive places. This is completely consistent with talentship, as we've seen.

When the logic is faulty or nonexistent, efficiency considerations may swamp very important but less tangible implications, and cost savings may mask the damage done to talent value.

Conclusion

Efficiency is, and will remain, a vivid and readily available element of a complete decision framework. We often have the opportunity to work with very progressive organizations with highly regarded HR functions and HR leaders who are valued strategic contributors. Even in those situations, a frequent reaction to our description of talentship is "We'd love to move in this direction, but our board and executive committee first insist on seeing us reduce our costs." It's not unusual to encounter HR functions that have been charged with reductions in their budgets of 10 percent per year for many years running, even in organizations that value talent and respect HR's contributions. It is a simple fact that business leaders have not yet had enough time to learn frameworks for considering talent and organization programs that go beyond accounting and cost efficiency.

With all due respect to our very talented colleagues in leading organizations, we can't help but wonder whether HR is really all that well respected if organizational leaders are willing to consider continual cost savings to be so important year after year. There are likely a number of organizations in which the right decision is to look beyond efficiency, to stop cutting and start investing in talent.

Efficiency must be acknowledged and it must be done well, but the emergence of a true decision science requires a more complete perspective. It's tempting to assume that high-quality talent and organization decisions can be supported by ever-less-expensive programs and practices, but at some point there is little waste to be cut. It seems quite likely that organizations probably underinvest in talent and organization programs simply because the costs are so tangible and the value is so intangible. Moreover, it's probably dangerous to take the position that attention to the effectiveness and impact of talent and organization investments can wait until HR gets its cost structure in line with benchmarks. Yet we often hear precisely that logic from otherwise very astute organization leaders.

Our view is that efficiency should be part of a broader and complete logical framework and that organizations shouldn't wait to consider impact and effectiveness until they have mastered efficiency. Frankly, by then it may be too late because competitors that took a more complete view will have already discovered so many ways to compete with and for talent through prudent, if costly, investments.

Throughout this chapter, we have seen how the focus on efficiency is driven in part by the prominence of accounting measures that track it. So it is important to consider how talent measurement systems can contribute to the emergence of the talentship decision science and how the HC BRidge framework can guide that process. That's the topic of chapter 9.

9

Talent Measurement and Analytics

Beyond Measures to the LAMP

How many times have you heard that the reason HR doesn't get the respect it deserves is because it's soft and doesn't have the measures that accounting, marketing, and other areas have? It is very common for experts to assert that decisions about talent and organization would be dramatically improved if only the HR profession would develop more or better "numbers," usually designed to provide objective evidence that HR investments pay off. This chapter applies the principles of talentship to measurement and illustrates that many popular notions about HR measurement are simply wrong, beginning with the idea that more measures equal better decisions.

A great deal of the earliest work attempting to connect HR activities to organizational outcomes was motivated by the goal of developing measures to calculate the costs and benefits of specific HR programs, such as staffing, training, and pay.[1] In the 1980s and 1990s our own experience was similar, in that we approached the task of enhancing talent and organization decisions by developing and understanding HR measurement.

We were frequently asked to help HR leaders develop more and better HR measures, because HR was seen as soft and the key to getting support for HR investments was more measures that would be accepted by business leaders using accounting and finance models. The paradox was that in organization after organization, the problem wasn't a lack of measures at all. In fact, these HR organizations had amassed hundreds of measures of their activities, some of which even quantified effectiveness outcomes such as learning, attitudes, and turnover. What we found was that HR measurement is useful, but a fixation on measurement can prove to be very dysfunctional.

Developing more measures wasn't going to solve the fundamental issue. The real need was for decisions about talent and organization investments to become more systematic, consistent, and shared between HR and non-HR professionals. It was understandable that HR leaders would believe that the problem was that HR measures couldn't compete with more well-developed measures from accounting and finance. Yet, as we have seen, the fundamental power of those decision sciences emanates not just from their measures but, more important, from the logic on which they are developed and presented.

As we discussed earlier, one hallmark of a well-developed decision science is when the measurement and data systems work synergistically with the decision framework and the alignment of processes and competencies inside and outside the particular function. The framework provides the logic that identifies what measures are needed and where measurement can most affect decisions that have a large impact on sustainable strategic success. The measures populate the logical framework, that framework evolves based on the findings from the measures, and so on. At the same time, the measurement framework provides the data for tracking processes and teaching competencies so they are aligned with the decision framework. Later in this chapter we'll present a detailed example of precisely this kind of evolution applied to talent and organization measurement.

The HC BRidge model provides a useful logical framework for designing and refining measurement systems so that measurement development is focused where it can have the most impact. In this chapter we will show how you can use the HC BRidge framework to diagnose and better understand how to improve HR measurement. More important, we will suggest a perspective that recognizes HR measurement as a catalyst for organizational effectiveness through better talent and organization decisions where they matter most. That requires looking well beyond the measures, to uncover the elements of a more complete system of decision support and organizational change.

Hitting the Wall in HR Measurement

Type "HR measurement" into a search engine, and you will get over nine hundred thousand results. Scorecards, summits, dashboards, data mines, data warehouses, and audits abound. HR organizations lament that their measurement efforts are stymied by limited budgets, but even among those with significant resources (in fact, *especially* in these cases), the array of HR measurement technologies is daunting. The paradox is that even when HR measurement systems are well implemented, organizations typically hit a wall.[2] Despite ever more comprehensive databases, and ever more sophisticated data analysis and reporting, HR measures only rarely drive true strategic change.[3]

As figure 9-1 shows, over time the HR profession has become more and more elegant and sophisticated, yet the trend line doesn't seem to be leading to the desired result. Victory is typically declared when business leaders are held accountable for HR measures. HR organizations often point proudly to the fact that top leaders' bonuses depend in part on the results of their scorecard measures, such as turnover, employee attitudes, bench strength, and performance distributions. For example, some incentive systems make bonuses for business-unit managers contingent on reducing turnover to a target level, raising average engagement scores, or placing their employees into the required distribution of 70 percent in the middle, 10 percent in the bottom, and 20 percent in the top.

Yet having business leaders manage to such numbers is not the same as creating organizational change. HR measures must create a truly strategic difference in the organization. As we have seen, turnover reductions, increased engagement, and performance differences are not equally pivotal everywhere. Understanding the nuances is often the key to avoiding costly mistakes based on well-meaning but misguided talent goals.

FIGURE 9-1

Hitting the wall in HR measurement

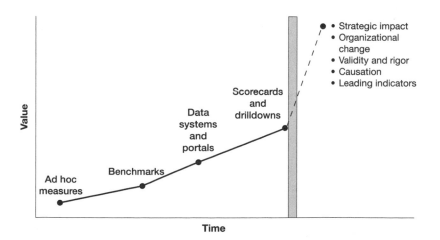

Many of the organizations we work with are frustrated because they seem to be doing all the measurement things right yet see the gap between the expectations for the measurement systems and those systems' true effects.

Why do HR organizations hit the wall? As we have seen, the HR profession is on the cusp of extending its paradigm from focusing only on compliance and services to including a specific focus on talent and organization decisions. Recognizing the implications of this paradigm extension provides clues to how HR measurement systems can learn valuable lessons from measurement systems in more mature professions like finance and marketing. In these professions measures are only one part of the system for creating organizational change through better decisions.

Beyond Proving the Value of the HR Function

Here is a question we commonly ask HR audiences: "Would you like to have HR measures as powerful as accounting measures?" The answer is invariably an enthusiastic yes. Then we ask the follow-up question: "How many of the accounting measures tell you about how the accounting department is doing?"

The implication is clear. Many HR measures originate from a desire to justify the investments in HR processes or programs. Typically, HR seeks measurement not to improve decisions but to increase the respect for (and potentially the investment in) the HR function and its services and activities. Talent measurement is often a search for validation of the HR function more than a quest for better talent and organization decisions.

In financial measurement it is certainly important to measure how the accounting or finance department operates. Measures—such as transaction-processing time, benchmark staff levels, and so on—are important for internal functional control. The vast majority of measures used for financial decisions, however, are not concerned with how finance and accounting services are delivered. Financial measures typically focus on the outcomes—the quality of decisions that impact financial resources.

One of the implications of the traditional HR measurement approach is that it often puts HR professionals in a bind. If the measurements show that HR is doing well, no one cares. If the measurements show that there is a problem, even when the problem is not caused by the HR function, it is still assigned to HR to fix. A classic example is turnover. If it is low, HR gets no credit; and if it is higher than it should be, it becomes an HR issue rather than a business issue. This stands in significant contrast with financial measures. When a division is behind budget, the accounting department is rarely responsible for fixing the problem. Rather, accounting and finance are tasked with providing the insight, measures, and frameworks that highlight the issue and provide the mental models for the business leader to craft an appropriate response.

Most HR measures today focus on how the function is using and deploying its resources. Satisfaction with the department is also measured. Some HR organizations actually measure satisfaction with different programs as a first step in deciding what the HR department should and should not do. We have proposed that the paradigm shift toward the talentship decision science requires HR to be accountable for improving talent decisions throughout the organization. That requires a framework for connecting those investments to organizational effectiveness, but it also requires taking a more holistic perspective on how measurements can drive strategic change. We describe that framework next.

The LAMP Framework

We believe that a paradigm shift toward a talent decision science is key to getting to the other side of the wall. Incremental improvements in traditional approaches are not adequate. HR measurement can move beyond the wall using what we call the "LAMP model."[4] The letters in *LAMP* stand for four critical components of a measurement system that drives strategic change and organizational effectiveness. As shown in figure 9-2, the letters stand for logic, analytics, measures, and process. Measures represent only one component of this system. Though they are essential, without the other three components, measures are destined to remain isolated from the true purpose of HR measurement systems.

LAMP is more than an acronym; it's also a metaphor for today's HR measurement dilemma. Consider this illustration: one evening while strolling, a man encountered an inebriated person diligently searching the sidewalk below a street lamp.

"Did you lose something?" he asked.

"My car keys. I've been looking for them for an hour," the person replied.

The man quickly scanned the area, spotting nothing. "Are you sure you lost them here?"

"No, I lost them in that dark alley over there."

"If you lost your keys in the dark alley, why don't you search over there?"

"Because this is where the light is."

ROI Is Not the Holy Grail

Is the path to a decision science for human capital paved with evidence that HR produces a positive ROI? This is certainly one of the most frequent propositions we hear from business leaders and HR measurement consultants. It has been a common assertion that calculating the ROI for HR programs and practices is the Holy Grail of strategic HR decisions and that the ultimate goal of a decision science is to create valid and credible ROI numbers. Understanding the returns and investments in HR programs and practices is useful, but the quest for ROI will not provide the entire solution to the need for a decision science or to the dilemma of talent segmentation.

Most ROI calculations fail to change decisions about vital human capital and organization resources. They are used primarily to demonstrate the value of HR investments after the fact. ROI creates the wrong focus. An ROI is a specific estimate, but for virtually all decisions, the necessary information is whether the return exceeds some minimum required hurdle rate or threshold.[a] Once the effects of an HR investment exceed that return on a risk-adjusted basis, it's irrelevant for most decisions whether they exceed it by 1 percent or 100 percent. Yet we have seen many good HR investments shot down because the accuracy of the ROI estimate wasn't perfect. Often that imprecision doesn't change the fact that even with the most conservative assumptions, the investment would pay off.

It is often falsely believed that when ROI is positive, the program has achieved maximum impact. This isn't necessarily so. If the value produced by better trained or better selected employees is greater than the cost of the training or selection, that doesn't mean that this is the highest potential payoff of those resources. It doesn't mean that the HR program was applied where it could make the greatest difference. It's the same with marketing. An advertising campaign might increase sales among those who see the ads, but it doesn't mean that population was the right customer segment for maximum sales or profits.

Typical ROI calculations focus on one HR investment at a time and fail to consider how those investments work together as a portfolio. Training may produce value beyond its cost, but would that value be even higher if it were combined with proper investments in individual incentives related to the training outcomes?

Thus, understanding ROI and putting it into a decision context requires a framework that distinguishes and integrates efficiency, effectiveness, and impact.

a. John W. Boudreau, "Decision Theory Contributions to HRM Research and Practice," *Industrial Relations* 23 (1984): 198–217.

FIGURE 9-2

Lighting the LAMP

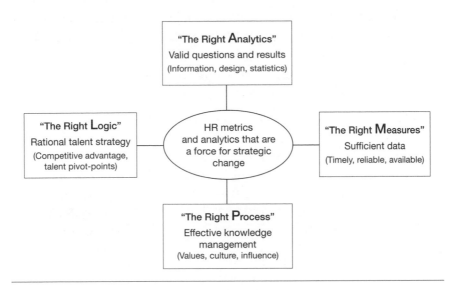

In many ways, talent and organization measurement systems are like the person looking for his keys where the light is, not where he is most likely to find them. This has been accelerated by advancements in information technology that often provide technical capabilities that far surpass the ability of the decision science and processes to properly use them. So it is not uncommon to find organizations that have invested significant resources constructing elegant search and interactive presentation technology around measures of efficiency or measures that largely emanate from the accounting system.

The paradox is that the real insights probably exist in areas where there are not standard accounting measures. Significant growth in HR outsourcing, where efficiency is often the primary value proposition and IT technology is the primary tool, has exacerbated these issues. Even imperfect measures aimed at the right areas may be more illuminating than very elegant measures aimed at the wrong place. As it's been said, "Even a weak penlight in the alley where the keys were lost is better than a very bright streetlight directed somewhere else."

As figure 9-2 shows, HR measurement will advance most quickly if it focuses on the ultimate objective of measurement in a decision science framework. Ultimately, measurement systems are only as valuable as the decisions they improve and the organizational effectiveness to which they contribute. Measures must enhance talent and organization decisions where they most affect strategic success and organizational effectiveness. Let's examine how the four components of the LAMP framework define a more complete measurement system. In doing so, we will present the elements in the following order: logic, measures, analytics, and finally, process.

Logic: Implementing the HC BRidge Decision Framework

Throughout this book we have illustrated the significant power of a logical framework that connects talent and organization investments to strategic success. Such a framework provides a language for systematic and consistently in-depth conversations about how to improve the way organizations compete with and for talent and how organizations are designed. Once the logic is clear, measures emerge that were not obvious before. Recall two of our examples. Boeing measured the behavioral performance of its engineers differently when it realized that the pivotal aligned actions included facilitating global teams. Starbucks measured engagement of its baristas differently from fast-food outlets that rely on standardization because of the strategic importance of employee trust and discretion. The point is that measurement systems, like so much of HR and talent management, are most powerful when logic precedes measurement and when measures are closely tied to the logical pivot-points that make the biggest difference to strategic success and the organization's unique position in its talent markets.

Measures: Counting What Counts

As noted earlier, the measures part of the LAMP model has received the greatest attention in HR. Lists of HR measures abound, often categorized into scorecards and dashboards. Much time and attention is paid to enhancing the quality of HR measures, based on criteria such as timeliness, completeness, reliability, and consistency. These are certainly important standards, but lacking a context, they can be pursued well beyond their optimal level or applied to areas where they have little consequence.

Measuring turnover offers a good example. HR organizations have spent countless hours debating the appropriate formula for turnover and the precision and frequency with which it can be calculated. One HR data warehouse team we worked with said, "We have built the most sophisticated turnover-tracking data and Web interface ever. Now we'll put it out there and see what our managers do with it. They are strategic leaders, so they will help us understand how to analyze turnover data."[5] What happened is that managers began to slice and dice the data in a wide variety of ways, each pursuing his or her own pet theory about turnover and why it mattered. Some generated reports on turnover by ethnicity, others based on skill levels, others based on performance, and so on. Having no common logic about the role of employee turnover in affecting business or strategic success, well-meaning managers were drawing conclusions that might be misguided or dangerous.

As we've seen in earlier chapters, the implications of turnover rates or any other HR measure are very different depending on strategic and business context. Where talent is quality-pivotal, because applicants are well qualified and quickly master the job, turnover is important because of its costs and its effect on talent shortages. Turnover affects the organization mostly through the lack of a full complement of employees. Thus, filling vacancies more quickly addresses the business issue.

A completely different situation is where turnover creates a capability shortage in a position that is quality pivotal, such as where it takes time to learn the job and experienced individuals are being replaced by inexperienced ones. Reducing turnover or filling vacancies more quickly may not address the problem. Turnover can be reduced without increasing overall workforce experience if the number of departures among experienced employees rises and the number of departures of inexperienced employees falls by an equal or greater number. Here, the effects of turnover on workforce learning and quality is key, so reducing turnover levels and time to fill may be much less important than keeping experienced employees or speeding the learning among new employees.

Finally, as important as turnover is, we only rarely see organizations measure the destinations of the employees who leave. For many roles, this is actually the greatest economic impact of turnover. The most common distinctions are between voluntary and involuntary turnover and the reason someone leaves. However, knowing where people are going is often critical. For example, it is far different if someone voluntarily leaves to work for a competitor (perhaps taking valuable knowledge—or even key clients—with them) versus leaving the industry entirely.

Precision alone is not a panacea. There are many ways to make HR measures more reliable and precise, but an exclusive focus on measurement quality can produce little more than a brighter light shining in a place other than where the keys are! Measurement quality must be considered in the context of decision support. Improved measures require investment, which should be directed where it has the greatest return, not simply where improvement is most feasible.

Diagnosing Measurement Systems

The logical elements of the HC BRidge framework—efficiency, effectiveness, and impact—also provide a template for building measurement systems. Organizations can use the HC BRidge framework to determine whether their measures are properly representing the three anchor points. Conference Board research suggests that the vast majority of HR measures fall in the efficiency anchor point.[6] The organization measures the resources spent on HR programs, the frequency or existence of HR programs, or in some cases the demographic characteristics of the workforce, as table 9-1 shows.[7] Turnover and resignation rates are among the most common measures.

Recent research at the Center for Effective Organizations shows that having measures in all three areas—efficiency, effectiveness, and impact—is correlated with the degree to which HR leaders play a significant role in strategy formation. Table 9-2 shows that there is a significant correlation between the existence of HR measures in every category and the degree to which HR leaders perceive a stronger role in strategy.[8]

The data in table 9-2 shows measures ordered with impact at the top, effectiveness in the middle, and efficiency at the bottom. The averages show that organizations in the survey more often reported that efficiency measures existed now (numbers closer to four, on the four-point scale), while effectiveness and impact measures were more likely "being considered" (closer to one on the scale). However, when the existence of each

TABLE 9-1

Highest-frequency human capital measures

Turnover	96%
Voluntary resignation	84
Average compensation	82
Average workforce age	77
Diversity	76
Compensation/total cost	76
Average seniority	75
Work accident frequency	74
Percentage with variable compensation	71
Percentage with stock options	71

Source: Stephen Gates, *Measuring More Than Efficiency,* Research report r-1356-04-rr (New York: Conference Board, 2004).

TABLE 9-2

Measuring the anchor points and strategic partnership

Anchor point	Does your organization currently . . .	Avg.	Correlation with HR role in strategy
Impact	Collect metrics that measure the business impact of HR's programs and processes?	2.7	.20*
Effectiveness	Use dashboards or scorecards to evaluate HR's performance?	2.9	.31**
Effectiveness	Use measures and analytics to evaluate and track the performance of outsourced HR activities?	2.7	.30**
Effectiveness	Have metrics and analytics that reflect the effects of HR programs on the workforce (i.e., competence, motivation, attitudes, behaviors, etc.)?	2.7	.29**
Effectiveness	Have the capability to conduct cost-benefit analyses (also called "utility analyses") of HR programs?	2.5	.19
Efficiency	Measure the financial efficiency of HR operations (e.g., cost per hire, time to fill, training costs)?	3.1	.29**
Efficiency	Collect metrics that measure the cost of providing HR services?	3.0	.24*
Efficiency	Benchmark analytics and measures against data from outside organizations (e.g., Saratoga, Mercer, Hewitt, etc.)?	3.0	.11

Response scale is 1 = "Not currently being considered" to 4 = "Yes, have now."   *p ≤ .05   **p ≤ .01

Source: Edward E. Lawler III, John W. Boudreau, and Susan Mohrman, Achieving Strategic Excellence (Palo Altc, CA: Stanford University Press, 2006).

category of measures was compared to the responses on a question of HR's role in strategy, for almost every measure there was a relationship between its existence and HR's stronger strategic role. Measures throughout the decision framework are needed; no one area is more related to strategic partnership than others. So it is important for HR organizations to consider carefully how well their measurement systems map the elements of the HC BRidge framework.

In our work with organizations, we have found that using the anchor points as a diagnostic framework moves attention from simply listing measures or organizing them using standard scorecard categories to considering how each measurement element connects to others to tell the story about the logical connections embodied in the framework. We ask HR leaders where most of their measures lie. They usually conclude that the preponderance of their measures, and thus the focus of their key constituents, is in the efficiency part of the framework.

They also realize that there are many measures that already exist in other management systems that could be usefully incorporated into their talent and organization measurement approach, to reflect effectiveness and impact. For example, many measures exist for the vital processes and resources from the impact part of the HC BRidge framework, but they are the purview of other functions, such as the supply chain, information systems, manufacturing, and R&D.

When leaders inside and outside the HR function begin to have in-depth conversations about the constraints and vital pivot-points that we illustrated earlier, they usually discover that process owners can connect their key process measures with the more typical HR measures in the efficiency part of the HC BRidge framework. We'll see the power of this connection in the example from Limited Brands later in the chapter.

Finding Talent and Organization Measures in Organizational Databases

The anchor points of the HC BRidge framework also provide a useful lens for understanding the connections between the structure of organizational databases and the talentship decision science. As we have seen, it is useful to consider how to populate the HC BRidge framework with measurements. It is also important to understand the structure of organizational databases and where those measures are likely to reside. Data warehouse technology can integrate data from different systems and processes. The HC BRidge framework can provide an organizing structure that applies such databases to talent and organization decisions.

The framework also provides a useful perspective on the typical maturity curve of measurement. HR and organizations must realize that connecting measures to a decision science takes time and that what's feasible will depend on the existing measures and data. Few organizational measurement systems were designed to reflect a talent and organization decision science. They are much more likely to reflect financial, operations, marketing, or other perspectives. Thus, the measures available to support the HR decision science will vary with the system's maturity. Figure 9-3 captures this relationship.

FIGURE 9-3

Metrics' maturity over time

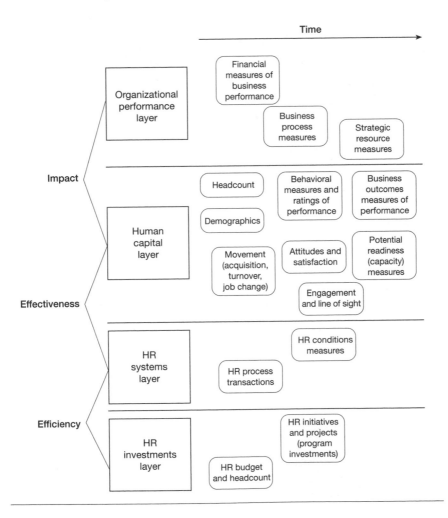

On the left side of figure 9-3 are the familiar anchor points of the HC BRidge framework. Here the framework is matched to the typical categories, or layers, of data as defined by most organizational data systems. The idea is to provide a map that organizational leaders can use to integrate the HC BRidge elements with the structure of the data they encounter in their existing information systems. Within each layer there is also a progression of data sophistication or maturity, which the diagram shows as moving from left to right within each layer.

Organizational Performance Layer

At the top is the organizational performance layer. Data in this layer reflects standard organizational performance measures, such as assets, cash, sales, and overall cost levels. Basic data systems typically contain information for financial reporting at the enterprise, business-unit, and functional levels. Such measures are important and useful, particularly for external financial reporting and for most management reporting. As we have noted, however, the data necessary to uncover the strategic pivot-points is often deeper, embedded in measures of organization and business processes and resources, such as manufacturing, supply chain, R&D, sales, and customer relations. This sort of data often exists in the managerial accounting system that tracks these processes and resources, but it is not always readily available in the organizational data systems until they reach a later stage of maturity, as the diagram shows.

Human Capital Layer

The next row shows the human capital layer. The data in this layer is generally located in the HR information system. In the most basic systems, the data in this layer tends to reflect information necessary for government and financial reporting, largely focused on demographics and headcount in different jobs or organizational units. Closely related to data on demographics and headcount is data on employee movement into, out of, and between organizational positions.

As HR information systems mature, they typically incorporate the data that is collected through employee surveys, including attitudes. Such surveys eventually tap employee engagement and perceptions of the line of sight from their work to the larger organizational mission. Next, data systems will incorporate the data from the performance measurement system, including performance ratings and perhaps information on specific performance behaviors. Once it is possible to gather data from the performance management system, it is also possible to gather data on employee potential and readiness, particularly when those ratings are done through the same process as performance ratings (such as the common two-dimensional format with performance on one axis and potential on the other). Finally, sophisticated systems will track individual-level behaviors directly related to business outcomes. For example, some of the more sophisticated systems track specific sales and patents for particular individuals.

Connecting the organization performance layer and the human capital layer supports the impact element of HC BRidge. An example would be to correlate observed behaviors (such as performance scales based on behavioral anchors like "sharing information" or "completing customer relations paperwork on time") with business outcomes (such as individual sales revenue or customer satisfaction scores). The relationship provides one way to measure the performance yield curves described earlier.

HR Systems Layer

The third data layer is the HR systems layer, which is also often found in the HR information system. This is focused on data about the performance and activity level of HR processes rather than measures connected to individuals. Basic data at this layer includes HR activities such as training, staffing, development, and rewards. It reflects such elements as the number of process transactions (requisitions filled, performance ratings completed, training days delivered, etc.). As data systems mature, we encourage collecting data on the necessary conditions for system success that we described in earlier chapters.

Refocusing measurement on these conditions has a powerful effect on the decision processes and accountability relationship between HR and its clients. For example, early learning management systems might measure the number and types of training provided or attended. A more advanced system might develop measures of the conditions required for learning to occur and be used. These conditions might include readiness for the learning experience (such as being motivated and understanding how the learning will relate to one's work); learning (the actual level of knowledge or skill attained); and transfer (the degree to which opportunities are provided to apply the learning after the learning experience). As we noted earlier, the readiness and transfer conditions are largely affected by the immediate supervisor of the learner and less by the learning experience itself.

To see how the measurement system supports elements of talentship, recall our earlier example in which employee performance is low due to a lack of readiness or transfer. The typical measurement system reflects only the training provided. So, when the employees' manager complains that the training isn't effective because the trained employees are not per-forming better, the HR measurement system shows that those employees were appropriately trained.

Now consider what happens if the system contains data on the relative levels of readiness, learning, and transfer for different managers. Such data might reveal that this manager's employees are learning as much as those of other managers but that they are significantly lower on readiness and/or transfer. While the HR function has a great deal of influence on learning, the manager has the greatest influence on readiness and trans-fer. We believe that more advanced HR systems measures will increasingly distinguish between conditions that are primarily under the control of leaders outside of HR (such as preparing participants to learn and provid-ing opportunities to apply the learning) versus those that are under the control of the HR function (such as the quality of a training program).

Many of the conditions that most significantly affect the success of HR systems are more controlled by leaders outside rather than inside the HR function. Just as accounting shows which units are performing above or below budget, more advanced measures at the HR systems layer will show the relative performance of units on important conditions defined by a decision-based approach to those systems.

Connecting the HR systems layer to the human capital layer often pro-vides data to inform the effectiveness anchor point of the HC BRidge framework.

HR Investments Layer

The final data layer is the HR investments layer. Such systems virtually al-ways begin with a focus on the resources used in the HR function, includ-ing the accounting budget and HR headcount. As the systems mature, they expand to include the basic HR deliverables, such as the number of programs, the number of employees using them, their frequency, and the time and money expended on specific HR initiatives.

Connecting the data in the HR investments layer with the data in the HR systems layer supports the efficiency anchor point of the HC BRidge framework.

A full treatment of the measurement implications of the HC BRidge framework is beyond this book's scope. Our purpose here is to illustrate how the HC BRidge framework provides an alternative to scorecards or other systems that focus on only one part of the logic connecting talent to strategic success. Using the four layers, organizations can begin discus-sions about how they would actually measure the HC BRidge linking elements in a way that uniquely captures the vital connections between talent, organization, and strategic success.

Analytics: Finding Answers in the Data

Even a very rigorous logic with good measures can flounder if the analysis is done incorrectly. For example, it is logical to suggest that when employee attitudes are positive, employees convey those attitudes to customers, who in turn have more positive experiences and purchase more. Many organizations test that logical premise by correlating employee attitudes with customer attitudes across different retail locations. If customer attitudes and purchases are higher in locations with higher employee attitudes, that is interpreted to mean that improving employee attitudes will improve customer attitudes. Many organizations have invested significant resources in programs to improve frontline employees' attitudes based precisely on this sort of correlation evidence.

Of course, this conclusion may be wrong, and such investments may be misguided. A simple correlation between employee and customer attitudes does not prove that one causes the other, nor that improving one will increase the other. For example, a high correlation between employee and customer attitudes can occur because stores that are in locations with more loyal and committed customers are a more pleasant place to work. Customer attitudes can actually cause employee attitudes. Or the relationship could be due to a third factor: location. Perhaps stores in better locations attract customers who buy more and who are more enthusiastic about new offerings. Employees in those locations may like working with such customers better and be more satisfied. Store location turns out to cause both store performance and employee satisfaction.

How Analytics Supports Better Decisions

Analytics builds on the science of determining the right conclusions from data. It draws on statistics and research design and then goes on to include identifying and articulating key issues, gathering and using appropriate data inside and outside the HR function, setting the appropriate balance between statistical rigor and practical relevance, and building analytical competencies throughout the organization. Analytics transforms HR data and measures into rigorous and relevant insights.

The more abundant data becomes, the more essential is analytical capability. Without sufficient analytical capability, HR and business leaders can fall victim to improper conclusions or be misled by superficial patterns and make poor human capital decisions. Analytics ensures that insights from HR data provide legitimate and reliable foundations for human capital decisions. Thus, analytics is an essential addition to rigorous logic. Analytics often provides a prominent way to connect the decision framework to the scientific findings related to talent and organization resources and decisions, which we noted earlier as an important element of a mature decision science. Frequently, the most appropriate and advanced analytics are found in scientific studies.

Finding the Talent Analytics in Organizations

Increasingly, organizations are devoting specific resources to improving analytics applied to talent and organization decisions. Analytical methods have long been a standard part of training social scientists in areas such as psychology, sociology, and economics. Many HR organizations already employ research teams. Such teams often comprise social scientists with PhD-level training in designing and carrying out research.

Other organizations rely on analytical capability outside the HR function. For example, organizations with very strong capabilities in customer and market analysis often engage their analysts on HR issues. It is not unusual to find market researchers called in to look for patterns of employee attitudes and to identify employee types, just as they might identify customer segments. Engineers may be adept at data mining and identifying patterns in things as varied as oil deposits, customer demographics, and flows through the supply chain; they are sometimes asked to find useful patterns in data on employee demographics, movement patterns between jobs, turnover, or attitudes. And some HR organizations call on the analytical capabilities of a wide variety of commercial vendors or universities.

HR analytics teams are also often called on as subject matter experts to support other HR professionals and are asked to educate their peers to help raise the level of analytical awareness in the HR function. For example, Sun Microsystems created an R&D laboratory for HR, and over time this laboratory evolved from a source of very specific research on the effects of HR programs, to a source of analytical expertise for others in HR, and finally to a source of forward-looking research on issues deemed to be critical to the strategic future of the organization, such as virtual work.[9]

Whether the analytical skills reside within the HR function, in other parts of the company, or with an outside organization, HR analytical teams today are typically focused on fairly narrow HR domains. It is not unusual for internal HR research groups to attend exclusively to attitude surveys, to compensation market data, or to mapping flows of employees through different roles and positions. These skills are increasingly valuable outside these rather specialized areas. Analytical skills are even appearing in competency models.[10] The challenge is to create an HR measurement system and organizational structure that successfully engages these skills where they can have the greatest effect. As we have seen, the most interesting and important decisions in HR span the functional specialties of HR and often require understanding relationships between talent and organization elements such as resources, processes, and differentiators. Thus, future talent and organization analysts will increasingly integrate and build cross-organizational databases and design research that incorporates business, economic, and strategic contexts.

The talentship perspective allows us to envision a future in which talent and organization analytics are much more closely tied to mainstream analytics in areas such as marketing, finance, operations, and information systems. Today's talent analytics are often separate from the more mature functional analyses and are often completed only after other analyses are finished. As we have seen throughout this book, there is no need for such a separation. Rather, traditional strategy and business analysis will be enhanced by incorporating insights from talent and organization and will be aimed at improving talent and organization decisions.

Process: Making the Insights Motivating and Actionable

The final element of the LAMP framework is process. In talentship the ultimate criterion for HR measurement is how it affects organizational effectiveness and sustainable strategic success. Measurement affects these outcomes through its impact on decisions and behaviors, and those decisions and behaviors occur within a complex web of social structures, knowledge frameworks, and organizational cultural norms. Thus, a key component of effective measurement systems is that they fit within a change-management process that reflects principles of learning and knowledge transfer. HR measures and the logic that supports them are part of an influence process.

For example, research shows that if managers don't perceive HR issues as strategic and analytical in the first place, they may simply ignore numerical and analytical information about HR.[11] They seem to place HR into a soft category of phenomena that are beyond analysis and therefore are only really addressable through opinions, politics, or other less analytical approaches.

So an initial step in effective measurement is to get managers to accept that HR analysis is possible and informative. The way to do that is often not to present the most sophisticated analysis right away. The best approach may be to present relatively simple measures that clearly connect to the mental frameworks that managers already use. In some organizations calculating the costs of turnover reveals that millions of dollars might be saved with turnover reductions. Organizational leaders have told us that a turnover cost analysis was their first realization that talent and organization decisions had tangible effects on the economic and accounting processes they were familiar with.

Of course, measuring only the cost of turnover is insufficient for good decision making. As we noted earlier, overzealous attempts to cut turnover costs can compromise candidate quality in ways that are far more significant to cost savings. Yet the best way to start a change process may be to first present turnover costs to create needed awareness that the same analytical logic used for financial, technological, and marketing investments can apply to HR.

We noted earlier that a significant element of the evolution of a talent and organization decision science will be a shift from creating influence by responding to client requests or telling constituents what is required, to enhancing HR's influence through educating constituents about the principles and logic they can use to make better decisions.[12] Education is also a core element of change processes. The ROI formula from finance is actually a potent tool for educating leaders in the key components of financial decisions. In the same way, as the talentship decision science takes hold, HR measurements will educate constituents and become embedded within the organization's learning and knowledge frameworks.

Let's turn to a comprehensive example of the principles we've discussed, at a global retail organization: Limited Brands.

Limited Brands' Store-Level Measurement Evolution

Limited Brands is a globally known retailer that operates a balanced portfolio of retail brands, including intimate apparel (Victoria's Secret), general apparel (The Limited), and personal care (Bath & Body Works).[13] A core process for Limited Brands is store operations, and the company uses a decision science approach to allocating scarce resources, such as real estate, technology, money, and talent.

Typical of many retailers, Limited Brands had sophisticated measurement systems and decision frameworks for many of its key resources in stores, but the models and measures used for talent and organization were rudimentary. In 2004 the organization set out to change this. Its experience vividly illustrates the power of adopting a decision science approach to talent and organization measurement, connecting measures with a shared and logical decision model and developing measures that deeply reflect the core processes and resources, not just the top-level outcomes.

From "Accounting for Payroll" to "Deploying Talent Resources"

Toyin Ogun, a VP of HR at Limited Brands, observes that the motivation for the talent and organization measurement makeover was the realization that decisions about talent and organization were founded largely on an accounting-based system of payroll tracking and allocation. Figure 9-4 shows the contrast between the existing system on the left and the aspiration on the right. Notice that both systems can be described as based on measurement, facts, and evidence. Indeed, in many organizations a scorecard that could track the allocation of payroll to stores would be regarded as a business-relevant measurement of human capital. Comparing the left to the right sides of figure 9-4 shows that although different measures would populate the new system on the right, the essence of the change was to literally reverse the measurement logic from top-down to bottom-up. Instead of starting with payroll and allocating it across stores based on activity, the objective was to begin with an in-depth decision model of optimal store activity and use that to make decisions about talent and organization, which would then determine the necessary resources, such as payroll, and their return.

FIGURE 9-4

Reversing the measurement logic at Limited Brands

Top-down Financially controlled: Labor hours	Bottom-up Operationally driven: Zero-based
1. Determine how much payroll we can spend	5. Deploy labor using scheduling tools
2. Subtract cost of management	4. Reconcile cost with financial metrics to understand potential trade-offs
3. Calculate number of dollars and hours left	3. Determine compensation practices by position
4. Allocate extra hours to stores that need them (subjective)	2. Determine skills and positions necessary to perform work and deliver customer expectations
5. Allocate remaining hours to remaining stores	1. Determine what should be done and how much effort it will take (store-by-store)

Source: Toyin Ogun, "Limited Brands Talent Measurement" (Metrics and Analytics Executive Program, Center for Effective Organizations, University of Southern California, 2005). Reprinted with permission.

Making the Subjective More Objective

As Ogun observes in figure 9-5, much of the decision making about talent in the existing system was subjective and not based on data or a shared logic. Store and business leaders were working hard to make good decisions, but a lack of measures, analytics, logic, and a repeatable process all contributed to potentially less-than-optimal decisions. As with so many talent decisions, well-meaning business leaders were using their own logical algorithms, such as catering to stores that asked first, sending talent to stores with the fastest-growing sales, or providing more labor hours to stores that were open the most hours. Each has some logical justification, but none was based on a deep and logical connection between talent and business success.

Seeing Store Operations Through the Lens of Talent Decisions

Limited Brands set out to develop a decision science about the right roles, aligned actions, and capacities that were connected to vital store processes and resources. Figure 9-6 shows the logic the company developed. Notice how this is not an HR diagram at all. Rather, it is an actual overhead perspective of the floor of a retail space, used to depict the vital processes and potential talent contributions. For example, salespeople at the front of the store are scheduled according to each store's unique traffic forecast (Point 1 in the diagram), while selling experts are deployed at

FIGURE 9-5

Limited Brands' traditional allocation of payroll within stores

- Labor hours today are allocated to stores using a variety of methods:
  - ○ Percentage of sales
  - ○ Last year's actual hours spent
  - ○ Store open hours
- These methodologies may not provide the hours necessary to perform the required tasks
- Incremental hours are also allocated to stores using a variety of methods:
  - ○ First come, first served
  - ○ Sales increases
  - ○ Extra floor sets
- These approaches limit the visibility to the trade-offs between selling hours and tasks
- These approaches fail to allocate hours based on the true work required to deliver the experience expected by customers

Stores are forced to make decisions that may not be in the customer's best interest

Source: Toyin Ogun, "Limited Brands Talent Measurement" (Metrics and Analytics Executive Program, Center for Effective Organizations, University of Southern California, 2005). Reprinted with permission.

FIGURE 9-6

Limited Brands' science of right people/place/time/role/skills

2. Add cashiers and wrap-desk support based on forecasted transactions by hour, labor standards, and queueing rules

3. Deploy selling experts at high-fashion locations and during peak sales hours

4. Layer in sales support (runners, "go-backs," etc.) to increase leverage of sales associates and experts

1. Schedule selling labor based on each store's unique customer traffic forecast and traffic per labor hour sweet spot

5. Determine true management hours using labor standards and protect this amount of time (i.e., do not schedule as selling)

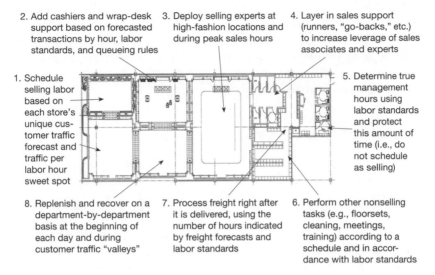

8. Replenish and recover on a department-by-department basis at the beginning of each day and during customer traffic "valleys"

7. Process freight right after it is delivered, using the number of hours indicated by freight forecasts and labor standards

6. Perform other nonselling tasks (e.g., floorsets, cleaning, meetings, training) according to a schedule and in accordance with labor standards

Source: Toyin Ogun, "Limited Brands Talent Measurement" (Metrics and Analytics Executive Program, Center for Effective Organizations, University of Southern California, 2005). Reprinted with permission.

the high-fashion locations during peak sales hours (Point 3). The pivotal contribution of store associates is different at the front of the store than at the expert-driven locations that involve high fashion. Freight processing activities are driven by a set of more specific labor standards based on the time it takes to unload trucks (Point 7).

The fact that this diagram looks like a store is important in subtle ways. The process element of the LAMP model emphasizes that the best talent and organization measurement systems will not only get the story correct and measure it well; they will embed it within the organization's mental models so that it is an effective decision support system both inside and outside the HR function. We will return to this idea in chapter 10.

Notice how differently the measurement question is framed when it is depicted this way. It is no longer simply an issue of allocating payroll or even of implementing HR programs. The connection between decisions about store performance and talent deployment is now seamlessly obvious to leaders inside and outside the HR function. The decision framework and the measurement model now fit with the processes that the organization naturally uses in its planning, budgeting, and strategy analysis.

In our work with organizations, we have found this to be a significant opportunity. We routinely coach HR and organizational leaders to use talentship and the HC BRidge framework to logically and systematically identify, measure, and analyze where talent decisions can make the biggest difference—and then to consider the organization's mental models and to present the findings within those frameworks. The framework in figure 9-6 was a perfect metaphor for a retail store, but we have seen frameworks based on brand management, materials flow diagrams, and other evocative metaphors, in different situations.

Allowing the Logical Model to Drive Measures

At this point Limited Brands has used logic and process to frame the talent measurement and decision question in a way that makes the former payroll-up system clearly obsolete. Now the task is to develop or find measures to populate the model. Figure 9-7 shows how Toyin Ogun describes the company's measurement approach.

Limited Brands realized that the measures necessary to populate its new decision framework lay both inside and outside the usual HR layers of its data systems. In fact, the measurement system would require constructing measures that could track actual in-store movements of customers and employees.

FIGURE 9-7

Limited Brands' science of right skills

The importance of understanding our customers' needs has traditionally been a merchant activity. To effectively model the optimal store experience, we need our stores to understand customer needs (at a minimum, stores need to have execution models or behavior built from customer insight); we also need to match customer needs with the right skills.

Finding the optimal customer service model and skills:

- Study customer behavior
  - Tracking software
  - In-store observations

- Analyze customer data
  - Customer relationship management
  - Point-of-sale data—conversion, trans, ads
  - Demographic data
  - Psychographic data

- Interview the customer
  - Exit interview

- Compile integrated data to develop a fact-based customer-centric model

Source: Toyin Ogun, "Limited Brands Talent Measurement" (Metrics and Analytics Executive Program, Center for Effective Organizations, University of Southern California, 2005). Reprinted with permission.

Notice the "In-store observations" notation under "Study customer be-havior." The next time you enter a Limited Brands store, look up at the ceiling, and you'll notice small, round units with cameras inside. These are used to record real-time data on the volume, distribution, and movement of customers and employees. Limited Brands combined this data with information from its standard sales tracking system (customer relationship management, point of sale, customer interviews, and customer demographics), as shown under the "Analyze customer data" bullet in figure 9-7. In terms of HC BRidge, the result was the ability to statistically connect very in-depth information about the actions and interactions of store talent and the process outcomes that mattered most. This is a far cry from simply measuring the HR practices used in a store and relating them to store sales, and it is much more detailed than relating the general HR practices of Limited Brands with the company's overall financial performance. The depth of the data here allows much deeper and competitively unique insights.

Making Analytics Interactive

Finally, Limited Brands developed a new approach to analytics by construct-ing a mathematical simulation tool. The tool integrates and combines data about customers, talent, employee behaviors, and store performance, al-lowing planners to run what-if scenarios that seamlessly integrate talent and organization decisions with decisions about other vital store re-sources and that examine what elements and combinations really move the needle in store performance. Figure 9-8 shows the architecture of that simulation. Notice the focus on optimization, not just maximization. No-tice that the model emphasizes mitigating risk through modeling different scenarios. This sounds like operations engineering, and that's no coinci-dence. Limited Brands drew on the expertise of its operations engineers to apply analytical logic to talent. This integration of mental models and logi-cal frameworks across disciplines is a hallmark of a mature decision science.

Competing Better

Limited Brands combined logic, analytics, and measures. What did the company learn? One lesson is that once customers decide to enter the fit-ting room, they are much more likely to purchase something. This led to investments in talent systems that inform store associates and managers about how often they succeed in getting customers into fitting rooms. By directing this information to store associates and managers, Limited Brands increases the opportunity for those employees to make decisions about their own talent, actions, and interactions that can enhance the store's

FIGURE 9-8

Limited Brands' labor scheduling architecture

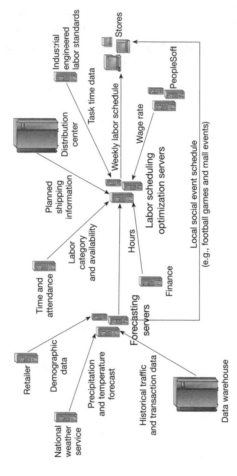

Optimization

- Dramatically improves business responsiveness to changing circumstances and ability to test "what if" scenarios
- Determines the best possible utilization of resources (e.g., people, money, time, equipment, etc.)
- Simultaneously analyzes all variables and multiple, conflicting objectives

- Mitigate risk and reduce uncertainty by modeling different scenarios
- Optimization at Limited Brands
  - Holiday register deployment   ○ Real estate location selection
  - Labor scheduling   ○ Pricing/revenue management

Source: Toyin Ogun, "Limited Brands Talent Measurement" (Metrics and Analytics Executive Program, Center for Effective Organizations, University of Southern California, 2005). Reprinted with permission.

success. With logic supported by measures, this clear line of sight from actions to store performance becomes a reliable part of store operations, not just a matter of luck.

Limited Brands also learned that a significant amount of its sales were on weekends. Before this analysis some stores had offered their best employees time off on weekends as a reward, perhaps hoping to reduce turnover by providing the best associates with something they wanted. These are worthy goals, but a deeper decision-based logic reveals the fallacy in what might have appeared to be logical reasoning.

In fact, data showed that this was exactly the opposite of what was optimal for the store and exactly opposite of what should be done to maximize commissions for the best associates. It turned out that many of the best associates were quite happy to work weekends once the relationship between weekend work and higher commissions through bigger sales was made clear. Moreover, having the best store associates working during the highest traffic times for shopping malls enhanced store performance.

This is also a very good example of the synergy between demand and supply that we discussed in earlier chapters. If competitors continue to operate with less rigorous logic, it creates a competitive opportunity for Limited Brands to attract, retain, and deploy the best store associate candidates.

Conclusion

The Limited Brands example illustrates how a holistic approach to talent and organization measurement must encompass all elements of the LAMP framework. It also shows how systematic development of a logic that connects talent and organization investments to vital organization processes is the key to making sense of the thousands of available measures that could connect talent and organization decisions to strategic success. Limited Brands' logic is consistent with the HC BRidge framework, while the application of that logic reveals relationships that are unique to Limited Brands' own strategies, competitive intent, processes, and resources.

This chapter showed how the talentship decision science provides an approach to talent and organization measurement that emphasizes decisions, organizational effectiveness, and using measures to articulate and teach a systematic logical connection between talent and organization decisions and the vital elements of strategic success. Measurement has been termed the "Achilles' heel" of HR management, but as we have seen, the real solution goes well beyond merely improving measures. In chapter 10 we will extend this theme to show how leading organizations are making talentship real by integrating it deeply into their strategy, performance, planning, and budgeting systems.

10

Making Talentship Work

How the HR Evolution Becomes a Practical Reality

In the previous nine chapters, we made the case that talent decisions are vital to organizational effectiveness and strategic success. We also highlighted key elements of talentship and the HC BRidge decision framework that supports it. We believe that the evolution of a truly strategic decision-based approach to talent and organization is imminent and that we will soon see leaders accomplish the long-touted goal of making talent decisions, not just HR, more strategic. Talentship and HC BRidge describe the frameworks for revealing the connections, but our work with organizations repeatedly shows that the process of connecting talent and organization decisions to business and strategy is typically too unsystematic to support lasting change.

Talentship and HC BRidge have potentially significant implications for HR leaders. Beyond just encouraging them to be at the table, it equips them to be proactive members of the leadership team with a unique perspective, supported by rigorous and reliable logic. Earlier we showed that a decision science requires shared mental models and management systems integration. HR and business leaders need to go beyond just identifying the logical talent and organization connections to strategies and the unique opportunities they reveal. Discovering the right answer isn't the same as motivating the organization to change based on that answer. *Change agent* has shown up in virtually every HR leadership competency model for years, yet research shows there is still a stubborn gap between the reality and the aspiration. We believe that change agent competencies are important, but talentship means creating change within a decision science. Talentship means change happens best when leaders inside and outside the HR function are skilled at asking the right questions, facilitating the vital conversations, and building the mind-set of their colleagues to see the strategic implications of talent and organization decisions more logically and insightfully.

In this concluding chapter, we describe what decision-science-based change looks like and how leading organizations are using that process to make talentship a tangible part of their approach to strategy and decisions. Of course, a complete description of the change process is beyond the scope of a single chapter. Here we will focus on what experience reveals to be the most significant elements of change. We offer guidelines to make talentship a systematic part of an organization's strategic planning, budgeting, performance management, and succession planning. Armed with both the decision logic and the tools for change, the essential evolution can get under way.

Engage Leaders Where They Are

We facilitate both strategy and leadership development discussions with line executives, and it's common for these senior leaders to say something like "As I think about the process we use to select and launch projects, I realize we do all this analysis of the customer requirements and build sophisticated financial models. Yet as soon as the project is awarded, we scramble like crazy to find the people, which causes us to miss our projections." Even when talent needs are based on deep and logical insights, organizational change often depends most on how well those insights are integrated into the existing decision processes.

Leaders need to consider talent implications at every stage of the decision cycle and have the discipline to define and refine the strategy until it is sufficiently clear to determine the talent implications. It's not enough to follow the more typical approach that fits talent decisions into the strategy after it is formed and when it is only deep enough to determine that it will meet the financial requirements. Throughout this book we have shown many examples of strategies that are simply not in-depth enough to clearly identify the strategic pivot-points around which talent and organization decisions must align. It would not be enough for Disneyland merely to know it had to be "The Happiest Place on Earth" or for Boeing to know that it needed to deliver a large-capacity airliner on time. The change process almost always requires both improving the strategy as well as connecting it to talent and organization decisions. This means that any lasting change must engage leaders who formulate and analyze strategy, and those leaders are often outside the HR organization. In fact, the very observation that HR leaders may require a deeper definition of strategy than other fields is a change process in itself—one that both HR leaders and line leaders need to be willing to address.

Talentship Cannot Be Just Another HR Program

Here's what we know will not work—creating a new HR program-based strategic talent analysis, launched and driven by HR, and added on to or run independently from the existing decision and planning processes. Very few line managers are looking for a new HR program to help them improve their strategic processes. Even fewer have the time to invest in new processes that are not directly relevant and connected to the work they are already doing. Inevitably, it will feel more like control or another HR hoop to jump through rather than help—no matter how well-intentioned the initiative or how valid the strategic talent and organization insights.

Equally unlikely to succeed are processes to identify strategic talent requirements that are completed by HR professionals or consultants and do not engage key business leaders to consider the business issues and the talent implications together. Business leaders may be grateful to HR for doing the work for them, but the analysis is often too superficial and static to lead to optimal decisions. Most leaders have experienced HR planning processes that produce a report that took a lot of work but isn't used much.

Leaders Know That People Are Important, So What Is Next?

Ten years ago a significant barrier to talentship was that leaders did not see people issues as important ones. That is rare today. Our experience has shown that most line leaders welcome the type of rich and robust insights that can result from deeper analysis of their strategy's talent implications. In fact, they often see such issues as even more important than decisions about money, technology, and so on. At the same time, they are often frustrated that their analysis frameworks, their strategy processes, and/or their HR leaders fail to meet the need. The issue is not a lack of motivation or willingness to get better at talent and organization decisions but rather the lack of a logical and specific process to actually make it happen. The logical frameworks in this book can serve as the platform to go beyond simply recognizing that talent matters. That recognition is a great motivator, but it's not the same as a plan of action. Organization leaders can go further by ensuring that the questions we've provided become an accepted and consistent part of their strategic and business planning.

Next, we describe some ways to make that a reality and the vital and exciting new role that HR leaders can play.

Connect Talentship to Organizational Change Efforts

Much has been made about the need for organizations to be more agile, flexible, and ready for change. The ability to change may be more valuable than the ability to defend the status quo.[1] The need to change rapidly and continuously often leads organizational leaders to presume that the kind of deep strategy analysis we have described is obsolete or irrelevant. They ask, "Why analyze talent and organization pivot-points within a deep strategy framework when the competitive environment and the strategies are always changing?" We illustrated some of the challenges with dynamic strategy issues when we described the competitive dynamics between Boeing and Airbus.

In fact, talentship is not only applicable; it is even more valuable in fast-changing environments. Major organizational change initiatives may provide a place to pilot the implementation of talentship concepts. In fast-changing environments, it is not enough simply to change. Organizations that survive and thrive learn to consistently change in directions that are strategically valuable, and they do so faster than their competitors. As a result, a common language for understanding the impact of talent and organization decisions becomes even more valuable. It is the only way organizations can anticipate and understand when changing strategic circumstances requires changes in talent and its organization. Suboptimal investment in talent and organization is as wasteful in fast-changing environments as in stable ones. In fact, resources are more scarce when change is rapid, so suboptimal investment may be even more harmful.

Other fields have learned the importance of going slow to go fast. It is foolish for an IT department to dive into a project and begin the programming as quickly as possible. Rather, the goal should be to accomplish the mission as quickly as possible, which very well might mean spending additional effort on the front end to fully understand the system requirements and priorities. The IT team may adapt and change along the way, but they also know that without a good systems analysis, the risk of missing the budget or the deadline (likely, both!) is far greater.

In a similar way, a decision science approach like talentship can play a vital role in defining, communicating, and improving change readiness and results. The logical analysis that underpins talentship provides the language, discipline, and frameworks to communicate the change. Often organizational change falters because those deeply entrenched in the organization simply don't understand how their actions and interactions affect strategic imperatives. Even well-meaning and motivated organization members will stumble without such an understanding.

Thus, a key opportunity to initiate and enhance the evolution toward talentship is to connect frameworks like HC BRidge to the organization's specific change priorities and to use them to reveal deep insights about the pivot-points for successful strategic change. As a starting point, try making a list of the top change priorities for your own organization. Then, use the talentship principles to consider what talent pools or organization structures would be most pivotal to really making that change happen, and test whether the list of talent programs is really as unique and logically specific as it could be. We often find that such an exercise quickly reveals ways to shape the talent agenda and doesn't require a deep strategy analysis because it focuses on the change priorities that have already been identified.

Integrate Talentship with Other HR Change Efforts

The HR function is changing on many different dimensions today. The types of change may include a new information system infrastructure, outsourcing, mergers and acquisitions, restructuring and downsizing, and globalization. It seems that the change agenda for the HR function itself is accelerating and increasing in scope.

It is a common reaction for some HR leaders to say, "I would be interested in talentship, but right now it seems that I have to work on the control and service delivery aspects of HR. I will consider talentship when we are ready for it." Our experience is that this is indeed sometimes the case—the HR function is simply not mature or sophisticated enough in its basic control and service requirements to consider extending its paradigm to include talentship. Doing so is the equivalent of introducing capital planning into an organization that does not have a general ledger or do basic budgeting well. There is certainly a minimum foundation of compliance and programs that must be in place before the HR function introduces talentship.

Yet, our experience suggests that organizations more typically err by waiting too long to introduce talentship. In HR functions where there is frustration with the service delivery elements, a talentship-based approach to the mission and organization of the HR function itself is actually the key to solving the perceived issues with service delivery and quality. For example, the barriers and friction between the corporate-office and business-unit HR professionals are more easily solved through a perspective that sees HR as a value chain to support decisions rather than in endless discussions over centralizing and decentralizing services without any foundational framework for those discussions. So while there does need to be some basic level of HR to implement talentship, these capabilities exist in most organizations; they just haven't been tapped yet.

Finally, we find talentship to be a useful framework for other significant and necessary HR changes. We worked with one organization that had recently announced a major merger. Rather than using the traditional approach of integrating HR functions by reviewing and allocating services across the two heritage organizations, in a new approach, leaders used the talentship concept as a way to join together as a unified organization. Another organization was preparing to outsource. In this second case, talentship frameworks not only helped inform the outsourcing itself, it provided a framework for designing the strategic work for the HR organization that remained after outsourcing. This included roles as diverse as business-unit HR, COE, and HR operations. Finally, another organization had historically managed HR in a highly decentralized way across three divisions. For cost and service consistency reasons, its leaders decided that certain elements of HR needed to be shared and that a more centralized approach was appropriate. The talentship framework and tools helped guide the reorganization and more clearly define the roles that would be retained in the business units and those that would be consolidated.

Those change efforts—merger integration, outsourcing, and restructuring—would have occurred with or without talentship. Each of them, however, benefited by leveraging the talentship concepts and used the change process to accomplish the original goal and to create incremental value by having a more decision-focused and sophisticated HR function.

In your own organization, consider the most prominent changes that your HR organization faces (outsourcing, restructuring, strategic mission, etc.), and use the talentship principles to identify how to make those changes in a way that enhances decisions about organization and talent where they are most important, rather than only considering the efficiency or effectiveness of the HR function. We find that when framed in terms of strategic talent decisions, organizations often uncover insights about the true value in large-scale HR organization change and a more logical and compelling case for the change is required.

Integrate Talentship with Existing
Management Systems and Processes

Timing is everything. The discussions created by considering the anchor points of efficiency, effectiveness, and impact all have their place. If they are too aggressively pursued at the wrong point in the organization's existing planning, budgeting, and performance processes, they will not be effective.

For example, it seems obvious that the right time to consider the talent and organization implications of the strategy is when strategic issues are first being discussed. Yet, in many organizations, the initial strategy discussion focuses on resources such as technology, advertising, or money, while the people issues are treated as a separate process, often occurring after, and in reaction to, the earlier strategy analysis.

One reason this happens is the failure to distinguish effectiveness and efficiency from impact. Impact connects most to strategy discussions, while effectiveness and efficiency are often better addressed in planning the HR function. It is the impact discussion that is appropriate at the point where business strategy is being created and this is where the talent implications should be drawn out to help clarify and refine the strategy.

The implications for HR (largely in effectiveness and efficiency) can be addressed later. If line leaders make a deep and logical connection between success and talent implications during the strategy process, they will be much better prepared to hear HR's recommendations regarding its programs and practices, as well as the investments necessary for the HR function. In fact, we encourage HR leaders to carefully distinguish the appropriate leaders for these different discussions. Line leaders should lead strategy discussions, with HR helping ensure that the talent implications are clear (impact). At the same time, HR should lead the discussion about how to create the necessary unique talent pool strategies to compete in the talent market and the programs and practices that should be implemented to create that unique market position. This professional expertise should not be delegated to non-HR leaders. Lacking a good basis for these distinctions, organizations can rely too heavily on non-HR leaders to define the HR policies and practices so that they receive the systems they want. As we have seen, however, there is great value in having strong professional HR expertise involved in the design of HR systems, processes, and the HR organization, while the more appropriate role for non-HR leaders is to work in close partnership with HR leaders, through the existing planning processes, to better identify the talent-strategy connections.

We find that four prominent areas provide opportunities to integrate impact analysis and talentship more broadly into existing planning processes:

- Strategic planning
- Succession planning

- Operational planning and budgeting

- Performance management and goal setting

Our experience suggests that in each process there are significant opportunities to inject the logic, language, and frameworks of talentship. Yet the appropriate elements of talentship and the significant contribution of the talentship logic vary with each process. So it is very important to consider carefully how to engage with each of the four processes.

Strategic Planning

Strategic-planning processes vary widely between organizations. Some organizations strongly coordinate their strategy processes across business units while others leave the processes to the business units' discretion. Still others do very little strategic planning internally, choosing to rely on external consulting firms. Organizations also vary widely on the role of HR leadership within the strategy process, although increasingly it is common to have HR leaders participate directly, which we believe should be the norm.

Many organizations have processes that they call "strategic planning" but that are actually more operational and financial, focused on building financial projections and justifying requests for resources (typically capital, discretionary spending, and headcount). Unfortunately, strategic plans that merely allocate financial resources or focus only on improving operations are often not sufficient to identify the kind of game-changing talent and organization pivot-points we have described here. So the first challenge in building a stronger connection between strategy and talent is for HR leaders to understand the strengths and weaknesses of the organizational strategic-planning processes as they consider the path toward talentship.

To make this assessment, consider where the strategies that currently guide the firm were created. Who drove the process? Who participated? What strategy, marketing, and finance frameworks guided the processes? What review process occurred?

To find the most vital strategic issues (versus the operational issues that are called "strategy"), look for situations where the following information is discussed and analyzed:

- External trends within the industry

- Relative market position versus competitors

- Market segments and value propositions

- Strengths and weaknesses versus competitors

- Product line strategy

When issues like these are discussed, the pivot-point lenses we discussed in chapter 4 are a natural fit. When addressing market positions, market segments, and/or value propositions relative to competitors, it is a natural extension to be more explicit about differentiators. For example, if the strategy discussion evolves toward the organization's distinctions compared to competitors, a useful question is this: "For those areas where we have strong differentiators, is it more important to get customers to place greater value on our advantages, or is the critical issue protecting the advantage from competitive attack?" As we have already seen, solving these issues provides direct line of sight to typically overlooked talent and organization implications.

Succession Planning

Like strategic planning, succession planning is a process focused on long-term organizational implications. HR often takes the lead in designing the systems, frameworks, and tools that support the process. As a result, succession planning can be an excellent system to introduce many talentship concepts. Because HR plays such a significant role in succession planning, our experience shows it is a formidable opportunity to encourage a deeper consideration of pivotal talent and organization issues. A key is to extend the goal of succession planning beyond having a slate of ready leaders (simple replacement planning). Rather, the purpose should be to have an in-depth and strategic discussion about the strengths, weaknesses, and optimal development plans for key talent resources. We find that few organizational leaders will dispute this assertion, so it opens the door to approach succession planning in this more strategic way. For example, we recommend that a succession-planning process should include at least five key elements:

- Talent requirements (demand)

- Talent resources (supply)

- Individual development and deployment planning

- Addressing the implications of the talent resources on the business plan

- Reviewing and refining the talent pool strategy

We won't discuss the tools and frameworks for each of these elements here, but you can see how the HC BRidge anchor points can impact these elements of an effective succession plan. Many succession-planning processes reflect an implicit assumption that the leadership competencies and behaviors that served in the past and serve today are the ones that will be needed tomorrow. They imply that "what got us here will get us there." This is why succession-planning processes tend to reflect the profiles of successful current and past leaders. Future leaders often appear quite similar in background, experience, and competencies to existing leaders. Most organizations know this may be a problem, but few have a systematic way to connect this awareness back to tangible succession-planning changes that better reflect future leadership needs.

In contrast, succession planning based on talentship ultimately strives to identify what's pivotal for the future strategy and what changes in future leadership will be most pivotal and aligned with those strategy pivot-points. Talentship offers an alternative to merely cataloging the traits of today's successful leaders by providing a logic that answers the question "What will our future leaders need to do that will make the biggest difference in our strategic success?" A great question to ask is "Given our strategy, how will our leaders need to be different than our competitors'?"

For example, in the Boeing/Airbus example, the analysis we provided might suggest that future Boeing leaders will increasingly be pivotal for their effect on accurate market predictions and for facilitating alliances with suppliers and other partners who possess vital intellectual capital. This could easily be different from the current profile of many aerospace leaders, whose careers may have reflected an era with less volatile markets and less strategic reliance on partnerships.

We find that the career paths in many organizations have been honed to produce leaders who were adept at an earlier model, one that emphasized success through a set of skills and competencies that made previous leaders successful but that may be far different from what is required for future success. A talentship-based succession process would go beyond asking whether there is a sufficient supply of successors in the traditional career paths and instead encourage attention to focus on the changing nature of the successors, as well as their availability. Succession-planning discussions rarely fail to pose the question "Are we preparing the leaders we need for the future?" Unfortunately, the typical answer is "Certainly, because we have deep bench strength in all our leadership pipeline positions." By now it is clear that this is an effectiveness answer to an impact question. The critical issue often is not the depth of the traditional bench as much as anticipating the need to change the nature of leadership succession to reflect changing competitive opportunities and strategy pivot-points, and to recognize the needed changes before the competition.

Because succession planning is recognized as a vital strategic, long-term process driven by HR leaders, those leaders often have more freedom to shape the process toward talentship discussions. Non-HR leaders are more comfortable when HR leaders raise these issues in the context of succession planning and leadership development.

Operational Planning and Budgeting

Strategic- and succession-planning processes vary widely from one firm to another, but budgeting processes typically are far more mature and consistent. Budgeting processes typically focus on one-year planning cycles. They are usually a significant tool for management control of key resources and performance management for key leaders and many others. Organizations check their performance against budget more often than they check results against strategic-planning projections or succession-planning goals.

This all means that the budgeting process will typically be well developed and that it will actively engage key organizational leaders, even in companies where strategy processes and succession planning may be more rudimentary or not as engaging to organizational leaders. In fact, where the strategic-planning processes are weak and the strategic competencies of the line leaders are low, we have found that the budgeting process is often the most effective place to begin engaging the strategy's talent implications. The operational budgeting and planning process is often an excellent initial opportunity to build a deeper understanding of talent and organization implications. Connecting talentship to the budgeting process is often the most viable alternative in such situations.

Of course, budgeting processes seldom engage the long-term questions of strategy and leadership preparedness, so the engagement process must be different.

Pivot-point logic and analysis can be powerful tools to expand the sophistication of the analysis within the budgeting cycle. For example, a common budgeting subprocess with immediate talent and organization implications is headcount planning. "How many people will be required?" is a question virtually always considered during budgeting. This can be the jumping-off point for a deeper discussion that integrates impact and effectiveness. Natural follow-on questions are:

- What talent issues (open positions, turnover, positive performance, etc.) had the largest impact on the budget in the year we just completed?

- What do you think are the most important new hires in this year's plan? What makes hiring them so pivotal?

- Where do we need to hire people who are significantly different from those we hired in the past?

- In what jobs would turnover be a significant problem in this year's plan? Why is it so important?

The key is to reframe the task beyond merely completing the budget (often a daunting process in itself!) and to use the context of the budgeting process to motivate a deeper exploration of the strategy-talent connection. More deeply considering the logic behind the resource allocations and the implications of budget assumption variances for future strategic positioning can improve the level of talent discussions, even without using all the strategy lenses described earlier. We often find that such discussions gently demonstrate to business leaders the need to establish a strategy process, because those leaders realize that they are allocating resources without a common understanding of the long-term plan and its implications.

So asking talentship questions can help leaders use the budgeting process to question or clarify key strategy assumptions. More directly, we often find that budget issues themselves often reveal talent pivot-points, when those issues are analyzed using impact questions. Examples include:

- Which business process constraints most affect the budget? (This question helps find the talent and organization alignments that will most relieve that constraint.)

- What are the biggest differences between the new budget and our current level of performance? (The answer here points to areas where large changes are required, which is a good place to find talent and organization pivot-points associated with the change.)

Performance Management and Goal Setting

The performance management and goal-setting process is another place to uncover talent and organization issues in an existing process. Performance management and goal-setting processes in particular have a powerful effect on capacity, culture, interactions, and actions. Virtually every organization invests significant time and effort in creating line of sight, or a very clear and deeply understood connection between the company's strategic goals and how they are translated into work group and individual performance expectations. Performance management systems strive to ensure that the sum of the subunit and individual goals add up to the firmwide goals and that there are systems in place to monitor and reward performance where it matters most.

HR leaders have significant influence in the logic and structure of performance management conversations, so we often see that this is an excellent, and often untapped, opportunity to use that influence to better focus on the strategic questions that support goal setting and performance management. For example, a useful question is "Are our performance management processes and systems focused and aligned on the strategic pivot-points?" Performance measures are often financial, which aligns them with the financial aspects of strategy. A talentship perspective encourages performance goals and measures that align with the strategy and where actions and interactions are most pivotal to success.

Dig Below the Financial Numbers. We find this often means digging below typical financial objectives. Such objectives often cascade down from high-level financial reporting goals and sometimes represent little more than allocating cost, revenue, and profit goals across business units. It is difficult for individuals at the operations level to connect what they do to such broad financial goals.

For example, in one customer service organization that involves driving trucks on routes, route drivers were held accountable for cost per mile. That's a perfectly legitimate financial goal, but the route drivers controlled neither the largest cost (truck maintenance) nor the number of miles they drove (which was determined by the logistics and dispatching system). We see this pattern surprisingly often in performance goals for frontline employees. By gently inviting business and operational leaders to consider how performance goals connect to the actions and interactions that most affect the strategic differentiators, processes, and resources—and what alternative goals might be more closely related to the human capacity of frontline employees—HR leaders can elevate the conversation on the performance management process. They will begin to uncover pivot-points such as the customer interactions of Disney sweepers and Starbucks baristas that we discussed earlier.

Make Good Strategies Even More Executable. Not only does the performance management process offer opportunities to elevate conversations when the strategy is not well developed; it can also be useful in organizations with well-developed strategies as a way to clarify the connections between the strategy and the talent and organization issues. When the strategy is deep and logical enough to connect to talent and organization, the performance management process provides a natural opportunity to examine whether goals and performance measures emphasize the strategy, talent, and organization pivot-points. Performance management measures can be used as natural diagnostics to see whether there is shared understanding about what aspects of talent, organization, and behavior are important.

An interesting way to turn the logic around is to start with the policies and practices and use them as a perspective on strategic intent. We encourage HR leaders to ask, "What do our performance measures and rewards imply are the important and pivotal interactions and actions, processes, resources, and differentiators? Do we all agree with those implications?" Leaders often recognize the need to revise the performance measures, which presents an opportunity to use talentship logic to direct that discussion toward the strategic context and then to use the lenses and pivot-point processes discussed earlier to enhance performance alignment and improve execution.

Another important area to consider in defining the performance management goals is to focus on the *what* and the *how* of performance management. It is not just about which goals must be accomplished but which methods are appropriate. These are increasingly critical aspects of performance management systems and relate to the interactions and actions element of the HC BRidge framework.

Finally, a powerful purpose of performance management is to provide employees with a clearer line of sight between their actions and the organization's mission. Yet, as the effectiveness chapters showed, traditional performance measures are often derived from generic job descriptions, broad financial measures, and goals that may or may not reflect a shared understanding of the strategy pivot-points. We often encounter organizations where performance management goals are set very carefully and diligently but are based on factors that are important or frequent, not pivotal. Recall how effectiveness improves line of sight through greater attention to the pivotal elements of performance and human capacity.

Indeed, the game-changing performance elements are often those that fall outside traditional job descriptions, as our Disney sweepers and Boeing engineer examples showed. Performance management focuses naturally on questions of which goals are vital and whether employees have true line of sight to their most significant contributions, so the performance management process provides a powerful opportunity to use impact logic to enhance the connections between talent, organization, and strategy.

As we noted earlier, too often engagement is measured only with respect to very high-level or generic objectives. When performance measures are developed through a deep and logical talent decision science, both performance and engagement can reflect the kind of unique and strategically vital elements that truly drive strategic success.

Integrate Talentship with Existing Mental Models

The HC BRidge framework provides a common logic and language that enables HR and business leaders to streamline and refine their strategic conversations about talent and organization decisions. We built the HC BRidge framework on efficiency, effectiveness, and impact because these three anchor points have much in common and naturally connect to most existing business frameworks in finance, accounting, marketing, operations, and information management.

Each business, and even each operational function, has its own set of mental models that are used to guide discussions, establish measures, and make decisions. Some of these are common across most organizations, such as operating profits, return-on-net assets, and economic value added. Others are unique and specific to a particular industry or even a particular organization. Examples include route scheduling for airlines or underwriting for insurance companies.

These frameworks define the mental models that leaders learn and use for financial assets; typically, they are fully integrated into core processes such as strategic planning, budgeting, and performance management. So they are a natural starting point for conversations about what talent and organization decisions most affect the elements of these mental models. The talent and organization implications of business and strategy are directly related to the strategic and business context, and that business context is usually described with a particular language.

Additional frameworks that span all businesses are shown in table 10-1. Because these frameworks (both generic and specific) guide so many thinking processes, they form the organization's mental models. They structure the vast amounts of data, and they are the first-level filter through which most information is processed.

Tools to create talent insights are more powerful when they are engineered into the language and logic that already exist within the organization. Today's efforts to hold leaders accountable for HR measures and scorecards, and to present a new HR planning process designed to make HR more strategic, often require that leaders learn a new language. Not only is this often difficult to sell; it misses a powerful opportunity to engage leaders where they already have tremendous energy and expertise. As we explained earlier, it is surprisingly powerful—and often easier—to frame the logic connecting strategy to talent and organization decisions so that it is compatible with the leaders' current mental models. Virtually all business models are in some way grounded in economic or financial logic. In fact, virtually all such models have elements that map to efficiency, effectiveness, and impact.

TABLE 10-1

Frameworks that span all businesses

Functional area	Management processes	Common frameworks
Finance	• Operational budgeting • Financial reporting • Capital budgeting	• EVA, ROIC • Revenue and expense reporting • IRR, incremental EVA
Marketing	• Customer segmentation • Product line management	• Customer attribute models • Product life cycle models
Strategy	• Long-range strategic planning	• Competitive environment (such as "five forces" from Michael Porter) • Competitive positioning
Product development and engineering	• Product development	• Product development processes • Product development review cycles
Operations	• Inventory management • Production planning • Quality improvement	• Process mapping standards • Economic order quantity • Material requirements planning • Six Sigma

Note: EVA (economic value added), ROIC (return on investment capital), IRR (internal rate of return).

Framing Talent Logic like Business Logic at Allstate

We find that HR leaders make great progress in elevating leaders' talent savvy by first uncovering the logic that is expressed in the business and then framing the talent logic to correlate with it. For example, when we work with organizations where engineering logic dominates, we use concepts such as failure rates (turnover), redundancy (overstaffing), and constraints. In organizations where a marketing logic dominates, we use concepts such as brand image (employment value proposition), customer segmentation (talent segments), and customer response functions (pivotal talent contributions). We find situations within the organization where the economic principles that drive talentship are used to manage a different resource and extend those principles to apply to the talent and organization resource.

For example, at Allstate, Joan Crockett, senior vice president of HR, helped line leaders understand a new approach to measuring staffing decisions by making an analogy between staffing decisions and the underwriting processes for new insurance policies.[2] Underwriting includes gathering information about the performance and risk factors of the insured organization or individual, relating those factors statistically to the probability of default or significant claims, and then determining the appropriate policy features to maximize the return-risk trade-off. Applying this to staffing, she described how staffing is talent's underwriting. It involves gathering information about the known performance and risk factors of applicants, relating that information statistically to applicants' performance after they are hired, and then determining the appropriate selection decision rules to maximize the return-risk trade-off in hiring.

Success Is When the Language of Business Becomes a Talent Language

In the most advanced organizations that we know, the business logic and the talent logic have become fundamentally intertwined. For example, in one software applications organization, the conversation about talent and organization evolved to the point where business leaders began to seamlessly connect their natural process logic with talent pivot-points.[3] Rather than being satisfied with talent goals, such as hiring more software developers and testers, they began to ask questions such as "We know that our business model requires that our search engine must be the first to search e-mail and blogs on both the hard disk and the Web. What kinds of designers and testers do we need to make that happen fast? Do we offer a unique proposition in the labor market to get and keep them? Are we deploying the best ones we have to this task?"

This was not the result of a mandate from HR or the CEO requiring that business leaders become accountable for HR and talent measures. Instead, it was a natural result of HR leaders posing insightful questions about the business model, questions that were informed by a logical framework for talent and organization implications. Over time, business leaders began to see such insight's value and how they could incorporate the questions into their existing mental models.

Sustainable Change Is the Goal, Not a Single Program or Event

There is a recurring theme within the techniques we've described here. The objective is not the adoption of a particular program, nor the successful completion of a strategy event. The process we have described here takes time, and it occurs through multiple learning cycles. Perhaps the best phrase to describe effective change management using talentship has come from several organizations we've worked with. As their HR and business leaders more deeply understand and use the techniques, they have told us, "Your approach is like a stealth bomber because we don't introduce it with a lot of flash and attention. We just start asking better questions, digging for the right pivotal information in the existing processes, and encouraging our leaders to think differently within the models they already use. In fact, the best outcome is when our business leaders begin to think of talentship logic as their idea!"

Change processes that are seen to emanate too much from the HR department are unfortunately often resisted and not respected. Talentship and HC BRidge represent new thinking in a world where everyone is already overtaxed. Virtually no organization believes it cannot benefit from a deeper and more strategic approach to talent and organization decisions. The problem is that the processes to make this happen often impose such significant additional demands that they are crushed under their own weight. Stealthy and incremental changes are often much more effective.

To create this change, there does need to be a specific and concentrated effort on the skills and capabilities of leaders in all parts of the HR function. We find that the key is to systematically develop HR collectively in the new language and concepts. This is challenging because many HR professionals operate fairly independently within the HR function. They define their value through their relationship with their line leaders, and they often hesitate to give up that independence and align around a common professional decision model. Yet, as we have seen, such alignment around a logical framework has been the hallmark of the evolution of decision sciences like marketing and finance, and is vital to success in talentship.

We designed the HC BRidge framework and the talentship decision science to be naturally compatible with the underlying logic of existing financial and business models. The concepts of pivot-points, constraints, resources, differentiators, efficiency, effectiveness, and impact all have counterparts in existing models, at all levels of the organization. They apply as well to a single business process as they do to high-level questions about global organizational design. That allows leaders at all levels to apply these ideas to the issues at hand and to have tangible successes at a basic level that can build to more complex or novel decisions.

A final key to successful implementation is managing the learning and change process in cycles. The goal is not to make perfect talent decisions, just as the goal of finance and marketing is not to make perfect decisions about money and customers. Rather, talentship strives to systematically improve talent decisions over time. Treating learning and change as an integrated process, and taking a multicycle approach that starts with small effects and builds on them, produces significant cumulative change and improvement in talent and organization decisions, well beyond what can be achieved with flashier and more dramatic approaches that require large immediate changes to existing organizational systems.

HR and the Line Learn and Use Talentship Differently

Our work has shown that a vital success factor in implementing talentship is to recognize that HR leaders and non-HR leaders begin the learning journey at very different points. HR leaders are often more familiar with the effect of talent and organization decisions on business performance because they see those effects daily. They often hold positions that demand that they be effective advocates for employees, so they more readily accept and search for logical connections. At the same time, HR leaders are often far less familiar with strategy and operational management processes and less adept at finding the strategic and operational pivot-points within them. This is where non-HR leaders often shine. Line managers are typically very familiar with strategy and operations and thus their development opportunity is to translate these insights into talent implications.

HR leaders understandably are more willing to invest time and resources in their talentship development, and we strongly recommend starting with HR in any type of talentship transformation. Evidence shows that HR leaders recognize that deeper strategy analysis skills are vital to their strategic role and impact on the business. Talentship provides a direct connection to what they often perceive as a critical business need. In contrast, the same evidence suggests that line managers may overestimate their skills in strategic talent and organization analysis and that they typically don't make a strong connection between their capabilities and the strategic role of their HR leaders.[4]

One approach that has proved highly effective for line managers is action learning, rather than classroom training. Effective organizations use talentship concepts in the deployment of a new strategy or change initiative. The newness of the initiative often conveys legitimacy for trying something a bit different. Business leaders, often guided by HR colleagues, find the pivot-points and focus the organization's energy on the critical elements required to execute the new strategy or change. In this way they not only develop new skills; they achieve important business objectives at the same time. Although action learning takes time, it is a powerful way to provide the real-world practice that's so important for success, and the investment in learning is directly linked to important business outcomes.

A common starting point is to develop HR professionals, who then apply the new skills and concepts to existing opportunities in strategic planning, operational planning and budgeting, succession planning, and performance management. Talent and organization decision models should be customized to fit the company's existing decision models. That way, the most effective conversations about talent and organization alignment occur so naturally that organizational leaders begin to think of them as their own idea. Finally, the best learning often comes through experience, so the most effective approach is a patient one that recognizes that learning will occur in steps.

Conclusion

Talentship does little good if it is merely a new set of analytical tools that are never used or if it is a one-shot analysis that gets brief attention but then is soon forgotten. Like finance and marketing, it must become an integral element of the mental models that HR and business leaders use to advance the organization's competitive success.

We began this book with the example of Corning seeing talent opportunities that others overlooked because Corning used a logical and systematic approach to talent strategy that others lacked. Throughout this book we've described the elements of that logic and techniques for making this approach a reality in any organization.

Organizations that make a commitment to improving the quality of decisions that depend on or impact talent by using the concepts described in this book will find the effort challenging at times but worthwhile in the long run. The payoff will be to illuminate the uncharted strategies quicker than your competition, and to thrive, rather than perish, through the essential evolution.

Notes

Chapter 1

1. Kurt Fischer, Vice President of HR, Corning, interview by Pete Ramstad and John Boudreau, Corning, New York, March 2001.

2. John W. Boudreau and Peter M. Ramstad, "Where's Your Pivotal Talent?" *Harvard Business Review*, April 2005, 23–24.

3. Jeffrey Pfeffer and Robert I. Sutton, *Hard Facts, Dangerous Truths, and Total Nonsense* (Boston: Harvard Business School Press, 2006).

4. See, for instance, Edward E. Lawler III, John W. Boudreau, and Susan Mohrman, *Achieving Strategic Excellence* (Palo Alto, CA: Stanford University Press, 2006); Frederick Frank and Craig Taylor, "Talent Management: Trends That Will Shape the Future," *Human Resource Planning Journal* 27, no. 1 (2004): 33–41.

5. James O'Toole, Edward E. Lawler III, and Susan R. Meisinger, *The New American Workplace* (Hampshire, England: Palgrave Macmillan, 2006).

6. Lawler, Boudreau, and Mohrman, *Achieving Strategic Excellence*.

7. Orlando C. Richard, Thomas A. Kochan, and Amy McMillan-Capehart, "The Impact of Visible Diversity on Organizational Effectiveness: Disclosing the Contents in Pandora's Black Box," *Journal of Business and Management* 8, no. 3 (2002): 265–291.

8. John W. Boudreau and Peter M. Ramstad, "Talentship and the New Paradigm for Human Resource Management: From Professional Practices to Strategic Talent Decision Science," *Human Resource Planning Journal* 28, no. 2 (2005): 17–26.

9. Keith H. Hammonds, "Why We Hate HR," *Fast Company*, August 2005, 40–48.

10. "Writer Defends 'Why We Hate HR' Article," Compensation.BLR.com, November 29, 2005, http://compensation.blr.com/display.cfm/id/154876.

11. Wickham Skinner, "Big Hat, No Cattle: Managing Human Resources," *Harvard Business Review*, September–October 1981.

12. Andrall E. Pearson, "Muscle-Build the Organization," *Harvard Business Review*, July–August 1987.

13. Ed Gubman, "HR Strategy and Planning: From Birth to Business Results," *Human Resource Planning Journal* 27, no. 1 (2004): 13–23.

14. James Mead (former manager of worldwide sales recruiting, Procter & Gamble), interview by John W. Boudreau, October 2006.

15. Interview with financial services organization by John Boudreau and Peter Ramstad, October 2003.

16. Eric Abrahamson, "Management Fashion," *Academy of Management Review* 21, no. 1 (1996): 254–285.

17. Jack F. Welch and John A. Byrne, *Jack: Straight from the Gut* (New York: Warner Business Books, 2001).

18. Stephen W. Pruitt, T. Bettina Cornwell, and John M. Clark, "The NASCAR Phenomenon: Auto Racing Sponsorships and Shareholder Wealth," Cambridge Journals, January 31, 2005, http://journals.cambridge.org/action/displayAbstract? fromPage=online&aid=274889.

19. "Coca-Cola Shakes Up Wireless Vending Plan," Discovery Channel, October 19, 1999, http://www.exn.ca/Stories/1999/10/29/57.asp; Constance L. Hays, "What Wal-Mart Knows About Customers' Habits," *New York Times*, November 14, 2004, http://www.nytimes.com/2004/11/14/business/yourmoney/14wal.html?ex=1258 088400&en=0605d1fc88b8ab98&ei=5090.

20. Sunmee Choi and Anna S. Mattila, "Impact of Information on Customer Fairness Perceptions of Hotel Revenue Management," *Cornell Hotel and Restaurant Administration Quarterly* 46, no. 4 (2006): 444–452.

21. H. Thomas Johnson, "Management Accounting in an Early Integrated Industrial: E. I. DuPont de Nemours Powder Company, 1903–1912," *Business History Review* 49, no. 2 (1975): 184–204.

22. H. Thomas Johnson and Robert S. Kaplan, *Relevance Lost: The Rise and Fall of Management Accounting* (Boston: Harvard Business School Press, 1991).

23. Robert Bartels, *The History of Marketing Thought* (Columbus, OH: Grid, 1976).

24. John A. Howard, *Marketing Management: Analysis and Decision* (Homewood, IL: R. D. Irwin, 1957).

25. Neil H. Borden and Martin V. Marshall, *Advertising Management: Text and Cases* (Homewood, IL: R. D. Irwin, 1959).

26. Brian E. Becker and Mark A. Huselid, "High-Performance Work Systems and Firm Performance: A Synthesis of Research and Managerial Implications," *Research in Personnel and Human Resources Management* 16 (1998): 53–101.

27. Michael E. Porter, "What Is Strategy?" *Harvard Business Review*, November–December 1996, 61–78.

28. "Sarbanes-Oxley Act of 2002," http://www.sarbanes-oxley.com/section.php? level=1&pub_id=Sarbanes-Oxley.

Chapter 2

1. Mike Lossey, Dave Ulrich, and Sue Meisinger, eds., *The Future of Human Resource Management: 64 Thought Leaders Explore the Critical HR Issues of Today and Tomorrow* (New York: Wiley, 2005).

2. John W. Boudreau and Peter M. Ramstad, "Talentship, Talent Segmentation, and Sustainability: A New HR Decision Science Paradigm for a New Strategy Definition," in *The Future of Human Resource Management: 64 Thought Leaders Explore the Critical HR Issues of Today and Tomorrow*, eds. Mike Lossey, Dave Ulrich, and Sue Meisinger (New York: Wiley, 2005).

3. Roger G. Schroeder, Kevin Linderman, and Dongli Zhang, "Evolution of Quality: First Fifty Issues of *Production and Operations Management*," *Production and Operations Management* 14, no. 4 (2005): 468–481.

4. Amy E. Colbert, Sara L. Rynes, and Kenneth G. Brown, "Who Believes Us? Understanding Managers' Agreement with Human Resource Research Findings," *Journal of Applied Behavioral Science* 41, no. 3 (2005): 304–325.

5. John W. Boudreau, "Strategic Knowledge Measurement and Management," in *Managing Knowledge for Sustained Competitive Advantage*, eds. Susan E. Jackson, Michael A. Hitt, and Angelo S. DeNisi (San Francisco: Jossey-Bass/Pfeiffer, 2003), 360–396.

6. Wayne F. Cascio, *Costing Human Resources: The Financial Impact of Behavior in Organizations*, 4th ed. (Cincinnati, OH: South-Western, 2000).

7. H. Thomas Johnson, "Management Accounting in an Early Integrated Industrial: E. I. DuPont de Nemours Powder Company, 1903–1912," *Business History Review* 49, no. 2 (1975): 184–204.

8. In accounting the *chart of accounts* is a listing of all the accounts in the general ledger, with each account accompanied by a reference number. Examples might include assigning numbers 1000–1999 to asset accounts, 2000–2999 to liability accounts, and 3000–3999 to equity accounts. Source: "Chart of Accounts," NetMBA, http://www.netmba.com/accounting/fin/accounts/chart/.

9. John S. Bronson (former executive vice president of HR, Pepsicola Worldwide), interview by John W. Boudreau, August 2006.

10. Interview with HR professional by John Boudreau, March 2002.

11. Customer relationship management (CRM) is a corporate-level strategy that focuses on creating and maintaining lasting relationships with customers. CRM enables organizations to better manage their customers through the introduction of reliable systems, processes, and procedures. Source: "Customer Relationship Management," *Wikipedia*, http://en.wikipedia.org/wiki/Customer_Relationship_Management.

12. Conjoint analysis is a tool that allows a subset of the possible combinations of product features to determine the relative importance of each feature in the purchasing decision. Source: "Conjoint Analysis," QuickMBA, http://www.quickmba.com/marketing/research/conjoint/.

13. Johnson, "Management Accounting."

14. John W. Boudreau and Peter M. Ramstad, "Human Resource Metrics: Can Measures be Strategic?" In Patrick Wright et al., eds., *Research in Personnel and Human Resources Management*, Supplement 4, *Strategic Human Resources Management in the Twenty-First Century* (Stamford, CT: JAI Press, 1999), 75–98.

15. John W. Boudreau and Peter M. Ramstad, "Where's Your Pivotal Talent?" *Harvard Business Review*, April 2005, 23–24.

16. "Press Kit: History & Timeline 1930s," Allstate, http://www.allstate.com/Media/PressKit/PageRender.asp?page=1930s.htm.

17. Adrienne Carter, "Telling the Risky from the Reliable," *BusinessWeek*, August 1, 2005, http://www.businessweek.com/magazine/content/05_31/b3945085_mz017.htm.

18. Interview with Matthew Brush and Kurt Fischer, in Corning, NY, by John Boudreau, November 2003.

19. Interview with Shawn Lancaster by Peter Ramstad, March 2005. Lynn Farrell, "Turning HR Cost Reduction Into Opportunity at The Hartford" (Presentation in *Beyond the Bottom Line* executive program, Center for Effective Organizations. April 2004).

Chapter 3

1. John W. Boudreau and Peter M. Ramstad, "Talentship, Talent Segmentation, and Sustainability: A New HR Decision Science Paradigm for a New Strategy Definition," *Human Resource Management* 44, no. 2 (2005): 129–136.

2. Information regarding the Walt Disney Company came from Disney executives, interviews by John W. Boudreau, July through September 2006.

3. "Disneyland Resort," Disney Online, http://disneyland.disney.go.com/disneyland/en_US/home/home?name=HomePage.

4. "Cedar Point Amusement Park, The Roller Coaster Capital of the World," http://www.cedarpoint.com.

5. "Fan Mail," *Eyes and Ears*, March 30–April 12, 2006.

6. "Jobs, Cedar Point," http://www.cedarpoint.com/public/jobs/index.cfm.

7. "Imagineers scale massive heights to create thrilling experience," *Eyes and Ears*, March 30–April 12, 2006.

8. Ibid.

9. Michael Lewis, *Moneyball: The Art of Winning an Unfair Game* (New York: Norton, 2003).

Chapter 4

1. "Merkel Clinches It, but the Price Is High," *The Economist*, October 12, 2005, 1.

2. Information regarding Airbus comes from many documented sources. See, for instance, Ken Vadruff, "Spirit Gets First Shot at Non-Boeing Job," *Wichita Business Journal*, October 14, 2005, http://wichita.bizjournals.com/wichita/stories/2005/10/17/story1.html; "Airbus Innovation Will Give the A350 XWB Family Its Competitive Edge," Airbus, July 18, 2006, http://www.airbus.com/en/myairbus/headlinenews/index.jsp; "The A380 Enters Production," Airbus, January 23, 2002, http://www.airbus.com/en/presscentre/pressreleases/pressreleases_items/01_23_02_A380.html; Irene L. Sinrich, "Airbus Versus Boeing (A): Turbulent Skies," Case 9-386-193 (Boston: Harvard Business School, 1990), 1–23.

3. Information regarding Boeing comes from many documented sources. See, for instance, Suresh Kotha et al., "Boeing 787: The Dreamliner," Case 9-305-101 (Boston: Harvard Business School, 2005), 1–18; "Where Is Boeing Going?" The Travel Insider, http://www.thetravelinsider.info/2003/boeing5.htm; "Major Assembly If First Boeing 787 Dreamliner Starts," Boeing, http://www.boeing.com/news/releases/2006/q2/060630a_nr.html; Irene L. Sinrich, "Airbus Versus Boeing (A): Turbulent Skies," Case 9-386-193 (Boston: Harvard Business School, 1990), 1–23.

4. Multiple models exist for many of the aircraft shown in figure 4-3. In those cases we plotted the model with the longest range. The models depicted are: 747-400ER, 767-400ER, 777-300ER, 787-9, A330-300, A340-600, A350-900 (as proposed), and the A380. The A350 specifications were not finalized before the project was replaced by the A350-XWB, so the positioning shown for the A350 is based on the preliminary specifications that were released as Airbus explored the concept. All other specifications are from the respective company Web sites.

5. Michael E. Porter, "What Is Strategy?" *Harvard Business* Review, November–December 1996, 61–78.

6. Jay B. Barney, "Integrating Organizational Behavior and Strategy Formulation Research: A Resource-Based Analysis," *Advances in Strategic Management* 8 (1992): 39–61.

7. "Thirsty Long-Term Investors Should Take a Sip of PepsiCo," Bull and Bears Top Stocks to Watch, http://www.thebullandbear.com/digest/0105-digest/0105-stocks.html.

8. Porter, "What Is Strategy?"

9. Barney, "Integrating Organizational Behavior."

10. Eliyahu Y. Goldratt, *Theory of Constraints* (Great Barrington, MA: North River Press, 1999).

11. John W. Boudreau and Peter M. Ramstad, "Measuring Intellectual Capital: Learning from Financial History," *Human Resource Management* 36, no. 3 (1997): 343–356.

Chapter 5

1. Berkshire Hathaway, http://www.berkshirehathaway.com.

2. General Electric, http://www.ge.com/en/.

3. For sources on information about Boeing and Airbus, see notes 2 and 3 of chapter 4 above.

4. Dinah Deckstein et al., "Berlin Mulls Purchase of EADS Shares," Spiegel Online International, http://www.spiegel.de/international/spiegel/0,1518,442783,00.html.

5. Daniel Michaels, "Airbus CEO Resignation Reflects Company's Deep Structural Woes," *Wall Street Journal*, October 10, 2006, A1.

6. Information regarding the Walt Disney Company came from Disney executives, interview by John W. Boudreau.

7. Robert S. Kaplan and David P. Norton, "Measuring the Strategic Readiness of Intangible Assets," *Harvard Business Review*, February 2004, 52–63; John W. Boudreau, Peter M. Ramstad, and John S. Bronson, "The HC BRidge: Linking Business Imperatives to Human Capital Strategies" (paper presented at the Balanced Scorecard Collaborative Best Practices Conference, Naples, FL, February 27, 2002).

8. Randy Bassler, Randy's Journal, http://www.boeing.com/randy.

9. Mark A. Huselid, Richard W. Beatty, and Brian E. Becker, "'A Players' or 'A Positions'? The Strategic Logic of Workforce Management," *Harvard Business Review*, December 2005, 110–117.

10. The three conclusions are cited in John W. Boudreau and Peter M. Ramstad, "Measuring Intellectual Capital: Learning from Financial History," *Human Resource Management* 36, no. 3 (1997): 343–356; John W. Boudreau and Peter M. Ramstad, "Strategic I/O Psychology and the Role of Utility Analysis Models." In Walter C. Borman, Daniel R. Ilgen, and Richard J. Klimoski, eds., *Handbook of Psychology*, vol. 12, *Industrial and Organizational Psychology* (New York: Wiley, 2004), 193–221; and John W. Boudreau and Peter M. Ramstad, "Where's Your Pivotal Talent?" *Harvard Business Review*, April 2005, 23–24.

11. Huselid, Beatty, and Becker, "'A Players' or 'A Positions'?"

12. M. Bichler et al., "Applications of Flexible Pricing in Business-to-Business Electronic Commerce," IBM, http://www.research.ibm.com/journal/sj/412/bichler.html.

13. J. Boudreau and P. Ramstad, "Strategic I/O Psychology and the Role of Utility Analysis Models," in *Handbook of Psychology*, vol. 12, *Industrial and Organizational Psychology*, eds. Walter C. Borman, Daniel R. Ilgen, and Richard J. Klimoski (New York: Wiley, 2004), 193–221.

14. Interview with large Midwest bank by Peter M. Ramstad, October 2005.

15. See, for instance, "Northrop Grumman Elects Wesley G. Bush Chief Financial Officer, Succeeding Charles H. Noski," Northrop Grumman, January 17, 2005,

http://www.irconnect.com/noc/press/pages/news_releases.mhtml?d=70968; "Condit Announces Changes to Strengthen Boeing Leadership," Boeing, May 8, 2000, http://www.boeing.com/news/releases/2000/news_release_000508a.html.

16. Mary Bellis, "The History of Pepsi Cola: Caleb Bradham," About.com, http://inventors.about.com/library/inventors/blpepsi.htm.

17. "People & Events: The Business of Direct Selling," *American Experience*, PBS, http://www.pbs.org/wgbh/amex/tupperware/peopleevents/e_direct.html.

18. See, for instance, "Amway Business Opportunity," Amway, http://www.amway.com/en/BusOpp/business-opportunity-10092.aspx; "Start a Business," Mary Kay, http://www.marykay.com/startabusiness/default.aspx.

19. Liza Featherstone, "Wal-Mart's Women—Employees and Customers—in Unhealthy Relationship," *Seattle Post-Intelligencer*, January 2, 2005, http://seattlepi.nwsource.com/opinion/205768_focus02.html.

Chapter 6

1. Erico Guizzo, "Winner: Carbon Takeoff," *IEEE Spectrum*, January 2006, http://www.spectrum.ieee.org/print/2606.

2. See, for instance, Robert S. Kaplan, "How the Balanced Scorecard Complements the McKinsey 7-S Model," *Strategy and Leadership* 33, no. 3 (2005): 41–46; Mark A. Huselid, Richard W. Beatty, and Brian E. Becker, "'A Players' or 'A Positions'? The Strategic Logic of Workforce Management," *Harvard Business Review*, December 2005, 110–117.

3. James O'Toole, Edward E. Lawler III, and Susan R. Meisinger, *The New American Workplace* (Hampshire, England: Palgrave Macmillan, 2006).

4. Geoffrey Colvin, "Managing in Chaos," *Fortune*, October 2, 2006, 76.

5. Edgar H. Schein, "Culture: The Missing Concept in Organization Studies," *Administrative Science Quarterly* 41, no. 2 (1996): 229–235.

6. Peter Pae, "Japanese Helping 787 Take Wing," *Los Angeles Times* [HOME EDITION], May 9, 2005, p. C1. Copyright, 2005, *Los Angeles Times*.

7. Eric Raimy, "Cyber Move," *Human Resource Executive*, September 2000.

8. Ibid.

9. Interview with technical person at Williams-Sonoma by John Boudreau and Peter Ramstad, February 2002.

10. Denise Rousseau, "The Shifting Risk for the American Worker in the Contemporary Employment Contract," in *America at Work: Choices and Challenges*, ed. Edward E. Lawler III and James O'Toole (New York: Palgrave MacMillan, 2006), 153–172.

Chapter 7

1. John W. Boudreau and Peter M. Ramstad, "Tapping the Full Potential of HRIS: Shifting the HR Paradigm from Service Delivery to a Talent Decision Science;" Chapter 2 in PeopleSoft, *Heads Count: An Anthology for the Competitive Enterprise* (Pleasanton, CA: PeopleSoft, 2003), 69–88.

2. Sue Shellenbarger, "In Their Search for Workers, Big Employers Go to Summer Camp," *Wall Street Journal*, February 23, 2006, D1.

3. John W. Boudreau and Chris J. Berger, "Decision Theoretic Utility Analysis Applied to Employee Separations and Acquisitions," *Journal of Applied Psychology* 70 (1985): 581–612.

4. "The Pros and Cons of Online Recruiting," *HR Focus* 81, no. 4 (2004): S2.

5. Shalini S. Dagar and Archna Shukla, "Soaring Salaries . . . Vanishing Workers," *Business Today*, September 24, 2006, 66.

6. Patrick F. McKay and Derek R. Avery, "What Has Race Got to Do with It?" *Personnel Psychology* 59, no. 2 (2006): 395–429.

7. Mary Dee Hicks and David B. Peterson, "The Development Pipeline," *Knowledge Management Review*, July–August 1999, 30–33.

8. James Combs, Yongmei Liu, Angela Hall, and David Ketchen, "How Much Do High-Performance Work Practices Matter? A Meta-Analysis of Their Effects on Organizational Performance," in *Personnel Psychology* 59, no. 3 (2006): 501–528.

9. Wayne F. Cascio and John W. Boudreau, *Costing Human Resources*, 5th ed. (New York: Prentice Hall, forthcoming).

10. Peer C. Fiss, "A Set-Theoretic Approach to Organizational Configurations," *Academy of Management Review* (forthcoming).

11. Eric Abrahamson, "Managerial Fads and Fashions: The Diffusion and Rejection of Innovations," *Academy of Management Review* 16, no. 3 (1991): 586–612.

12. Jack F. Welch and John A. Byrne, *Jack: Straight from the Gut* (New York: Warner Business Books, 2001).

13. Bethany McLean and Peter Elkind, *The Smartest Guys in the Room* (New York: Penguin, 2003).

14. For sources on information about Boeing, see note 3 of chapter 4 above.

15. Michael Cieply, "Pivotal Property: Disney's Plan to Build Cities on Florida Tract Could Shape Its Future," *Wall Street Journal*, July 9, 1985, 1.

16. Information and quotations regarding Starbucks came from an interview with David Pace by John Boudreau, "Human Resource Strategic Excellence" (teleconference series from the Center for Effective Organizations, University of Southern California, 2006).

17. Ibid.

18. Matt Richtel, "The Long-Distance Journey of a Fast-Food Order," *New York Times*, April 11, 2006, A1.

19. Kristina Goetz, "The Diva of Starbucks," *Cincinnati Enquirer*, May 6, 2001, http://www.enquirer.com/editions/2001/05/06/loc_the_diva_of.html.

20. Brooke Locascio, "Working at Starbucks: More Than Just Pouring Coffee," Tea & Coffee Trade Online, January–February 2004, http://www.teaandcoffee.net/0104/coffee.htm.

21. John S. Bronson (former senior vice president of HR, Williams-Sonoma), personal communication with John Boudreau and Peter Ramstad, September 2006.

Chapter 8

1. James O'Toole, Edward E. Lawler III and Susan R. Meisinger, *The New American Workplace* (Hampshire, England: Palgrave Macmillan, 2006).

2. Information in this chapter regarding SAS was provided by Gale Adcock (director of corporate health services, SAS), interview by John W. Boudreau, September 2006.

3. Jeff Chambers, "Human Resource Strategic Excellence" (teleconference series from the Center for Effective Organizations, University of Southern California, 2006).

4. Useful formulas for calculating such costs can be found in Wayne F. Cascio, *Costing Human Resources*, 4th ed. (Cincinnatti, OH: South-Western, 2000); and in Wayne F. Cascio and John W. Boudreau, *Costing Human Resources*, 5th ed. (New York: Prentice-Hall, forthcoming).

5. Jack F. Welch and John A. Byrne, *Jack: Straight from the Gut* (New York: Warner Business Books, 2001).

6. John W. Boudreau, "Effects of Employee Flows on Utility Analysis of Human Resource Productivity Improvement Programs," *Journal of Applied Psychology* 68 (1983): 396–407.

7. Wayne F. Cascio and John W. Boudreau, *Costing Human Resources*, 5th ed. (New York: Prentice Hall, forthcoming).

8. Wayne F. Cascio, *Responsible Restructuring: Creative and Profitable Alternatives to Layoffs* (New York: Berrett-Koehler, 2002).

9. Sherry Kuczynski, "Help! I Shrunk the Company!" *HR Magazine* 44, no. 6 (1999): 40–45.

10. Douglas P. Shuit, "Passing the Bucks," *Workforce Management* 82, no. 9 (2003): 30–34.

11. Edward E. Lawler III et al., *Human Resources Business Process Outsourcing* (Hoboken, NJ: Jossey-Bass, 2004).

12. Interviews by John Boudreau with Six-Sigma experts in several companies, July 2002.

Chapter 9

1. See, for instance, John W. Boudreau, "Utility Analysis for Decisions in Human Resource Management," in *Handbook of Industrial and Organizational Psychology*, vol. 2, 2nd ed., eds. Marvin D. Dunnette and Leaetta M. Hough. (Palo Alto, CA: Davies-Black, 1991), 621–745; John W. Boudreau and Peter M. Ramstad, "Human Resource Metrics: Can Measures Be Strategic?" in *Research in Personnel and Human Resources Management*, Supplement 4, *Strategic Human Resources Management in the Twenty-First Century*, eds. Patrick Wright et al. (Stamford, CT: JAI Press, 1999), 75–98; Wayne F. Cascio and John W. Boudreau, *Costing Human Resources*, 5th ed. (New York: Prentice Hall, forthcoming); Jac Fitz-enz, *How to Measure Human Resource Management*, 3rd ed. (New York: McGraw-Hill, 2001).

2. John W. Boudreau and Peter M. Ramstad, "Talentship and Human Resource Measurement and Analysis: From ROI to Strategic Organizational Change," *Human Resource Planning Journal* 29, no. 1 (2006): 25–33.

3. Edward E. Lawler III, Alec Levenson, and John W. Boudreau, "HR Metrics and Analytics: Uses and Impacts," *Human Resource Planning Journal* 27, no. 4 (2004): 27–35.

4. Boudreau and Ramstad, "Talentship and Human Resource Measurement and Analysis."

5. John W. Boudreau and Peter M. Ramstad. "Tapping the Full Potential of HRIS: Shifting the HR Paradigm from Service Delivery to a Talent Decision Science." Chapter 2 in PeopleSoft, *Heads Count: An Anthology for the Competitive Enterprise* (Pleasanton, CA: PeopleSoft, 2003), 69–88.

6. Stephen Gates, *Measuring More Than Efficiency*, Research report r-1356-04-rr (New York: Conference Board, 2004).

7. Stephen Gates, *Value at Work: The Risks and Opportunities of Human Capital Measurement and Reporting*. Conference Board Report #r-1316-02-rr (New York: Conference Board 2002).

8. Edward E. Lawler III, John W. Boudreau, and Susan Mohrman, *Achieving Strategic Excellence* (Palo Alto, CA: Stanford University Press, 2006).

9. California Strategic Human Resource Partnership, *Sun's HR Labs: Driving Decisions with Data* (Palo Alto, CA: California Strategic Human Resource Partnership, 2002).

10. National Academy of Public Administration, *HR in a Technology-Driven Environment* (Washington, DC: National Academy of Public Administration, 2002).

11. G. Johns, "Constraints on the Adoption of Psychology-Based Personnel Practices: Lessons from Organizational Innovation," *Personnel Psychology* 46, no. 3 (1993): 569–592.

12. See, for instance, John W. Boudreau and Peter M. Ramstad, "Tapping the Full Potential of HRIS: Shifting the HR Paradigm from Service Delivery to a Talent Decision Science." Chapter 2 in PeopleSoft, *Heads Count*; Boudreau and Ramstad, "Talentship and Human Resource Measurement and Analysis."

13. Information regarding Limited Brands came from Toyin Ogun, "Limited Brands Talent Measurement" (Presented at the *Metrics and Analytics Executive Program*, Center for Effective Organizations, University of Southern California, September 23, 2005).

Chapter 10

1. Edward E. Lawler III and Christopher G. Worley, *Built to Change* (Hoboken, NJ: Jossey-Bass, 2006).

2. Joan Crockett (senior vice president of HR, Allstate), interview by Peter M. Ramstad, January 2006.

3. Interview with software applications organization by John Boudreau and Peter Ramstad, June 2004.

4. Edward E. Lawler III, John W. Boudreau, and Susan Mohrman, *Achieving Strategic Excellence* (Palo Alto, CA: Stanford University Press, 2006).

Bibliography

Abrahamson, Eric. "Management Fashion." *Academy of Management Review* 21, no. 1 (1996): 254–285.

———. "Managerial Fads and Fashions: The Diffusion and Rejection of Innovations." *Academy of Management Review* 16, no. 3 (1991): 586–612.

Barney, Jay B. "Integrating Organizational Behavior and Strategy Formulation Research: A Resource-Based Analysis." *Advances in Strategic Management* 8 (1992): 39–61.

Bartels, Robert. *The History of Marketing Thought.* Columbus, OH: Grid, 1976.

Becker, Brian E., and Barry Gerhart. "The Impact of Human Resource Management on Organizational Performance: Progress and Prospects." *Academy of Management Journal* 39, no. 4 (1996): 779–801.

Becker, Brian E., and Mark A. Huselid. "High-Performance Work Systems and Firm Performance: A Synthesis of Research and Managerial Implications." *Research in Personnel and Human Resources Management* 16 (1998): 53–101.

Borden, Neil H., and Martin V. Marshall. *Advertising Management: Text and Cases.* Homewood, IL: R. D. Irwin, 1959.

Borman, Walter C., Daniel R. Ilgen, and Richard J. Klimoski, eds. *Handbook of Psychology.* Vol. 12, *Industrial and Organizational Psychology.* New York: Wiley, 2004.

Boudreau, John W. "Decision Theory Contributions to HRM Research and Practice." *Industrial Relations* 23 (1984): 198–217.

———. "Effects of Employee Flows on Utility Analysis of Human Resource Productivity Improvement Programs." *Journal of Applied Psychology* 68 (1983): 396–407.

Boudreau, John W., and Chris J. Berger. "Decision Theoretic Utility Analysis Applied to Employee Separations and Acquisitions." *Journal of Applied Psychology* 70 (1985): 581–612.

Boudreau, John W., and Peter M. Ramstad. "Measuring Intellectual Capital: Learning from Financial History." *Human Resource Management* 36, no. 3 (1997): 343–356.

———. "Talentship and Human Resource Measurement and Analysis: From ROI to Strategic Organizational Change." *Human Resource Planning Journal* 29, no. 1 (2006): 25–33.

———. "Talentship and the New Paradigm for Human Resource Management: From Professional Practices to Strategic Talent Decision Science." *Human Resource Planning Journal* 28, no. 2 (2005): 17–26.

———. "Talentship, Talent Segmentation, and Sustainability: A New HR Decision Science Paradigm for a New Strategy Definition." *Human Resource Management* 44, no. 2 (2005): 129–136.

———. "Where's Your Pivotal Talent?" *Harvard Business Review*, April 2005, 23–24.

Boudreau, John W., Peter M. Ramstad, and John S. Bronson. "The HC BRidge: Linking Business Imperatives to Human Capital Strategies." Paper presented at the Balanced Scorecard Collaborative Best Practices Conference, Naples, FL, February 27, 2002.

California Strategic Human Resource Partnership. *Sun's HR Labs: Driving Decisions with Data.* Palo Alto, CA: California Strategic Human Resource Partnership, 2002.

Cascio, Wayne F. *Costing Human Resources: The Financial Impact of Behavior in Organizations.* 4th ed. Cincinnati, OH: South-Western, 2000.

———. *Responsible Restructuring: Creative and Profitable Alternatives to Layoffs.* New York: Berrett-Koehler, 2002.

Cascio, Wayne F., and John W. Boudreau. *Costing Human Resources.* 5th ed. New York: Prentice Hall, forthcoming.

Choi, Sunmee, and Anna S. Mattila. "Impact of Information on Customer Fairness Perceptions of Hotel Revenue Management." *Cornell Hotel and Restaurant Administration Quarterly* 46, no. 4 (2006): 444–452.

Colbert, Amy E., Sara L. Rynes, and Kenneth G. Brown. "Who Believes Us? Understanding Managers' Agreement with Human Resource Research Findings." *Journal of Applied Behavioral Science* 41, no. 3 (2005): 304–325.

Combs, James, Yongmei Liu, Angela Hall, and David Ketchen. "How Much Do High-Performance Work Practices Matter? A Meta-Analysis of Their Effects on Organizational Performance. *Personnel Psychology* 59, no. 3 (2006): 501–528.

Dunnette, Marvin D., and Leaetta M. Hough, eds. *Handbook of Industrial and Organizational Psychology.* Vol. 2. 2nd ed. Palo Alto, CA: Davies-Black, 1991.

Fiss, Peer C. "A Set-Theoretic Approach to Organizational Configurations." *Academy of Management Review* (forthcoming).

Fitz-enz, Jac. *How to Measure Human Resource Management.* 3rd ed. New York: McGraw-Hill, 2001.

Frank, Frederick, and Craig Taylor. "Talent Management: Trends That Will Shape the Future." *Human Resource Planning Journal* 27, no. 1 (2004): 33–41.

Gates, Stephen. *Measuring More Than Efficiency.* Research report r-1356-04-rr. New York: Conference Board, 2004.

Gates, Stephen. *Value at Work: The Risks and Opportunities of Human Capital Measurement and Reporting.* Conference Board Report #r-1316-02-rr. New York: Conference Board, 2002.

Goldratt, Eliyahu Y. *Theory of Constraints.* Great Barrington, MA: North River Press, 1999.

Gubman, Ed. "HR Strategy and Planning: From Birth to Business Results." *Human Resource Planning Journal* 27, no. 1 (2004): 13–23.

Hambrick, Donald C., and James W. Fredrickson. "Are You Sure You Have a Strategy?" *Academy of Management Executive* 19, no. 4 (2005): 51–62.

Hicks, Mary Dee, and David B. Peterson. "The Development Pipeline." *Knowledge Management Review*, July–August 1999, 30–33.

Howard, John A. *Marketing Management: Analysis and Decision.* Homewood, IL: R. D. Irwin, 1957.

Huselid, Mark A., Richard W. Beatty, and Brian E. Becker. "'A Players' or 'A Positions'? The Strategic Logic of Workforce Management." *Harvard Business Review*, December 2005, 110–117.

Jackson, Susan E., Michael A. Hitt, and Angelo S. DeNisi, eds. *Managing Knowledge for Sustained Competitive Advantage*. San Francisco: Jossey-Bass/Pfeiffer, 2003.

Johns, G. "Constraints on the Adoption of Psychology-Based Personnel Practices: Lessons from Organizational Innovation." *Personnel Psychology* 46, no. 3 (1993): 569–592.

Johnson, H. Thomas. "Management Accounting in an Early Integrated Industrial: E. I. DuPont de Nemours Powder Company, 1903–1912." *Business History Review* 49, no. 2 (1975): 184–204.

Johnson, H. Thomas, and Robert S. Kaplan. *Relevance Lost: The Rise and Fall of Management Accounting*. Boston: Harvard Business School Press, 1991.

Kaplan, Robert S. "How the Balanced Scorecard Complements the McKinsey 7-S Model." *Strategy and Leadership* 33, no. 3 (2005): 41–46.

Kaplan, Robert S., and David P. Norton. "Measuring the Strategic Readiness of Intangible Assets." *Harvard Business Review*, February 2004, 52–63.

Kuczynski, Sherry. "Help! I Shrunk the Company!" *HR Magazine* 44, no. 6 (1999): 40–45.

Lawler, Edward E. III, et al. *Human Resources Business Process Outsourcing*. Hoboken, NJ: Jossey-Bass, 2004.

Lawler, Edward E. III, John W. Boudreau, and Susan Mohrman. *Achieving Strategic Excellence*. Palo Alto, CA: Stanford University Press, 2006.

Lawler, Edward E. III, Alec Levenson, and John W. Boudreau. "HR Metrics and Analytics: Uses and Impacts." *Human Resource Planning Journal* 27, no. 4 (2004): 27–35.

Lawler, Edward E. III, and James O'Toole, eds. *America at Work: Choices and Challenges*. New York: Palgrave MacMillan, 2006.

Lawler, Edward E. III, and Christopher G. Worley. *Built to Change*. Hoboken, NJ: Jossey-Bass, 2006.

Lewis, Michael. *Moneyball: The Art of Winning an Unfair Game*. New York: Norton, 2003.

Lossey, Mike, Dave Ulrich, and Sue Meisinger, eds. *The Future of Human Resource Management: 64 Thought Leaders Explore the Critical HR Issues of Today and Tomorrow*. New York: Wiley, 2005.

MacDuffie, John Paul. "Human Resource Bundles and Manufacturing Performance." *Industrial and Labor Relations Review* 48, no. 2 (1995): 197–221.

McKay, Patrick F., and Derek R. Avery. "What Has Race Got to Do with It?" *Personnel Psychology* 59, no. 2 (2006): 395–429.

McLean, Bethany, and Peter Elkind. *The Smartest Guys in the Room*. New York: Penguin, 2003.

National Academy of Public Administration. *HR in a Technology-Driven Environment*. Washington, DC: National Academy of Public Administration, 2002.

O'Toole, James, Edward E. Lawler III, and Susan R. Meisinger. *The New American Workplace*. Hampshire, England: Palgrave Macmillan, 2006.

Pearson, Andrall E. "Muscle-Build the Organization." *Harvard Business Review*, July–August 1987.

PeopleSoft. *Heads Count: An Anthology for the Competitive Enterprise*. Pleasanton, CA: PeopleSoft, 2003.

Pfeffer, Jeffrey, and Robert I. Sutton. *Hard Facts, Dangerous Truths, and Total Non-sense*. Boston: Harvard Business School Press, 2006.

Porter, Michael E. "What Is Strategy?" *Harvard Business Review*, November–December 1996, 61–78.

Richard, Orlando C., Thomas A. Kochan, and Amy McMillan-Capehart. "The Impact of Visible Diversity on Organizational Effectiveness: Disclosing the Contents in Pandora's Black Box." *Journal of Business and Management* 8, no. 3 (2002): 265–291.

Schein, Edgar H. "Culture: The Missing Concept in Organization Studies." *Administrative Science Quarterly* 41, no. 2 (1996): 229–235.

Schroeder, Roger G., Kevin Linderman, and Dongli Zhang. "Evolution of Quality: First Fifty Issues of *Production and Operations Management*." *Production and Operations Management* 14, no. 4 (2005): 468–481.

Shuit, Douglas P. "Passing the Bucks." *Workforce Management* 82, no. 9 (2003): 30–34.

Skinner, Wickham. "Big Hat, No Cattle: Managing Human Resources." *Harvard Business Review*, September–October 1981.

Welch, Jack F., and John A. Byrne. *Jack: Straight from the Gut*. New York: Warner Business Books, 2001.

Wright, Patrick, et al., eds. *Research in Personnel and Human Resources Management*. Supplement 4, *Strategic Human Resources Management in the Twenty-First Century*. Stamford, CT: JAI Press, 1999.

Wright, Patrick, et al. "The Relationship Between HR Practices and Firm Performance: Examining Causal Order." *Personnel Psychology* 58 (2005): 409–446.

Index

About the Authors

John W. Boudreau is Research Director at the Center for Effective Organizations and Professor of Management and Organization in the Marshall School of Business at the University of Southern California. He is recognized worldwide for breakthrough research on the bridge between superior human capital, talent, and sustainable competitive advantage. He is a strategy, HR, and talent management adviser to organizations ranging from early-stage companies to U.S. and global *Fortune* 100 organizations to government and nongovernmental agencies and nonprofit organizations. He is an executive educator with the University of Southern California, IMD, Wharton, and Cornell University. Dr. Boudreau has published more than fifty books and articles. His research received the Academy of Management's Organizational Behavior New Concept and Human Resource Scholarly Contribution awards and has been featured in *Harvard Business Review*, the *Wall Street Journal*, *Fortune*, *Fast Company*, and *BusinessWeek*, among others.

Dr. Boudreau is a fellow of the National Academy of Human Resources and helped establish and was Director of the Center for Advanced Human Resource Studies at Cornell University, where he was a professor for over twenty years. Dr. Boudreau is a member of the board of advisers of the Human Resource Planning Society and WorldatWork, and a trustee for the Foundation of the National Academy of Human Resources. He holds an undergraduate degree in business from New Mexico State University and a master's degree in management and a PhD in industrial relations from Purdue University's Krannert School of Management.

Peter M. Ramstad is the former Executive Vice President of Strategy and Finance for Personnel Decisions International (PDI). Over his sixteen-year career at PDI, he held a variety of leadership positions, including Chief Financial Officer and head of the Organizational Consulting Group. As the founder of PDI's strategy practice, he consulted with many organizations worldwide on strategy, organizational, and HR-related issues. He received his undergraduate degree in mathematics and accounting from the University of Minnesota, where he also attended graduate school. He was a certified public accountant and certified management accountant. Before joining PDI, he was a consulting partner with a major public accounting firm. He has been a faculty participant in executive education sessions and research center presentations with the University of Minnesota, the University of Southern California, Cornell University, and Texas A&M University. He has been a frequent speaker at academic, professional, and corporate conferences and programs where he is acknowledged for his unique ability to integrate financial, strategic, and organizational theory into unique, actionable insights. He is currently Vice President of Business and Strategic Development with The Toro Company.